I0025005

Salem Wilder

Life - its nature, origin, development and the psychical related to the physical

Salem Wilder

Life - its nature, origin, development and the psychical related to the physical

ISBN/EAN: 9783742867124

Manufactured in Europe, USA, Canada, Australia, Japa

Cover: Foto ©Thomas Meinert / pixelio.de

Manufactured and distributed by brebook publishing software
(www.brebook.com)

Salem Wilder

Life - its nature, origin, development and the psychical related to the physical

LIFE:

ITS NATURE, ORIGIN, DEVELOPMENT,

AND THE

PSYCHICAL RELATED TO THE PHYSICAL.

BY

SALEM WILDER.

———————◆———————

BOSTON:

PRESS OF ROCKWELL AND CHURCHILL, 39 ARCH STREET.

1886.

PREFACE.

THE writer is impressed with the idea that much more might be properly written concerning the Nature of Life and the duties which must accompany living. He does not expect to add much which is new; but the thoughts here recorded have remained after an extended reading of eminent authors who have written upon like subjects.

Moral questions receive special attention, and are discussed from a common-sense point of view; but a striking coincidence is to be noted in the fact that those nations which have done most to enlighten the world through biological, psychological and physiological investigations have been professedly Christian.

The sceptical as well as the believing have a right to know from what stand-point the writer urges his views; and both may ask why he speculates concerning matters beyond the comprehension of the human intellect.

The belief of an author cannot alter the significance of a single fact, nor can the disbelief of any other man affect the position of actual truth; yet our peculiar views upon moral and religious subjects do color our reasonings, even when dealing with matters not directly moral or religious.

Many passages have been wrought into the text which

others might have allowed to appear as notes. Certain
parts of the work consist of fugitive thoughts written
at various times during the past ten years, and in some
instances these thoughts are imperfectly interwoven, and
there will be found many digressions from the main line
of the argument.

Certain imperfectly understood teachings of nature have
been perverted by a class of eminent men, and some one
should restate these teachings from a different point of
view. The writer has endeavored not to state as fact what
does not rest upon good authority; but in writing what
follows he assumes a serious responsibility. In the border
lands of theory and speculation the lines of truth are not
always clearly defined. To mislead is easy, and to mislead
in important lines of thought may do harm; yet men must
bear the responsibility of their honest convictions.

If the following pages shall incline readers to think and
seriously inquire "What is truth?" the chief desire and expectation of the author will be realized.

S. W.

Boston, February, 1886.

CONTENTS.

CHAPTER I.

WHAT IS LIFE?

CHAPTER II.

WHAT IS LIFE?

CHAPTER III.

WHENCE IS LIFE?

CHAPTER VII.

THE DEVELOPMENT OF LIFE.

CHAPTER VIII.

DOES LIFE INHERE IN MATTER?

CHAPTER IX.

HISTORY OF DISCUSSIONS.

CHAPTER X.

INCREASING SIZE OF THE BRAIN.

CHAPTER XIV.

CONCLUDING SPECULATIONS.

LIFE.

CHAPTER I.

LIFE, WHAT IS IT?

In treating a subject concerning which so little is positively known the writer proposes to present a few significant facts and considerations.

Let us inquire concerning some of the general characteristics of that incomprehensible and invisible element or manifestation which we call life.

Life in its essence is a mystery; but the earth teems with numberless varieties of living creatures, and the phenomena of life are so common that we look upon them as part of the course of nature. We are not inclined to inquire concerning life's origin and extent except in meditative moments, or when impelled to serious thought by the vicinage of death. Then we are often disposed to inquire whence? whither? But when we attempt to push our inquiries into the nature of life we may read over the portals of its temple, "Walk softly here," for the ground on which we tread is under thickest mystery.

Why do we say of one that he is alive, and of another that he is dead? What is life? — and also its opposite, death?

For present purposes I assume that life is a manifestation of the vital energy or principle which preserves health and strength in living beings.

But in one sense this assumption does not bring us a just conception of the proper answer.   I however assume that a vital energy or principle exists, though well aware that biologists are in dispute upon this very point.

Dr. H. C. Bastian (p. 56, "Beginnings of Life ") says : —

"Two fundamentally opposite doctrines have been maintained again and again as to the nature of life, under one or the other of which all the views ever promulgated on this subject may be ranged.   According to the one school, life is to be regarded as the principle or cause of organization ; and, according to the other, life is the product or effect of organization."

H. C. Bastian and others regard life as the effect of organization.

Hunter, Huxley, and many other eminent physiologists regard life as the cause rather than the consequence of organization.

If life is merely the result of organization, then men and animals are simply organized machines brought together by and under the complete control of the mechanical forces of nature.

Chemists have labored to produce living matter, but so far have utterly failed in these endeavors.   Organic matter has been analyzed, and its chemical constituents, carbon, oxygen, nitrogen, sulphur, etc., are well known.   But when chemists combine these elements in the same proportions no breath comes,. no throbbing heart, no blood circulation ; in fact, not the slightest trace of what we distinguish by the name of life.

It should be borne in mind that living protoplasm has not been and cannot be analyzed. A chemist can say that dead protoplasm is compounded of carbon, nitrogen, oxygen, sulphur, etc. ; but, when he attempts to analyze living protoplasm, death takes place, and it is only dead protoplasm which he analyzes. What escapes in the passage from life to death cannot be recognized by chemistry, and probably it has no chemical quality.

By using poisons which would destroy all animal life chemists may produce certain substances like those produced in the animal system at normal temperature ; or, by using a degree of heat utterly destructive to animal life, something similar has been produced. But in animals these are produced with moderate temperature, and without poisons.

So radically different are the actions of chemicals in the laboratory and the chemical actions in living beings which produce like results. Yet some have asserted that the production of urea by chemists is an indication that life in animal organisms is the result of chemical action or chemical combinations.

Dr. Lionel Beale, the distinguished physiologist and microscopist, writing on this point, says (" Protoplasm, or Matter of Life," p. 270), " All the force, all the heat, all the motion, in the non-living universe is incompetent to develop a living monad; and this the physicists know. In their view of the construction of living beings they ignore the fact of the existence of an already existing organism ; but this existence is absolute. They ingeniously invest attendant circumstances and external conditions in the garments of causes, and persuade the public that these are all in all.

They then ignore, or deny, the inheritance of life, which is all in all, and without which all matter, all force, all possible attendant circumstances and external agencies are as nothing."

Huxley admits that carbonic acid, water, and ammonia cannot combine to produce protoplasm, or the matter of life, unless the principle of life presides over the operation. Even Hæckel, the monistic naturalist, admits that life cannot be produced by chemistry.

However, there is chemical action in the animal system, and the work of waste and repair of the animal tissues constantly goes on. But no chemist has ever been able to produce the simplest animal organism, much less intelligence, the distinguishing trait of all higher forms of animal life. Chemists may analyze and combine as they will, but something is still wanting. The germ of life must be *implanted* before the living active machine can be set in motion.

We confess that from the teachings of science we have no knowledge of life separate from matter; for all manifestations of life we have ever seen, whether animal or vegetable, have been connected with matter. But that is by no means proof that life cannot exist separate from matter, or that the vital principle is not something different from any material substance, and resident in matter, but not of it, and placed there by the eternal and life-giving intelligence.

Science gives us no positive light in regard to the origin of intelligence, though theories are abundant enough. Here, as in regard to the origin of life, we may "walk softly," for more is unknown than is known.

Yet I have no sympathy with those, on the one hand, who tell us it is irreverent to pry into the secrets of nature, for nature does not reveal her *secrets;* nor do I sympathize with those metaphysicians who tell us that we have no right to study what cannot be comprehended by our reason. The one would shut from us all matters of faith in the unseen ; and the other would prevent us from investigating whatever might tend to make us distrust authority in spiritual things.

The Duke of Argyll has, in substance, said, "When men tell me that I must not search for truth in a certain direction the fair inference is that they fear I may discover valuable truth hidden there."

When we try to describe life in the abstract we cannot do it with any degree of fulness or clearness.

Herbert Spencer defines life to be "The continuous adjustment of internal relations to external relations."

His definition has been much praised ; but it does not seem to convey a full and complete meaning, for life seems to comprise more than a "continuous adjustment" alone. The *life principle* appears to be the *cause* of this "continuous adjustment," for, if the life principle does not precede, this "continuous adjustment" never takes place. This adjustment seems to be the product or consequence of the life principle. With death this "continuous adjustment" ceases. In fact the ceasing of this "continuous adjustment" is what we call death.

Grindon says that Spencer's definition is not that of life itself, but it merely describes certain "phenomena of life." "A definite and clear definition of life itself is yet to be given."

The difficulty in defining the word "life" arises from the different conceptions of what life really is. One conception may be called the metaphysical, and another the physiological. Spencer's definition is chiefly physiological ; but it seems to me that the metaphysical view which arises from our own consciousness should be considered as important as the physiological. These differences of opinion doubtless arise from different points of observation.

Dr. Letourneau (in his Biology, p. 34) says: "The definition of H. Spencer, 'The continual agreement between interior and exterior relations' has the fault of being too abstract, and of soaring so high above facts that it ceases to recall them." "It would be better to descend nearer to the earth, and to limit ourselves to giving a short summary of the principal vital facts which have been observed." "Doubtless life depends upon a twofold movement of decomposition and renovation, simultaneous and continuous; but this movement produces itself in the midst of substances having a physical state, and most frequently a morphological state, quite peculiar to them. Finally, this movement brings into play diverse functions in relation with this morphological state of the living tissues, habitually composed of cells and fibres endowed with special properties."

Spencer's definition is not comprehensive enough nor clear enough to suit Dr. Letourneau, and he gives the following definition of life: "Life is a twofold movement of simultaneous and continual composition and decomposition, in the midst of plasmatic substances, or of figurate anatomical elements, which, under the influence of this indwelling movement, perform their functions in conformity to their structure."

Some assert that the tendency of present scientific thought is towards considering life to be the result of organization. Nevertheless I must question the rightfulness of this tendency. An authority no less than Herbert Spencer, in answer to the question, "Does life produce organization, or does organization produce life?" states, "that function is from beginning to end the determining cause of structure."

As above intimated there is a great lack of clearness in the various meanings which different writers attach to the word "life." Some regard life as an entity, or something like what the human soul is supposed to be, — a something which can exist separate from matter. This is the metaphysical view. Others regard life as a "condition," or a result of the union of a force, or something called vitality, with matter. In this connection the statement is often repeated, "Force cannot exist without matter, nor matter without force."

Thus, in regard to the question whether life is the cause or the result of organization, if life can exist separate from matter, surely life may, and doubtless should, precede organization. But, if life is "a condition," or simply a process of action, and cannot exist unless connected with matter, then organization may precede or be coexistent with the life.

Lawrence says (Lectures, p. 65), "Life presupposes organization, as the movements of a watch presuppose the wheels, levers, and other mechanism of the instrument." This statement is the physiological view, and regards life as simply a "condition" dependent upon organization. But life exists in absolutely structureless matter, and if there is no structure, where is the organization? Can there be organization without organs? Hæckel says there are "organisms without organs," strange as this may sound.

On the other hand, many believe that there can be no animal organization unless life precedes or is antecedent to the organization. Most of this difference of opinion arises (as above intimated) from the different ideas entertained as to what life in the abstract really is. Those who take the physiological view use the word life in a sense nearly equivalent to the verb "to live."

While we know little of the abstract principle of life we know that a certain amount of violence will deprive an ani-

mal of life. We also know that if the blood is drawn off
the life goes out with it. We also know that when the
life once leaves a plant or an animal it never returns.

We cannot tell the exact seat of the life. The ancient
Jews were commanded not to eat the blood, " for the blood
is the life." Strange as it may seem, the blood has life in
itself, and its white corpuscles are believed to be living organisms ; yet we cannot say that the blood is the life itself,
any more than we can say that the heart is the life. Life
permeates all the vital organs, and in fact is in every part
of a living body. We cannot definitely locate it in any particular part of the physical system. But, if there is no particular seat of life, where does death begin?   .

Dr. Papillon says, in his work, "Nature and Life" (pp.
309 and 310), " If life is everywhere ; and if, consequently,
death occurs everywhere, in all the elements of the system,
what must be thought of that point in the spinal marrow
which a famous physiologist styled the vital knot, and in
which he professed to lodge the principle of life itself? The
point which Flourens regarded as the vital knot is situated
nearly at the middle of the prolonged spinal cord — that is,
the middle of that portion of the nerve-substance which connects the brain with the spinal marrow. This region, in fact,
has a fine and dangerous excitability. A prick, or the penetra-
tion of a needle into it, is enough to cause the instant death of
any animal whatever. It is the very means used in physiological laboratories to destroy life swiftly and surely in dogs. That
susceptibility is explained in the most natural way. This
spot is the starting-point of the nerves that go to the lungs.
The moment that the slightest injury is produced in it there
follows a check on the movements of respiration, and ensuing
death. This vital knot of Flourens enjoys no sort of special

prerogative. Life is not more concentrated nor more essential in it than elsewhere ; it simply coincides with the initial point of the nerves animating one of the organs indispensable to vitality, the organ of sanguification ; and in living organisms any alteration of the nerves controlling a function brings a serious risk as to its complete performance. There is, therefore, no such thing as a vital knot, a central fire of life, in animals. They are collections of an infinity of infinitely small living creatures, and each one of these microscopic living points is its own life-centre, for itself. Each, on its own account, grows, produces heat, and displays those characteristic activities which depend upon its structure. Each one, by virtue of a preëstablished harmony, meets all the rest in the ways that they require, just as each lives on its own account, so on its account each dies; and the proof that this is so is found in the fact that certain parts taken from a dead body can be transferred to a living one without suffering any interruption in their physiological activity, and in the fact that many organs which seem to be dead can be excited anew, awakened out of their torpor, and animated to extremely remarkable vital manifestations."

Though life cannot be located specially in any particular part of the body, and thus we cannot say that it resides in any particular organ of the body, or that it especially resides in the blood, yet, as a part of the blood (the white corpuscles are by some anatomists supposed to be living organisms), it might naturally be supposed (as the fact really is) that there should be a live blood and a dead blood, just as really as there may be a live egg and a dead egg. Live blood has heat, and is generally in a fluid state. Dead blood is generally comparatively solid, though it often remains in a fluid state in the veins for some time after death. The fluidity of the blood has been shown generally to depend on its life, and not on its heat or circulation. If you draw off blood and keep it at the same temperature as the living blood, and also keep it in circulation by artificial means, it will still become partially solid, the same as if allowed to become cool.

Without blood there can be no life in any air-breathing animal; and yet we are no nearer to the answer to our question, "What is Life?" when we say it resides in the blood or in the heart, or in protoplasm, than we should be if asked what kind of men live in Boston, and we should answer that they live in brick or in stone houses. If the blood is life's house, that does not inform us what the life is.

It is wonderful how the principle of life can keep the human system so many years at a temperature just right for rapid decomposition; and yet this principle counteracts all this tendency to decay, keeps the system from putrefaction, and causes the whole work of increasing physical strength to go on till the man attains his highest vigor. How life is prolonged, or by what abstract principle vital action is carried on, has not been revealed to mortals.

In closing his address at Nashville, August, 1877, Prof. O. C. Marsh uses the following language: "In this long history of ancient life I have said nothing of what life itself is; and for the best of reasons: because I know nothing. Here, at present, our ignorance is dense; and yet we need not despair. Light, heat, electricity and magnetism, chemical affinity and motion, are now considered different forms of the same force; and the opinion is rapidly gaining ground that life, or vital force, is only another phase of the same power. Possibly the great mystery of life may thus be solved; but, whether it be or not, a true faith in science knows no limit to its search for truth."

Men have attempted to tell how life originated, and they talk of its ultimate principle, "protoplasm, or the physical basis of animal and vegetable life." But though protoplasm is called the ultimate, were not its original elements dead matter until they received new qualities from the principle of life? These questions have been discussed by profound students, but no voice has yet clearly answered the question, "What is Life?"

Some assert that all life, whether animal or vegetable, is of the same nature; and that plants as well as animals have nerve centres. Though this theory of nerve centres may not receive general assent, there are things which seem to indicate that some plants have organs of sensation.

For instance, the sensitive plant will close itself on the approach of an intruder, just as a rabbit will burrow on the approach of an enemy. If you touch a certain part of the blossom of the common barberry with a pin, the stamens will close tightly around the pin, as if to hold it a prisoner. There may be, however, reason to believe that these actions of plants are caused by electricity or a like force.

Hæckel represents the mimosa when it folds its leaves as acting from the same forces in nature and the same principles as men do when they think; but I venture the opinion that there is considerable difference in the quality of such action.

However, there appears to be something like instinct in plants and trees. Plant a tree that needs moisture near a stream of water, and it will send out its roots in the direction of the water. On the contrary, plant a tree that needs a dry soil in a similar position, and its roots will run away from the water, and towards a dry soil.

Life in the lower order of animals has a great similarity to that in the vegetable kingdom. In fact the animal and vegetable kingdoms seem to run together, or into each other.

There is an order of life which cannot with certainty be classed as either animal or vegetable, but which seems to partake of the nature of both. There is a considerable number of living organisms which may be either animal or vegetable, and I am not sure that some do not in certain respects partake of the nature of both. Some plants have motions like those of animals. Certain kinds of algæ, when the cases or bulbs which hold their seeds burst, scatter the seeds, and these seeds sometimes travel around an hour or two with a rapid motion through the water like living animals. But they afterwards settle upon a rock, and grow into a plant like the parent stock. These seeds are called zoöspores.

Huxley (p. 160, "Science and Culture") says : "At the present day, innumerable plants and free plant cells are known to pass the whole or part of their lives in an actively locomotive condition, in no wise distinguishable from that of one of the simpler animals, and while in this condition their movements are, to all appearance, as spontaneous — as much the product of volition — as those of such animals."

In regard to the supposition that some plants may have nervous centres and systems, Huxley says (p. 164, "Science and Culture"), of what is called Venus' fly-trap : "Touch one of them with the end of a fine human hair, and the lobes of the leaf instantly close together, in virtue of an act of contraction of part of their substance, just as the body of a snail contracts into its shell when one of its 'horns' is irritated." "The reflex action of the snail is the result of the presence of a nervous system in the animal."

It does not necessarily follow because contractility of muscle in animals shows a nervous system to exist in the animal that a nervous system also exists in plants when they have similar motions ; but Huxley says : " It suggests a suspicion of their identity which needs careful testing." He further says (p. 165) : " The question whether plants are provided with a nervous system or not', thus acquires a new aspect, and presents the histologist with a problem of extreme difficulty, which must be attacked from a new point of view and by the aid of methods which have yet to be invented."

" Thus it must be admitted that plants may be contractile and locomotive ; that, while locomotive, their movements may have as much appearance of spontaneity as those of the lowest animals ; and that many exhibit actions comparable to those which are brought about by the agency of a nervous system in animals."

He also mentions a case that occurred not long since which shows how extremely difficult it is to decide as to what kingdom certain active particles belong. Prof. Tyndall made an infusion of hay, and soon there appeared in the infusion what seemed to be living animals. He showed some of this infusion to Huxley, and asked him whether he thought the moving creatures were animal or vegetable. After examination, as they undoubtedly came from vegetable matter, Huxley decided that they were vegetable and not animal. Tyndall did not believe in Huxley's decision, and said he would as soon " think that a sheep was a plant." Huxley afterwards spent much time in making careful examinations, and finally states that he cannot " certainly say whether the creature is an animal or a plant." But he still believes it to be a plant.

He also quotes the eminent botanist, De Bary, when describing the zoöspores which cause the potato-rot, and the way they make their lodgements on the plants as they swim about : " Foreign bodies are carefully avoided, and the whole movement has a deceptive likeness to voluntary changes of place which are observed in microscopic animals."

Bear in mind that these moving zoöspores are vegetable, and not animal; and that they swim in the moisture on potato-leaves as a fish would swim in a mill-pond; and after a while a spear-like protuberance comes out from the side of the zoöspore and penetrates the potato-plant. Then they multiply so rapidly that in a day or so millions are grown on a single plant, and, being very minute, are carried by the winds whatever way they blow, and thus in a short time they spread over miles of territory, carrying disease, or perhaps death, to the potato-plants.

You can feed some minute animals (not one five-hundredth of an inch long) as well as you can feed cattle. Huxley states that you may put finely ground carmine into water in which certain kinds of animalcules live, and they will feed upon it, and when filled will become so tinged with carmine that it can readily be seen in their bodies. Their manner of feeding proves that such are animals and not vegetables.

The singular nutrimental peculiarity of all living animals is, that their nutriment is taken from without, and assimilated, and what they do not need to retain is generally thrown out through excretory ducts. The taking of food is like this even with the little infusoria, which are so low down in the animal scale that they have no mouths, but take food in on all sides. This food then goes towards their centres, and from the centre there is another action towards the outside, which carries out of the animal what it does not need for its nutrition.

Strange manifestations of life are found in those animals which look so much like vegetables that it is difficult to distinguish the one from the other.

Mr. Wallace, as quoted by Mivart (p. 45, "Gen. of Species"), says of certain butterflies found in Sumatra which look like leaves of trees: "These butterflies frequent dry forests, and fly very swiftly. They were seen to settle on a flower or a green leaf, but were many times lost sight of in a bush or tree of dead leaves. On such occasions they were generally searched for in vain, for, while gazing intently at the very spot where one had disappeared, it would often suddenly dart out, and again vanish twenty or fifty yards farther on. On one or two occasions the insect was detected reposing, and it could then be seen how completely it assimilates itself to the surrounding leaves. It sits on a nearly upright twig, the wings fitting closely back to back, concealing the antennæ and head, which are drawn up between their bases. The little tails of the hind wing touch the branch, and form a perfect stalk to the leaf, which is supported in its place by the claws of the middle pair of feet, which are slender and inconspicuous. The irregular outline of the wings gives exactly the perspective effect of a shrivelled leaf. We thus have size, color, form, markings, and habits all combining together to produce a disguise which may be said to be absolutely perfect; and the protection which it affords is sufficiently indicated by the abundance of the individuals that possess it."

"Some insects, called bamboo and walking-stick insects, have a most remarkable resemblance to pieces of bamboo, to twigs and branches."

Of these latter insects Mr. Wallace says: "Some of these are a foot long, and as thick as one's finger, and their whole coloring, form, rugosity, and the arrangement of the head, legs, and antennæ, are such as to render them absolutely identical in appearance with dry sticks. They hang loosely about shrubs in the forest, and have the extraordinary habit of stretching out their legs unsymmetrically, so as to render the deception more complete."

Thus, speaking of one of the walking-stick insects, Mr. Wallace says : " One of these creatures, obtained by myself in Borneo (Ceroxylus laceratus), was covered over with foliaceous excrescences of a clear olive-green color, so as exactly to resemble a stick grown over by a creeping moss or jungermannia. The dyak who brought it to me assured me it was grown over with moss, although alive, and it was only after a most minute examination that I could convince myself it was not so."

Again, of the leaf-butterfly, he says : " We come to a still more extraordinary part of the imitation, for we find representations of leaves in every stage of decay, variously blotched and mildewed, and pierced with holes, and in many cases irregularly covered with powdery black dots, gathered into patches and spots, so closely resembling the various kinds of minute fungi that grow on dead leaves that it is impossible to avoid thinking at first sight that the butterflies themselves have been attacked by real fungi."

There are certain grasshoppers which look almost exactly like leaves. Instances of a similar nature might be multiplied, showing in what wonderful ways nature exhibits the varieties of life. Probably the fact that animals or insects mentioned above look so much like vegetables may be the means of preserving their lives from natural enemies ; and hence be the indirect means of keeping the species in existence.

H. L. Fairchild, in "Popular Science Monthly" for September, 1882, writing of the means of defence, of which breaking apart may be an example, says: "Oddest of all defensive methods is that of snapping off the tail. The blind-worm, or the slow-worm, is a little, snake-like lizard, common to the Old World. When alarmed, it contracts its muscles in such a manner and degree as to break its tail off at a considerable distance from the end. But how can this aid it? The detached tail then dances about very lively, holding the attention of the offender, while the lizard himself slinks away. For a considerable time the tail retains its capability of twisting and jumping every time it is struck. The lizard will then grow another tail, so as to be prepared for another adventure. There are other lizards which have similar power, though in a less degree. The American glass-snake, so called, is one."

The limbs of certain reptiles, and of some other animals grow like vegetable shoots. If a serpent loses his tail he can have another by growth. If a lobster loses a claw, or a lizard a leg, another will grow to replace it. If a snail loses his head even, another will grow on in course of two or three months. Cut some animals into two or more pieces and each part will grow into a separate individual. Take the polype for instance, cut that into several pieces, and each piece will grow into an individual organism like the original one. If you cut off the part which may be called its tail from that piece will grow all the other parts of the body, till it completes itself, mouth and all, like the original animal.

Huxley states (p. 85, "Origin of Species"): "And so far does this go that some experimentalists have carefully examined the lower orders of animals, — among them the Abbé Spallanzani, who made a number of experiments upon

snails and salamanders, — and have found that they might
mutilate them to an incredible extent; that you might cut
off the jaw, or the greater part of the head, or the leg, or the
tail, and repeat the experiment several times, perhaps, cutting off the same member again and again ; and yet each of
those types would be reproduced according to the primitive
type ; nature making no mistake, never putting on a fresh
kind of leg, or head, or tail, but always tending to repeat, and
to return to the primitive type."

But if you cut off a man's finger one will not grow to
replace that.   Life in the lizard's leg, the lobster's claw,
and in the serpent's tail is like that pertaining to the very
lowest types of animals.   This also resembles life in the
vegetables, in the skin of the higher animals, and in the
nails or hoofs of certain animals.

Herbert Spencer remarks : " The highest animals repair
themselves to a very small extent, mammals and birds only
in the healing of wounds.   The power of reproducing
lost parts is the greatest where the organization is the
lowest."

The lowest animals are like certain plants which can be
divided again and again, and each separate part will grow into
a plant like the original one.   Plough through a horseradish
bed, and the pieces that are carried away by the plough and
left in other places will grow into perfect roots.   Often this
is the cause of considerable trouble to the gardener.

A strange thing connected with animal organisms is the
appearance of life excited by a galvanic battery after
death.

The length of time that these appearances of life will
continue is generally greatest in the lower animals.

Take a common frog, cut it in two, and hours afterwards,

on the application of the battery to the backbone, the part will jump as if alive.

Dr. Bastian says (p. 27, " Beginnings of Life ") : " During winter the muscles of certain fishes and certain reptiles have been known to contract for a week after death ; though in birds and mammals this property of the voluntary muscles disappears after a few hours." From the researches of Nysten upon the bodies of decapitated criminals, it appears that in man, as in the lower animals, a certain order is observed amongst the different muscles of the body in the loss of this vital property. Contractions from electrical stimuli ceased in the left ventricle of the heart after forty-five minutes ; in the muscles of the extremities, after seven hours ; and last of all, in the right auricle of the heart, which on this account had been previously spoken of by Galen as *ultimum moriens.* In one instance Nysten found that this portion of the human heart could be made to contract sixteen and a half hours after the death of the individual."

When a man is decapitated we consider him dead. But query : Has all life actually left the right auricle of the heart, so long as galvanism will cause it to contract ? A considerable portion of a man's body may be dead before the brain dies : why also may not one part of the vital organs even be dead before all the heart dies ?

Dr. Beale says (p. 261) : " The life of a man or the life of an animal is something very different from what is termed the ' life ' of a white blood-corpuscle, or of a mucus, or pus corpuscle ; inasmuch as many hundreds of white blood-corpuscles, or elemental units of the tissues, might die in the man, without the life of the man being affected. Moreover, the man himself might perish, and some of his living particles remain alive."

A man is not always dead when all outward signs of life have disappeared. Instances are not uncommon where persons are resuscitated after they are supposed to be dead, as in cases of persons apparently drowned. An acquaintance of mine once apparently died of a contagious disease, and preparations for burial were being made. The man told me that he was conscious of what was going on, but that he could not exhibit any signs of life. After a while one of the attendants thought he detected signs of life, and the preparations were postponed, and the man lived. In a case like this, decomposition only would seem to be certain evidence that the man was really dead.

In "Nature and Life" (pp. 325 and 326), Dr. Papillon says : "A zealous philanthropist quite lately gave a sum for a prize of twenty thousand francs to the discoverer of an infallible sign of death. Doubtless the intention is excellent, but we are safe henceforward in regarding the sexton's work without alarm ; the signs already known are clear enough to prevent any mistake, and to make the fatal risk of premature burial impossible."

" We must point out in the first place the immediate signs of death. The first and most decisive is the absolute stoppage of the heart's pulsations, noted for a duration of at least five minutes, not by the touch, but by the ear. ' Death is certain,' says the reporter of the Commission named in 1848 by the Academy of Sciences to award the prize of competition as to the signs of true death, ' when positive cessation of pulsation of the heart in the subject has been ascertained, which is immediately followed, if it has not been preceded, by cessation of respiration and of the functions of sensation and motion.' The remote signs equally deserve attention. Of these, three are recognized : corpse-like rigidity, resistance to the action of galvanic currents, and putrefaction. As we have already seen, rigidity does not begin till several hours after death ; while general and complete disappearance of muscular contractility, under the stimulus of currents, and last of all, putrefaction, are only manifest at a still later period. These remote signs, particularly the last, have this advantage, that they may be ascertained by those unacquainted with medicine ; and it is very well to pay some attention to them in countries where physicians are not charged with the verification of the disease, but they are of no importance wherever there are doctors to examine the heart with instruments, and to decide promptly and surely upon the death from the complete stoppage of pulsation in that organ."

The question, what death really consists of, is a very interesting and profound one.

Prof. Joseph Le Conte, in his treatise on the "Correllation of the Vital with the Chemical Forces," says (p. 200) : " As organic matter is so much matter taken from the common fund of the matter of earth and air, embodied for a brief space to be again by death and decomposition returned to that common fund, so also it would seem that the organic forces of the living bodies of plants and animals may be regarded as so much force drawn from the common fund of physical and chemical forces, to be again refunded by death and decomposition, — yes, by decomposition ! We can understand this. But death ! Can we detect anything returned by simple death ? What is the nature of the difference between the living organism and the dead organism ? We can detect none, physical or chemical. All the physical and chemical forces withdrawn from the common fund of nature, and embodied in the living organism, seem to be still embodied in the dead, until, little by little, it is returned by decomposition. Yet the difference is immense, it is inconceivably great. What is the nature of this difference, expressed in the formula of science? What is it that is gone, and whither is it gone? There is something here which science cannot yet understand. Yet it is just this loss which takes place in death and before decomposition, which is in the highest sense the vital force."

But equally great is the change from death to life. At one moment matter is inert, or dead, and in another it is alive, without the least chemical change that we can detect. This change is instantaneous. The line believed to exist between the living and the dead can be crossed instantly; but how wide is the gulf, and how immeasurably deep the chasm! Well may we ask in wonder, What is this force or energy which makes this wondrous transformation?

Life has many varied forms and strange shapes, especially when it is hard to tell whether it is animal or vegetable. Some animals are planted like vegetables. Others, like the clam, live and grow without seeming to travel; though I believe as a matter of fact, the clam does change its dwelling-place.

There are also other striking similarities between animal and vegetable life.

Trees grow by secretion, as well as animals. In fact, the white corpuscles in the blood of a man (which are about one twenty-five hundredth of an inch in diameter) are almost identical in chemical constituents with the corpuscles in the sap of certain trees. These white corpuscles in the blood of a healthy man are about one to three hundred of the red, and are somewhat larger than the red corpuscles. In some diseased persons, however, the white become equal in number to the red corpuscles. (Bastian, p. 225.)

Thus in such diseased persons the blood approaches in its chemical composition the sap in the trees.

Girdle a tree so that the sap cannot go up under the bark, and the tree will die, as an animal will die if you stop the circulation of its blood. The blood of the tree circulates under the bark, and the little tubes which carry the sap to its leaves correspond to the veins of a man. The leaves of a tree are its lungs, and they also take in some of its nutriment; they inhale carbonic acid gas, which man exhales.

There is a difference, however, in the way a tree shows its death. It does not fall down at once, like an animal; but the first sign of death is the withering of its lungs, or leaves, or their fall. Neither is the decay of a tree accompanied by that offensive odor which accompanies decaying animal matter; though in some decaying vegetables, as the cabbage and the potato, the odors are anything but sweet.

However, when you attempt to distinguish the lowest orders of animals from vegetables, it is very important that the odors of decay should be duly noted; for if they are not, it may be impossible to determine whether they are animal or vegetable. The sponge, for instance, on the rocks and shells where it grew, was for a long time supposed to be a vegetable; but when odors from decay and from burning were noticed they were so distinctly animal that the sponge is now conceded to be animal, and not a vegetable.

There is a similarity of construction between animals and vegetables. The tree has a bark for a covering, and the animal, a skin. Cut the bark of a tree, and the sap, or the tree's blood, will flow. So also, cut the skin of an animal, and some of the vital fluid, or blood, will flow. But cut the limb off a tree, and it may not injure its vigor. It may make it even more vigorous. Certain trees and vegetables thrive all the better for pruning.

Not so with the higher order of animals. By cutting off their limbs a definite loss of power occurs.

Cut a tree down, and it may sprout and become a vigorous tree again. But of man, Job said, " As the waters fail from the sea, and the flood decayeth and drieth up, so man lieth down, and riseth not : till the heavens be no more, they shall not awake, nor be raised out of their sleep."

Men and animals decay with age, and so also plants and trees. There is a turning-point in the lives of trees and animals.

Perhaps, after a vigorous life of from two hundred to five hundred years, the highest vigor of a tree may be reached, and then, like an old man, it may be on the down-hill of life. There are also health and disease in both plants and animals. Both need food. The tree must have earth and moisture, or it will die of hunger and thirst, like an animal deprived of nourishment.

How similar the origin of fowls and the oak ! The changes of the chicken in the shell, like the germ in the acorn, can be observed during its early development, and until it bursts its shell.

The chick has nutriment in its crop from the yolk of the egg to sustain it until it has strength to go in search of other food. Quite similar is the germ of the acorn before it bursts its shell. The acorn itself furnishes food to nourish it until its roots can go down into the earth in search of other nourishment. How similar this to the mammalian mother, who carefully nurses her young till it can take other food !

There is also in each of these cases an expenditure of energy, and this energy must be supplied by combustion from within until it can get nourishment from without. Thus, as we might suppose, the egg during the season of incubation grows lighter in weight. So likewise the acorn sprouting loses much of its solid substance in feeding the shoot. Likewise the caterpillar, when it comes forth a butterfly from its chrysalistic state, is much lighter than when, as a caterpillar, it entered the chrysalis. In some cases nine-tenths its weight is lost during development. The energy required for development in this case must be supplied from combustion within. So, also, all energy of development must be supplied from within when it cannot be had from without; for Nature will not be cheated out of her just dues; and she will supply no energy, no development, except it be paid for in a legal way. No human government can more strongly demand "legal tender" than Nature does.

How strangely, also, will Nature assert herself, even in the youngest creatures ! Place the eggs of a duck under a hen, and let her hatch them out. Why do the little ducks so soon take to the water, where the hen, their foster-mother, does not dare to go? Who taught the little duck that its foot was shaped just right for swimming? Why does it not heed the example and instructions of the only mother it has known, and keep away from water? Why is the whole nature contained in the egg from which it comes forth? "From a bad egg comes a bad crow," is a familiar quotation. Who but the great Author of all life can fully explain all the laws of heredity or descent?

Trees and animals have a similarity of structural organization. The animal has a bony skeleton, to give it form and strength. Even the tortoise has a skeleton; but that is on the outside instead of inside. So the tree has in every year's growth a part that is stronger and harder than the other part; and it has also cells, through which moisture and other nutriment circulate. Trees breathe through their leaves, and also gather some nourishment through them; and light and heat are as necessary to trees as they are to animals. If you keep a tree constantly stripped of its leaves, it will die, as surely as a man will if his lungs are so filled or so impaired that he cannot get oxygen to keep up the vital fires.

With man life means action. We speak, and justly too, of a man of no energy as a lifeless character; for he does not show qualities that we have a right to look for in a being endowed with life. Even a lazy man will speak slightingly of another lazy man.

Again, observe the similarity of physical structure in man and birds and quadrupeds : how the fore legs of quadrupeds and the wings of birds correspond to the arms of men.

Yet in some parts of anatomical structure there is a wide difference between birds and men, especially in the position and shape of their lungs, and in the construction of their bones. Bones of birds are more hollow, and thus are made as light as possible for the strength required.

Their breathing-apparatus is more generally distributed throughout the body than in men or quadrupeds. A considerable portion of the bird's lungs is near the outside, and directly under the wings; hence a pressure under the wings of a bird on each side of the body will stop its breath, and death will generally ensue within one minute.

But, unlike men, birds can breathe through the hollows in their bones.

H. L. Fairchild, in "Popular Science Monthly" for April, 1882, says : " Except in water-birds, the hollow bones also contain air, and by their connection with the lungs respiration can be continued through an opening in the arm or thigh bone, although the windpipe may be tied."

I will now mention some curious phenomena connected with the development of life through a mixture of races : —

One of the strangest characteristics of living things appears in what are called hybrids. These hybrids may be either animal or vegetable. They are the progeny of what appear to be two different species of plants or animals. I say appear to be different species, for I do not believe that radically different species can interbreed. Hybrids do not interbreed between themselves.

The offspring of the ass and the mare is called a mule. The horse will also interbreed with the zebra and the quagga. But horses, asses, quaggas, and zebras belong to different branches of the same family. Progeny from the intermixture of either of these are infertile among or between themselves, though they sometimes interbreed with the original stock.

The most singular trait of the cross between the horse and the ass is the difference between the mule and the hinny ; the mule being the offspring of a jackass and a mare, and the hinny the offspring of a stallion and a she-ass. Now one would naturally suppose that the offspring of a she-ass and a stallion, and a he-ass and a mare, would be alike ; but they are not : the mule has the head, ears, and tail of the ass, and the body of a horse, but brays like an ass ; while the hinny has the head, ears, and tail of a horse, and the body of an ass, but neighs like a horse ; — so strangely different in hybrids are the qualities transmitted by the male and female parents.

The dog and the fox will interbreed, but their offspring are infertile with each other, though they may interbreed with the parent stocks. The wolf and the dog, being of a nearer relationship, will interbreed, and their offspring are fertile, and rear a race of wolf-dogs.

This ability to propagate a race easily, in a great measure indicates the nearness of the relationship between races which seem to be different from each other.

CHAPTER II.

•

SIMILARITIES IN LIVING CREATURES.

I WISH now to call attention to certain similarities, both physiological and instinctive, which pertain to nearly every class of animals, and also to the harmonious and unvarying action of the laws of nature in connection with all animated existences.

General rules apply to many characteristics of nearly every variety of living beings. The brain, stomach, heart, liver, — how very similar their operations in different animals! But the heart and stomach in different orders of animals are very differently constructed.

Hunter, in his classification of animals, places,— first, " mammalia and birds; having a heart with four cavities. Second, reptilia and amphibia; having a heart with three cavities. Third, fishes and mollusks (pars); having a heart with two cavities. Fourth, articulated animals; having a heart with one cavity. Fifth, medusæ; having the heart and stomach identical."

Notwithstanding these radical differences of construction the circulation of the vital fluids and the action of the vital organs have a wonderful similarity.

How strangely alike are men and animals in their affections and in their anger! What strange variations of form and habits, and yet what similarity of tastes! Brutes appear to have their seasons of hilarity, depression, and even sorrow. How piteous the moans of a dog that has lost his master; how joyous at meeting an old acquaintance; how like, in some respects, a playful child and a playful kitten! Each will cry from a sense of loneliness, and each likes to be caressed.

How like in their industry are active human beings and bees! Each improves the time in active labor. Each has a disposition to accumulate against the time of need. Bees, like men, when they have accumulated property are disposed to keep and defend it. What a remarkable instinct (or shall I call it intelligence?) bees show in the construction of their comb, the house for their young, and the storehouse of their food! The mathematical proportions of these houses are as correct as those in any human habitation. Their hexagonal shape, and pyramidal bases placed as they are, make the strongest possible structure considering the amount of material used.

It has been stated that the bee is so made physically that it could not make its comb in any other shape; but I do not believe this statement, for I think the contrary can be shown. Obstructions have been purposely placed where bees would like to build their comb; and, to avoid these obstructions, on the one side they have built their cells larger externally than at the bottom of these cells; but on the other side they made the orifices of the cells smaller than the cells were at the bottom, and thus built the faces of the comb on a regular curve instead of straight, but still kept regular mathematical proportions. This seems to show intelligence of no mean order. But suppose the previous statement, that the bees' physical construction is such that they can build their comb in only one way, were true; then what intelligence so constructed the bees themselves that they can make their comb only in correct mathematical proportions? Did this happen fortuitously?

I do not suppose any man ever directed the construction of a public edifice, who more thoroughly adapted all its proportions to secure the proper strength, than do these bees, taught by the supreme intelligence, or by nature. Sometimes they show remarkable intelligence in the construction of defensive works to keep out moths that might destroy their young, and themselves even, if these moths could get access to their homes. It is a pity that human beings are not better imitators of the bees in this respect.

The organization of the bee is a very complex one, with a delicately organized nervous system; in fact the very anatomy of the bee indicates a high degree of intelligence.

If man has been evolved, or developed from lower animals, as Darwin supposes, we might reasonably expect, from the highly complex and intelligent organization of the bees, that they would be our near relatives. But Hæckel can find no common ancestors without going back through thirteen grades to the primitive worms, and rather despondingly remarks (p. 252, vol. 1, " Evolution of Man ") : " Unfortunately, we lose by this the relationship which might otherwise connect us with termites, ants, bees, and other virtuous members of the articulate class. Among these insects are many well-known patterns of virtue, which the fable-writers of old classic times held up as examples for men. In the civil and social arrangements of the ants, especially, we meet highly developed institutions which we may even yet regard as instructive examples. But unfortunately these highly civilized animals are not related to us."

Prof. Oscar Schmidt says (p. 28): " Hours do not

suffice to describe the structure of the bee. Even externally, its body, which possesses so highly complicated a structure, promises a rich development of the interior. The manducatory apparatus can be rendered comprehensible only by comparison with the oral organs of the whole insect world. The various divisions of the alimentary canal are each provided with special glands. The rich psychical life, all the actions which imply intelligence, calculation, and perception of external situation, are rendered possible by a highly developed nervous system, and the marvellously complex sensory organs with it, of which the eyes are especially remarkable. Independently of the generative organs, consisting of manifold parts of greater or less importance, the history of the multiplication and development of the bee demands a study of itself."

Thus, from the very complexity of the bee's structure, we might naturally look for the high degree of intelligence which bees manifest.

The higher order of animals seems to possess considerable intelligence. The ant (spoken of above) has been commended for its activity, and the sluggard has been advised to imitate it. But when we speak of intelligence in animals we are told that they work entirely by instinct. I am not, however, willing to admit that instinct accounts for all the manifestations of intelligence they exhibit. Ants appear to have a kind of language by which they communicate with each other, and in such a way as to be perfectly understood.

Who has not seen signs of intelligence among dogs, and to some extent reason? They also appear to have certain sense of right and wrong.

Some years since, at Rye, N.H., two large dogs went together about two miles from their homes, in the night-time, to where a flock of sheep was kept, and killed several of the sheep. They did this more than once; and these destroyers could not be detected for a long time, but were at last discovered; and the first thing that attracted attention and raised suspicion against them was their guilty appearance on days succeeding their bloody excursions. A watch was set, the dogs were detected, and paid the penalty with their lives.

It may be answered that these dogs did not have any sense of right or wrong, but that they feared punishment, and this made them appear guilty after their wrong-doing. But why this fear, when no one saw them kill the sheep? If we suppose they feared that some one saw them, does not this very fear imply a species of reason?

Instances of a similar nature might be multiplied, many of them coming under my personal observation, which show that dogs have in their mental make-up much that is akin to reason, and (without indorsing the Darwinian theory in every respect) I think that their actual relationship to the genus homo in their mental characteristics may be nearer than some are willing to acknowledge.

Agassiz goes beyond this in his book on the classification of animals (pp. 96 and 97), and writes as follows : —

"When animals fight with one another, when they associate for a common purpose, when they warn one another in danger, when they come to the rescue of one another, when they display pain or joy, they manifest impulses of the same kind as are considered among the moral attributes of man. The range of their passions is even as extensive as that of the human mind, and I am at a loss to perceive a difference of kind between them, however much they may differ in degree, and in the manner in which they are expressed. The gradations of the moral faculties among the higher animals and man are, moreover, so imperceptible that to deny to the first a certain sense of responsibility and consciousness would certainly be an exaggeration of the differences which distinguish animals and man. There exists, besides, as much individuality within their respective capabilities, among animals, as among men, as every sportsman, every keeper of menageries, and every farmer or shepherd can testify, or any one who has large experience with wild, tamed or domesticated animals."

If dogs had the gift of speech doubtless they would exhibit intelligence which would surprise us, for they might learn from each other facts of history, and a thousand other things of which we now suppose them to be profoundly ignorant.

Look at a human infant! If it was not for knowledge transmitted to it through spoken, written, or sign language, how high would it be likely to rise in the scale of intelligence? It is true its brain is large, but that very size of brain needs attention; and the child must have culture, else bad results will be likely to follow.

Notwithstanding what has been written to show that highly elaborated languages with nearly perfect grammatical structure, do not necessarily indicate any particular revelation of language to man (and while I am willing to admit that all languages in their inception may have been very simple), yet I am constrained to consider the power of speech to be a direct gift to man, as the crowning intelligent being on the earth. Moreover, the Creator has given to man vocal organs differing greatly from those of all other animals; so that, even if the dog or the horse had as large and as active a brain, and were as well constituted mentally as man, yet they would not be able to articulate any known human language. Thus the Creator has not only endowed men with large brains but also with suitable physical organs, through which their thoughts can be communicated, and thus the experience of one may be the guide of the many.

But though we may be complimentary to the intelligence of the higher animals, let us understand that the gulf which separates the brute from the human is very wide, deep, and in fact impassable, so far as any light from science has shown. The development of the highest order of the brute creation is upon a radically different basis. Take the young of the highest anthropoid races at the time of birth and compare it with the human infant. No one species of apes is in every respect nearest like the human species. In some respects the orang is nearest, and in other respects the chimpanzee, but for the purposes of comparison take the latter. At the time of birth, the infant chimpanzee looks (in some respects) more intelligent than the human infant. But as each develops in its natural way a wide divergence appears. The upper part of the forehead, which represents the reasoning faculties, fills out and becomes strongly developed in the human infant as it grows older, while in the infant chimpanzee, the forehead, instead of becoming fuller, begins to recede, and the shape of its brain seems to indicate a tendency towards less rather than more intelligence as its body becomes developed.

So very marked is this divergence between the infant chimpanzee and the human child as each grows older that it can be accounted for only by admitting that the great intelligence which presides over all nature, and over all the laws of birth and development, has from the very first fixed this radical difference. This filling out of the human fore-

head before the infant can talk shows that it has inherited
something through its very constitution which tends towards
thought and reflection ; while the receding forehead of the
anthropoids as they grow towards maturity show that they
inherit a constitution tending exactly in an opposite direction. This difference will doubtless forever remain.

M. Quatrefages, in his "Human Species," says (p. 379) :
"In drawing comparisons between men and apes, the sphenoidal angle, discovered by M. Virchow, studied by M.
Welker, and which, thanks to M. Broca, may be measured
without making a section of the skull, presents special interest." These experiments and measurements show that
in man the average sphenoidal angle measures, in infancy,
141 degrees, but in the average adult 134 degrees, showing
a decrease of seven degrees in the size of this angle, from
infancy to adult age.

But, on the contrary, in apes, — take the sajou for instance :
At birth this angle measures 140 degrees, or one degree less
than in the human infant ; but at mature age it measures
174 degrees, or an increase of 34 degrees. In the orang,
at birth this angle measures 155 degrees, and in the adult
174 degrees, or just the same as the sajou, but showing an
increase of 19 degrees between infancy and adult life, giving
an average increase of 26½ degrees of this angle in the apes.
But in the average human this angle decreases 7 degrees
from infancy to mature age.

But, notwithstanding human superiority to the speechless
animals, our domestic animals are entitled to kind and con-
siderate treatment. Life even in the brutes is a wonderful
thing. If life is merely a mechanical operation, as some
suppose, why should a horse flee from a wild beast on
account of fear ? What other mechanical operation has fear ?

Who ever knew a steam-engine to turn out of its course for any beast from fear? Still, there are many things about a steam-engine that much resemble museular action of animals. The active energies of each are supported by combustion. The combustion of a peck of oats in a horse develops power, just as really as a peck of coal burned under the boiler of a locomotive. But what a difference in the results ! The oats are turned not only into muscular and motive power but into tissues and nerves that have sensations ; and they also furnish food to repair wasted tissues. But the combustion of coal under a boiler repairs no wasted tissues, and builds up no body that can feel pain, or emotions of fear, joy, or sorrow. It takes the vital principle to make combustion perform this double duty.

As the physical system is supported through combustion, and largely receives its strength through this, several questions naturally arise.

First, Whence originates life-giving power? Can this power be derived from the purely mechanical laws of nature? Or is there a force, whether personal or impersonal, behind, or antedating the laws of nature, which originated and ordained these immutable natural laws, and from which comes this life-giving power in accordance with these immutable laws?

The varieties of plants and animals are almost infinite in number ; and yet all these can be arranged in a few classes, and in some respects they are all constructed and developed upon one general plan. Every variety of living thing seems perfectly formed for the purposes of its existence. How does all this happen to be so? Did all this happen without purpose, or without what (for want of a better term) we call intelligent direction?

Notwithstanding all the dust thrown by those who repeat the statement that the theory of evolution annihilates the idea of design in creation, the fact still remains that some power has acted in a manner which we are accustomed to call intelligent, and this power lies back of all the phenomena of evolution, and the process of evolution is one manifestation of the way in which this power has been and is still working. If we deny purposive direction in this, we might as well assert that Handel's grand oratorios or Beethoven's sublime symphonies were composed and arranged by throwing mud-balls at random on a musical staff, and then writing the notes where these mud-balls struck. More than 1,900 years ago, Cicero, in substance, asked what would be thought of a man who should assert that a valuable book could be written by throwing lettered blocks into the air and allowing them to fall at random, with the expectation that they would so fall and arrange themselves as to compose a nice poem or a logical argument? Nice poems and logical arguments are not produced without careful, intelligent thought; nor is it likely that as wonderful and complex things occur in nature without purposive direction. In nature there is everywhere as much harmony, and as real an exhibition of intelligent methods, as is seen in the production of great musical compositions or in logical arguments. Everywhere not only harmonious arrangements are found but also the nicest mathematical proportions, whether we look among plants and animals, or to the planetary systems. As much care seems to be given to the construction of tiny insects as to the balancing of worlds and systems of worlds, which go on their ceaseless rounds through the immensity of space, and always in perfect order.

If we doubt that these nicely harmonious arrangements

were made by an infinitely wise being, and suppose they do not indicate the intelligence and power of a creator, by what magical power do they happen to exist? Why may we not as well suppose that the telescope of Lord Rosse made itself, or that it was constructed without intelligent instruction, as to suppose that even the eye of a fly made itself, or was constructed by nature without a superintending, creative and intelligent power? Why may we not as well suppose that the finest coins ever struck off in a mint simply happened to fall in that shape without a die to give them shape or form?

There can never be an event under the laws of nature without a cause, and this cause must of necessity be of a nature related to this event, and must be powerful enough to produce it; and no effect can be greater than its cause. The less (except through outside help) can never produce the greater; so, not the smallest insect lives which was not caused to exist by a power capable of producing life, and also by a power above our comprehension; for, if we could comprehend the full action of this power, we might ourselves originate life. Scientific research has not yet demonstrated how life originally came into existence on the earth. But every man knows it does exist on the earth, and this not without a cause, and a cause also that is equal to the event, viz., the production of life.

Those who believe in the mechanical and chemical theory of life think they find in nature alone all the power necessary to evolve life, or to raise inorganic matter to the plane of organic, or living matter. Though to my mind it is extremely unphilosophical to attempt to account for the origin of life without recognizing the existence of an almighty, eternal, and intelligent being as the original

Creator, yet the Creator works so largely and so unerringly through secondary causes, or through the laws of nature, to such an extent, that in one sense I do not wonder that some never look beyond these secondary causes, but recognize them as existing eternally, and hence in their minds they dispense with any idea of an original great first cause. They do not recognize in this cause an acting, thinking, eternal intelligence.

The manifestations of life on the earth furnish us with all that we know for a certainty of any life. Vegetable life is largely dependent upon one of these secondary causes, viz., the sun. Blot out the sun, and all life on the earth would cease ; nay, more, the planets would rush into space no one knows where, nor to what ruin. The rays of the sun falling upon trees and plants contribute to their growth, and in fact to a considerable extent feed them. Then plants and vegetables furnish food to herbivorous animals, and these in turn furnish food to carnivorous animals. But notice this : carnivorous animals and birds of prey prefer to feed upon plant and grain eating animals. (They like to take food one remove from vegetables, but seldom desire to take it two removes from vegetables.) Thus, flesh-eating animals are not generally accustomed to feed upon other exclusively flesh-eating animals.

A singular and distinguishing trait or characteristic of nearly every species of birds of prey is that the female is considerably larger and stronger than the male. In almost every variety of hawks the spread of the wings of the female is from two to four inches greater than that of the male, and they are correspondingly stronger. The female eagles weigh, on the average, about a pound more than the male eagles, and they are in a corresponding degree more powerful. I

have never heard of eagles feeding upon the flesh of other
flesh-eating birds; but they rob fish-hawks of fishes which
they have caught for their own use. Ben. Franklin did not
like this habit, and was much opposed to putting the eagle
on our national coat-of-arms, for, said he, "the eagles do not
get an honest living."

However, the eagles are a type of the rapacity, heartless-
ness, and cruelty of carnivorous animals. They live by the
seizure and death of others. But this again, in a figure, is a
type of the subsistence of living creatures in general.
Nearly all live by the destruction or assimilation of other
orders; and some will even eat others of their own species.
Plants live upon inorganic, and animals upon organic
nature. It may be said that when big fishes eat little ones
this is a general type of the subsistence of all animated
existence.

The large tree, "monarch of the forest," overtops and
stunts all other vegetation within its reach. It must be fed,
and hence withholds nutriment and sunshine from weaker
vegetation. So with animals, even to the highest, — man.
The great and strong generally take from the small and
weak; and there is no reasonable hope that a similar condition of things will not remain so long as the present
order of things exists. We dream of the millennium, and
indulge other fond hopes, and to some extent there may be
improvement, and Hope says, "there is a good time
coming." But the character of human nature will ever
remain substantially the same. The communist dreams of
the time when all men will have equal privileges, and all be in
a certain sense equal; but so long as nature favors one man
with more intelligence than another, just so long will one be
superior to another; and as long as one is superior, so long

will he not only claim a preëminence, but will obtain a certain eminence.

There are, however, some noble exceptions to this general rule, especially when the learned instruct the ignorant, the morally strong try to lift up and strengthen the morally weak, and the physically strong defend the defenceless, and the wealthy give of their abundance to comfort the indigent. Though a grasping nature inheres in all men, scarcely any are totally devoid of sympathy, and in some the spirit of kindness is very strongly developed. These show that, after all its defects, human nature is not entirely devoid of godlike sympathy.

But we must look facts squarely in the face ; and some of these facts are not of such an assuring nature as we might desire.

Philanthropists look forward to the blissful time when wars shall cease, and when the knowledge of the laws which govern health will be so well understood that there can be no wide-spread epidemics, and when the average life will be much longer than it now is. This is well as a sublime dream ; but what do stern facts indicate? If wars cease, and the average of life is greatly lengthened, population will wonderfully increase. Exceeding great numbers must be fed, and well fed too, or pestilence will stalk abroad, and again diminish the number of the living. But if pestilence does not come, and food is short, the hungry must and will have food, and the rule, get food "honestly if you can, but get it," will be applied. Man is a fighting animal, and will always so remain. Those in possession of fertile and pro-ductive fields will not give them up without a struggle ; hence wars will be inevitable.

When we consider what the present population of this

little globe would have been in the regular course of increase if none had lost their lives by accident, wars, or pestilence, we see that the present power of food production by the earth would not suffice to feed one-tenth of the number that would be here. Under favorable circumstances races of men increase very rapidly. Had it not been for untimely deaths from famine, pestilence, accidents, or wars, there would not be standing-room on the whole earth for the immense number of human beings which would now be in existence.

From one single pair, providing each couple should produce four children, — within thirty generations, or in less than one thousand years, — the living descendants would number near three thousand millions, or more than twice the present number of all the human inhabitants of this globe.

Doubtless food production can be increased greatly beyond our present needs; but let the present population be increased one hundred-fold, as it would be within a thousand years if the dreams of certain philanthropists could be realized, and then the bosom of mother Earth could not furnish the needed supply of food. There is such a thing as a balance of forces in nature, and a limit to the supplies for both vegetable and animal life. Certain birds and beasts of prey, which men are anxious to destroy, are doubtless very useful in the economy of nature. Take owls, for instance. What good do they do? They often destroy the farmer's chickens, and this is placed to their debit; but, if we credit them with the great numbers of mice and other injurious vermin which they destroy, we shall find a large amount to be placed to their credit. It is doubtful if any living creature has been made in vain, although some may question

what good can come from the existence of certain insects,
the mosquito for instance, or certain venomous serpents.

We talk of the survival of the fittest. Doubtless, in a
general way there is truth in the doctrine of such survival ;
but we might also say the survival of the most fortunate ;
for how often do the strongest succumb to accident, or un-
foreseen calamities? A large proportion of humanity is
carried along by force of circumstances, as wood is carried
by currents of water, or as straws are carried by the winds.
It is true, that some men seem superior to circumstances,
and appear to make circumstances serve their purposes, and
weave the web of life's actions according to their desires ;
and some work themselves into other currents ; but it is
doubtful if even the most fortunate reach anywhere near the
goal of their ambition. There are always other worlds to
conquer, or, if we cannot find them, — like Alexander, — we
weep because we cannot find others to conquer.

But it is asked, Why not make laws to restrain the grasping propensities of strong men, and so protect the weak that
all may stand financially upon a level?

When men can stop the natural ebbing and flowing of the
tides, then, and not till then, will they be able to turn back
the tide of the tendencies of human nature. Suppose, for
instance, laws were made for an equal distribution of property, and carried into effect, how long would it be before the
distribution would be as unequal as it is now? On account
of the improvidence of many who never before had any
spare money, and the freeness with which they would spend
it, doubtless there would be given to business an impetus
such as it never before received, and immense fortunes would
in a very short time be acquired by shrewd financial operators.
Probably within twenty years there would be men with

greater fortunes than any man now possesses. But why not make laws which will render such an accumulation impossible? When we make laws which prevent men from honest accumulation we shall take away the greatest stimulus to activity, and the remedy would be much worse than the disease. The lazy and the improvident will always be found in human society, and it is questionable how far it is the duty of the industrious and frugal to help the indolent, especially when such assistance tends to encourage indolence and shiftlessness.

Look at the immense numbers which society has to maintain on account of habits of inebriation.

By what law of right do the intemperate and slothful live upon the temperate and frugal?

It is said that whatsoever a man sows, that shall he also reap; and, if one will sow to rum, what can he expect to reap but drunkenness and the untold evils which it brings? Through habits of sloth, intemperance and sensuality, drunkards make themselves, in a measure, unfit to take proper care of themselves, and then, like carnivorous animals, they prey upon the benevolent community which supports them; but with this difference, viz., that carnivorous animals generally feed upon animals of other species, while the lazy, slothful and improvident live upon their own species. Some men are especially like the carnivorous animals to this extent, viz., that they consider everything which comes within reach of their claws to be lawful plunder.

Others may be likened to children who cannot understand, when they want a certain thing, why they should not have it, although they have not the shadow of a right to its possession.

But this is not all in regard to the intemperate and

criminal classes : they fasten upon the succeeding generation a lot of lazy, diseased, incompetent, and too often vicious descendants ; and such live upon the industry of their own species, and become parasites upon the substance of their own race.

From such views of nature and of life, the statement has been confidently made that the Creator cannot be an infinitely wise and benevolent being if He designed that the world of organic life should be as we now find it. The statement is also made, that if animals were created for the purpose of being destroyed to furnish food to other animals, this shows a cruel, instead of a benevolent, design. But this is by no means a logical conclusion. Even if one animal loses its life to give food to another, it by no means necessarily follows that there was no kindness in the creation of the animal thus destroyed ; for we must remember that death, in some way, is a necessity, or the production of life must be stopped, else, as stated above, no sufficient amount of food could be produced by the earth to feed the animals which would be brought into existence. But why could not the Creator have so formed His creatures that they could exist without food? We may ask a dozen other similar questions ; but, before we can convict the Creator of cruelty in creating animals, we must consider another fact which relates to the balance of existing happiness and unhappiness. If there is much more happiness than unhappiness enjoyed by animals as a whole, was not their creation a benevolent act? It is evident that most animals generally live without fear, and most, if not all, appear to enjoy themselves well, and the short fear that may exist previous to being destroyed cannot be an equivalent or offset to their comparatively long time of enjoyment.

Take even insects which are devoured by the birds, — who knows that in their brief lives they may not enjoy all that their natures are capable of? There must be suitable food for plants, animals, and men, or these cannot continue to exist. Until the objector can show that the animal creation in general does not enjoy more than it suffers, in consequence of its existence, then a balance of benevolence instead of malevolence must be credited to the creating or originating power.

But I assume, even in the case of men, who are gifted with the power of reason, and also of reflection upon both their sorrows and their joys, that in general they enjoy more than they suffer. A great proportion of the sufferings of men, however, is caused by unnecessary violations of the laws of nature, though many of these violations may be committed ignorantly. The laws of nature however do not suspend their regular operations to favor one who has ignorantly transgressed them. And the very fact that the laws of nature are invariable in their operations is a blessing; for, if they were not so, how could we with certainty calculate anything in regard to the results of our own or others' acts?

Even with men natural death is a benevolent reality; for, if no one ever died a natural death, murders would be the rule, since, as above stated, the earth would be so crowded that food enough to feed the human race could not be produced, and hunger would drive to madness, and madness to murder, to get those out of the way who were consuming the food which others needed.

But again, in regard to the assertion that an infinitely wise and benevolent power never could have originated the present order of nature, those making these assertions refer especially to the sufferings of men; but even in the case of men, if, as a general rule, they did not enjoy more than they suffer, suicides would be more common. Instead of suicides being one in five hundred, more or less according to the condition of the people, they would be the rule rather than the rare exception. It may be said, in answer, that fear of death or fear of an unknown future existence may so restrain men that many of the unhappy who otherwise might commit suicide now refrain from doing so.

Here arise two considerations : First, a man must have a conviction that there may be a future life, in which he may be less happy than here, otherwise such a fear would not restrain him. Second, why this fear, if there is not some ground for apprehension on this point? Those who do not believe in a creative power do not believe in a conscious future life ; so if the atheist thinks he has more unhappiness than happiness in consequence of his existence, why does he not put an end to his existence? The very fact that he does not argues one of two things : first, he either has some fears in regard to a future existence, or he is conscious that he enjoys more than he suffers in consequence of his existence. But some who claim to be very wise, and to see farther into natural causes than others, assert that blind, unconscious causes could produce all that we see of life ; and, further, they seem to think that they have relieved an intelligent designer of a great stigma by attempting to show that an intelligent being could not possibly have formed nature as it is. Such may be wise, but I cannot comprehend such wisdom.

I now call attention to another characteristic of life, viz., its uncertainty.

With ordinary machines, like watches, or mill-machinery, we can calculate very nearly how long they will last. Living organisms, however, have a recuperative or repairing power in case of injuries (unless they are of a fatal character), while mere mill-machinery has within itself no recuperative power; and in this respect the living machine is far above the merely mechanical; yet in the plant bearing the fairest flowers there may be an unseen worm gnawing its vitals. "Thou must decay!" is stamped on all living things.

While the presence of life lifts inorganic matter into organic, and thence up through plant into animal life, the departure of life sends this same matter back to its elements; and thus ever the ceaseless round goes on from death to life and from life to death again.

The sunlight acting on the elements causes the grass to grow, and the grass feeds the cattle, producing milk and flesh, and these in turn become food for men and other animals. Then again these higher organisms return to the elements, constantly going from lowest to highest, and back again to lower forms of matter.

How like are these changes to the emotions and feelings of living, loving, and intelligent creatures! Byron wrote,

"Man! thou pendulum between a smile and a tear."

So hearts exuberant and full of joy to-day may be sad or bursting with anguish to-morrow. Nothing on earth is stationary.

CHAPTER III.

WHENCE IS LIFE?

PROBLEMS which arise in connection with the origin of life and conscious existence are numerous and interesting. For more than two thousand years human intellects have wrestled with these questions, and, as history is said to repeat itself, so the theories advocated and taught by Zeno two thousand two hundred years ago find advocates to-day among highly intelligent men. Inasmuch as some prominent writers are now disposed to ridicule and treat as chimerical, ideas, which, for all that they have ever shown to the contrary, may be founded in truth, I will, before proceeding to the direct consideration of questions concerning the origin of life, give a short historical sketch of discussions, and also inquire whether all that is now declared to be scientific has just claims to that proud distinction.

Zeno contended that the vital force filled all things, and was ever ready to burst into animated existence whenever favorable conditions existed, and that this vital force controlled all things, but that it was an invisible principle, and not a personal God. Thus to worship this was simply an absurdity, which ignorant or illiterate men might indulge in without special harm.

So certain moderns contend that everything, even to our conscious existence, springs from eternal and unalterable laws of nature. While many are silent on the question of belief in the existence of a personal Deity, others, like the

Stoics, declare that matter is eternal, and that it has in itself
the power of originating life, and thus that the idea of a self-
existent and omniscient Creator is a delusion, a mere figment
of the imagination.

The Stoics contended that life in animals and men is only
a part of this everywhere-present vital flame, which simply
bursts into a new development in the individual; and, as
matter goes its ceaseless round, through inorganic to organic,
and from organic back again, so life is simply a phenomenon,
an emanation, followed by absorption through death, and
thus this vital flame or emanation goes back and forth
eternally from death to life and from life to death again.

We of the present age consider ourselves wonderfully
favored with knowledge of a great number of accurately
known facts ; but in this matter of life and its origin, if we
throw aside the reasonings of Plato, who taught before the
Stoics existed, and who acknowledged a Supreme intelligence
or intelligences, and build our knowledge, as Zeno did,
simply upon known facts, and pursue our inductive reasonings only from known facts, we may well come to the conclusion, from the paucity of such facts to build upon, that in
regard to the origin of our existence we can never know the
truth with any considerable degree of certainty.

Also in many other matters we can never know the
absolute truth, and thus well may we ask, as Pilate did,
" What is truth ? " It is very certain that those who are
most confident that they hold the truth in its genuineness
and purity as the only absolute truth are quite as likely to
be in error as those who modestly and sincerely ask, " What
is truth ? "

So the decidedly positive writers of the present time,
when speculating in regard to life's origin, are searching in

regions where no positive demonstrations exist in our present state of knowledge; and they may well moderate their pretension to positive knowledge. They will be wise if they admit that men who are not scientific, but who base their opinions concerning these points on simple statements of what they regard as a direct revelation from God, may really be as philosophical as the positive writers who reject all ideas of revelation, and attempt to reason not from known facts but from premises which have their bases in simple assumptions.

It is quite important that we be able to separate the known from the unknown, and ascertain what is fact, in opposition to what is assumed.

Examples are not wanting of men confessedly of high scientific attainments who have adopted theories to account for physical phenomena, and reasoned from premises of which neither they nor any other men ever had experimental knowledge. Sometimes such theories have been generally accepted; but subsequent experiments or observations have shown conclusively that these assumed premises could not be true, and not till then have these theories been abandoned. Take, for instance, the kinetic theory of the gases (which may or may not be true), and also that of a luminiferous ether, with which space is (very properly) supposed to be filled; how scientific men have theorized about them, when in neither case have these philosophers ever shown that anything actually demonstrable is known of the supposed facts on which these theories have been built.

Who ever saw the ultimate atoms of gases going in straight lines with inconceivable velocities, and either dodging or striking against each other when they happen to meet? Who knows whether these supposed atoms are elastic or non-clastic? Able scientists disagree here; yct men supporting such theories, while the question whether the atoms arc clastic or non-elastic, or, in fact, whether they actually cxist under thc conditions supposed, is uncertain, havc been called scientific. But when some unscientific speculator suggests that facts which no human philosophy has cver cxplaincd may possibly bc cxplaincd by divinc revelation, he is (by these philosophers) sct down as a victim of credulity, and no philosophcr. Of course no man who bascs his bclief on things demonstrably untruc can be a philosophcr. Let it also be fully understood that no in-telligent man has a moral right to put confidence in any theory or doctrine which contradicts wcll-ascertained and demonstrable facts.

Without attempting to decide whcther or not this belief in divine rcvelation is justified by fact from a scientific point of vicw, I do assert that it may be as philosophical to resort to revelation for an explanation of somc things which have never been otherwise explained as it is for a scientist to assume that the theory of the kinetic action of the gases is truc, or that an all-pervading ether must cxist, simply because he cannot otherwise explain certain phcnom-ena, when, in fact, neither has any ccrtain knowledgc as to whether his theories arc based on facts or not. I say this : that consistency may be considered in argument; and I also ask, how it happens that one speculator who rcasons from *supposed* facts is a philosopher, and another, reasoning from premises also unccrtain, is no philosopher?

It mattcrs not, so far as real philosophy is concerned, whether these supposed revclations are found in the Koran, or Book of Mormon, or in the Christian or Jewish Scripturcs, the believer in either (until thc contrary can be shown)

has just as good a claim to be considered a philosopher
as the scientist who founds his theory of the origin of life
on suppositions which he cannot prove to be facts; *e. g.*
"spontaneous generation."

Thus the men who take their opinions from and build
theories of life's origin on statements made by men eighteen
hundred, or even three thousand, years ago, — who claimed to
get their facts through direct revelation from the original
Creator of all things, — are as justly entitled to respectful consideration as Dr. Hæckel in his "Natural History of the
Creation;" for he draws his conclusions in many cases as
largely from the mysterious and the unknown as do the
most credulous supporters of the supernatural or miraculous
origin of life.   Granted that neither knows for a certainty
what the truth is in regard to questions at issue : it may be
well to remind these over-positive writers, who ridicule the
idea of direct revelation, that they do not hold all the wisdom or intelligence of this world, and that truths may possibly exist which they do not comprehend, and hence
refuse to acknowledge.

I am well aware that to certain men this language will
be offensive; but no man has a moral right to throw aside
supposed revelation from the Supreme Being as worthless
without first fairly and intelligently considering whether
such supposed revelation is really what it purports to be.
It is quite popular with some to scout the idea that the
statements of the Bible in regard to the origin of life are of
any value, and point to the utter unreliability of the Bible
when quoted on any ordinary scientific question.   Granted
that the Bible is of little value in regard to the common
scientific questions (since it is not a scientific book) : that
by no means shows that in matters beyond the domain of

positive sciences its utterances may not be of great value.
Of course there can be no need of any revelation concerning
matters of which men can obtain full knowledge by study;
for to make a divine revelation in such a case would not
only be unnecessary, but it would be a direct encourage-
ment to slothful mental habits.

Many who reject revelation, and throw it aside as unworthy
of notice, have never sufficiently studied its teachings to
comprehend what it professes to reveal. What would be
thought of a man, who, by learning that, two hundred and
fifty years ago, astronomers thought that the sun was not
over five millions of miles distant from the earth, should
now reject all present calculations of astronomers because
they teach that the sun is over ninety millions of miles
away?

This would be entirely parallel with the acts of those who
throw the idea of revelation aside without proper consideration because three hundred years ago, or even in later years,
ignorant men have claimed meanings for its teachings which
were never intended by its writers.

If one receives the Bible as a revelation from God, or the
Supreme Ruler of the universe, he should expect to find
many statements which the present generation will but
imperfectly understand; and many of its teachings will not
be thoroughly understood until, through the evolution of
events, or by the progress of scientific knowledge, light
bursts upon our imperfectly informed students of its mysteries.

No man has a right to throw aside such a book as worthless until he has first candidly studied it with the purpose of
harmonizing its apparent discrepancies, supposing such
apparent discrepancies to exist; and no man who studies

such a book while prejudiced against it can be an impartial judge either of its value or worthlessness.

Let me not be understood by this to attempt to discourage scientific research. True scientific inquiry is one of the noblest pursuits in which men can engage. What I am now objecting to is the egotism displayed by certain parties claiming to be scientific.

Having said this by way of explanation, I will now attempt to develop some ideas connected with the question " Whence is life? "

A book was written long ago not expressly to teach geography or astronomy, or any other physical science ; but that book does profess to teach us the origin of life and its final destiny, and makes positive assertions about matters which have long puzzled scientific men. Among these assertions are the following : —

"In the beginning God created the heaven and the earth."

" And God said, Let the waters bring forth abundantly the moving creature that hath life, and fowl that may fly above the earth." And farther on it says, " So God created man in his own image : in the image of God created he him ; male and female created he them." And, " God breathed into the nostrils the breath of life ; and man became a living soul."

How do these statements agree with the scientific teachings? Was there a beginning? Was there an original creation? Was life first developed in the waters? Was man made after the other animals? Was man the last creature into whom was breathed the breath of life? Does not geology indicate that successive races of animals lived before man existed on the earth? Does not natural history indicate that the earliest living creatures appeared in tho waters ?

The Duke of Argyll says, p. 113, "Primeval Man," " The evidence of geology has always been, that among all the creatures which have in succession been formed to live upon this earth, and to enjoy it, man is the latest born. This great fact is still the fundamental truth in the history of creation. That history, as geology has revealed it, has been a history of successive creations and of successive destructions, old forms of life perishing, and new forms appearing ; so that the whole face of nature has been many times •renewed."

Well, then, how about the other two assertions, viz., of an original creation ; and, that God was the Creator? Are these as likely to be true as the other two? The statements rest on the same original evidence, viz., the Book. This book, moreover, states that out of the ground " God formed every beast of the field and fowl of the air."

Can any one show that this is not also true? Certainly in the ground are found all the materials which enter into the bodily composition of men, beasts of the field, and the fowls of the air ; and who can show that they were not thus formed as above stated, even if the popular development theories prove to be true? or that it took millions of years to develop a perfect man from the original germs?

This book conveys the idea that God was the author and originator of all life. Do we know, or does any one know, to the contrary?

I do not introduce this inquiry to contradict anything which science has demonstrated ; but when the Book states truly all facts concerning which we have positive scientific testimony on this subject, is it not reasonable to presume that its other statements, which science cannot prove to be either true or untrue, may also be true? What right, in the absence of contrary information, has any one to assert that they are not true?

But some do not assent to this manner of statement, and, if it can be shown that this statement is not founded on actual fact, then it must be acknowledged that the origin of life is involved in obscurity; for when we leave this conclusion, and try to find this origin through scientific research, the most learned men disagree, and, if they speak freely, they admit that they have only suppositions for foundations of many of their hypotheses. My inquiries are now limited to the life which is on the earth. I do not attempt to inquire into the character or origin of life on the planets or stars (from want of proper information on this point), though the discussion of planet life might be as sensible and profitable as many of the discussions concerning evidence in support of certain modern scientific hypotheses. Yet searching inquiry into the foundation principles of scientific truth (if of a practical character) is one of the most noble occupations in which an intelligent being can be engaged.

Some, however, assert that all natural bodies are living, and that the distinction generally thought to exist between the living and the non-living does not really exist. But it seems to me that there is a distinct line between the living and the dead which should be evident to every one whose mind has not become befogged with speculative ideas. I propose to examine some of these philosophic speculations in relation to the origin of life, and see if we can deduce any useful or profitable conclusions concerning the same; and also bring to view as much real truth as may be gleaned from my means of investigation.

The most important question connected with man's origin
and destiny is one which science cannot demonstrate, viz.,
" If a man die shall he live again? " The question whether
man is to continue in a state of conscious existence after
death is much more important than how he happened to be
in existence, or whence his life came. As far as science has
been able positively to teach, both questions are involved in
mystery ; and they are not only intimately connected, but
that pertaining to a future existence (if it can be shown
that a future existence is probable) has a momentous
bearing upon man's highest welfare. But in writing thus
it is proper to remember that some do not believe in the
immortality of the soul, or in its spiritual existence, and
hence such must be approached from another direction, and
must be reasoned with on other grounds, if we are to have
satisfactory arguments with them. Materialistic doctrines
are preached, printed, and urged with vigor, and are read
far and wide, and it is unwise for those who claim to be
guided by reason to throw such thoughts and supposed discoveries aside without due consideration.

But that my readers who feel so great delight in the contemplation of a blissful future existence may not be disturbed
by the course of this discussion, it is proper to remark at
this stage that the questions which arise in discussions
between materialism and spiritualism run into each other to
a greater extent than the decided advocates of either theory
seem to imagine.

Suppose, for instance, that a materialist assumes that souls
of men (if they have any) are material : what then ? Does
he know that it is so, or does any one know to the contrary ? We can easily imagine that a material essence may
exist and yet be a thousand times more tenuous than the

most subtle gas we know of; it may still be material and
yet of such extreme tenuity that no human intelligence can
tell whether it is material or immaterial. Thus the discussions concerning the question whether the spirit of man
is material or immaterial are not of so essential importance
as many suppose, and the decision either way (which of
course no man can positively give) cannot touch the
question of all questions, the one of supreme importance,
viz., that pertaining to the continued conscious existence of
moral and intelligent beings after death; though I am
aware that some of the best men fear that the admission of a
doubt upon this immaterial question may be attended with
disastrous consequences to cherished beliefs and brightest
hopes. I do not share these fears; for, if assured of a continued conscious and happy existence, it is not of much
consequence whether this existence is continued in material
or immaterial garments.

But to return to our question : " Whence is life ? " We
may properly inquire, where do we discover the first
appearance of life? It is generally conceded that the basis
of all physical life is " protoplasm," or, as Dr. Beale more
properly calls it, "bioplasm." I shall, however, use the
term protoplasm, because it is so generally used by a large
class of writers on the point under consideration.

Protoplasm consists of minute particles of organic matter.
These particles, or molecules, enter into the composition of
all living plants and animals, and now two distinct theories
of the origin of life confront us.

As stated in a previous chapter, for ages past physiologists of two different schools have opposed each other on the
question whether life is a cause or an effect. One school of
physiologists claims that life is simply the result of the

organization of matter, and hence life cannot exist separate from matter. The other school asserts that life is not the result of organization, but is the cause of the organization of matter into living beings.

These two theories are as wide apart as the poles, and the whole question turns upon one actual fact, and this fact fixes, or determines, the position which life holds in connection with all animated existences upon earth. Briefly stated, it is whether life is the cause which precedes and regulates the formation of living organisms, or whether life follows and is added to the organization as a result.

Is the principle of life the cause which operates to produce or evolve living beings? Does it impel the particles of protoplasm or bioplasm to come together, and become distributed throughout the organism, so that bones and muscles grow and build themselves up into visible corporeal frameworks?

We must bear in mind that one distinguishing trait of living matter is motion. Many confound the action of living matter with that of crystallization, and represent their actions to be similar. But the action of living matter differs greatly from that of crystallization, from the fact that living matter moves by internal power, while crystallization never does this. Organic matter, or bioplasm, goes by its own motion to inorganic matter, and takes it up and assimilates it. Inorganic matter has no power itself to move, though it may be attracted by another body. Doubtless life exists in granules of protoplasm or bioplasm long before their molecules become large enough to be seen by or with the most powerful microscopes.

And a motion similar to that in the smallest particles which we can discover doubtless exists before we can by

any means discover any motion. Can we then conclude
that the corporeal system is brought together by chemical or
other causes, and life simply a concomitant, resulting from
the organization, brought in by natural causes, and thus
worked into the wonderful living mechanisms found in various
animals, and in the highest types of humanity?

In regard to the commencement of human physical existence and the acts which spring from inherited tendencies,
Dr. Maudsley says : " No power of microscope or chemistry,
no power which science can make use of will enable us to
distinguish the human ovum from the ovum of a quadruped ;
yet it is certain that the former has inherited in its nature
something whereby it develops under suitable conditions into
the form of a man, and that the latter has in like manner
inherited something whereby, under suitable conditions, it
develops into a quadruped." (p. 21.)

The nature of the man as well as of the beast is contained
in the ovum, even when it is less than one hundredth of an
inch in diameter, when no microscope can enable us to tell
the beast from the human, and yet, when but little enlarged
from this minute state, the living creature is already divided
into two sides, which resemble two leaves, and molecular
actions are then going on as surely as in the mature organism.
When more enlarged, minute specks representing beginnings
of arms and legs appear ; but even then it is impossible to
tell whether it is a biped or a quadruped, although the whole
peculiar nature is already there ; so true is it now, as in
the days of Adam, that " every living thing brings forth
after its kind." The nature being in the ovum, if we are to
look for the starting-point we must look for germs of life
antecedent to anything which we can detect with the microscope, even to the first atom of living matter, which attracts

to itself another congenial atom of like matter and then commences to build the physical framework of the living animal.
The ultimate principle of life must be then in these living
particles. But this does not explain when or where the
personal life of separate individuals commences.

To show that living action can be seen in minute specks
of bioplasm, I quote (second hand) from Dr. Beale. " One
characteristic of every kind of living matter is spontaneous
movement. This, unlike any movement of non-living
matter yet discovered, occurs in all directions, and seems to
depend on changes in the matter itself rather than on impulses from without. I have been able to watch the movements of small amœba under a magnifying power of five
thousand diameters. Several of these were less than a
hundred thousandth part of an inch in diameter, and yet
were in a state of most active movement. The alterations
in form were very rapid. They might be described as
minute portions of very transparent material, exhibiting the
most active movement in various directions in every part,
and capable of absorbing nutrient materials. A portion of
what was one moment at the lowest point would pass in an
instant to the highest. One part seemed, as it were, to pass
through the other parts, while the whole mass moved, now in
one, now in another direction. What movements in lifeless
matter can be compared with these? "

Doubtless the living principle commences to build the
ovum when it is as minute as these specks of living matter ;
and this is as really life, in one of its phases, as the life in
mature individuals. But the life of a separate individual as
a real personality commences when the seed, or male cell,
and egg, or female cell, coalesce and become one ; and this,
in most cases, doubtless occurs before these combined cells

are one hundredth of an inch in diameter. Then these combined cells commence to throw off other cells of two different kinds, and one kind goes to build up the outside framework of bones, muscles, limbs, skin, etc., and the other kind goes to form our inside organs, as heart, lungs, stomach, bowels, etc. ; and thus the framework goes on till the physical form is complete. Not only every beast, but every plant, brings forth after its kind, and the nature of the plant is contained in the seed.

Why should trees planted side by side, with their roots running in like soil, secrete juices so different from each other? Why should the maple secrete sugar, while by its side the deadly nightshade secretes poison? What power short of infinite intelligence could endow these trees with such wondrous powers of discrimination that none ever make a mistake, and secrete any nourishment which can change their distinctive characters?

Water is supposed to be the vehicle which carries nourishment over the tree or plant, and leaves it where it belongs. Water holds in solution various kinds of protoplasm, and carries them over the living tree to its smallest twig and the most tiny bud. Afterwards the water is evaporated, and passes into the air pure water; but it leaves in the tree some of the solid matter which it previously held in solution.

A large part of the living tree is water. So of our own bodies, over 70 per cent. is water, and about the same proportion of our blood is water. Without water there can be no living, active, physical existence. Water in our blood is believed to carry over our bodies the nourishment needed to sustain us, placing particles which make our bones and muscles and brains just where they belong.

We have said that living actions are in the ovum when it

is only a minute globule, and that life has distinguishing traits in the little embryo, though we cannot tell what kind of animal it is; but even at the very first existence the life principle is exercising its preserving influences; for let life be destroyed, and then what? The molecular action which is peculiar to life ceases instantly, and the very first chemical or molecular action that succeeds is that peculiar to dead bodies, and in the direction of decomposition. No chemical differences just before death and just after can be detected in the mature animal; but the ceasing of the living kind of molecular action is instantaneous at death (or really is death), though digestion or chemical action often continues in the stomach after death. But digestion is not a vital action.

Now what is the power which causes an instantaneous stoppage of living action? What is that which leaves the body that instantaneously produces a difference so radical? Is this change the result of disorganization? Or does the departure of the living principle cause this change? If organization is the cause of life, and life merely the result, would not the character of the organization instantly change at death? But can we detect any difference in the physical organization just before and just after death? So far as can be seen with the most powerful microscopes, the very commencement or beginning of every animal organism is accompanied by life. If organization is the cause of life, then life is its effect. As the cause must always precede the effect, so if organization is the cause of life, then organization must precede life. But, if this does so precede, why is it that no man with the most powerful microscope ever saw animal or vegetable organization beginning before life is in it? Are they coexistent? It is quite a different thing to suppose that life's principle is the cause of organization ; for the principle of life, if it has a real existence, is invisible, and hence could not be expected to be seen doing this work of organization. Its work can only be seen in its effects. Rapid vital action can be seen in the most minute amœba ; but no such action was ever seen in inorganic matter. If departure of life causes a change towards decomposition, why should not the entering in of life be the immediate cause of composition or organization?

It is true that those who understand that the original creation of man, as described in Gen. 2 : 7, is to be taken as a literal statement of fact will find that man was made out of the dust of the earth, and his physical organization completed before God breathed into him the breath of life. In this one case, as stated, organization preceded life. But there is little fear that those who contend that organization preceded life will cite the case of the original creation of man as an authority to which they would appeal in regard to the present manner of the production of life.

Prof. James Orton, in his work on comparative zoölogy, speaking of the lowest organisms, p. 30, says : "It has been supposed that muscular and nervous matter is diffused in a molecular form ; but all we can say is, that the highest power of the microscope reveals no organized structure whatever, i.e., there are no parts set apart for a particular purpose, but a fragment is as good as the whole to perform all the function of life. The animal series, therefore, begins with forms that feel without nerves, move without muscles, and digest without a stomach ; in other words, life is the cause of organization, and not the result of it. Animals do not live because they are organized, but are organized because they are alive."

Herbert Spencer says : " Does structure originate function,

or does function originate structure? is a question about which there has been disagreement. Using the word function in its widest signification, as the totality of all vital actions, the question amounts to this : Does life produce organization, or does organization produce life?"

" To answer this question is not easy, since we habitually find the two so associated that neither seems possible without the other; and they appear uniformly to increase and decrease together." . . . "There is, however, one fact implying that function must be regarded as taking precedence of structure. Of the lowest rhizopods, which present no distinctions of parts, and nevertheless feed, and grow, and move about, Prof. Huxley has remarked that they exhibit life without organization." (" Biology," pp. 153 and 154, vol. 1.)

" It may be argued that, on the hypothesis of evolution, life necessarily comes before organization. On this hypothesis, organic matter in a state of homogeneous aggregation must precede organic matter in a state of heterogeneous aggregation. But since the passing from a structureless state to a structured state is itself a vital process, it follows that vital activity must have existed while there was yet no structure : structure could not else arise. That function takes precedence of structure seems also implied in the definition of life. If life consists of inner actions so adjusted as to balance outer actions, — if the actions are the substance of life, while the adjustment of them constitutes its form, then may we not say that the actions to be formed must come before that which forms them? that the continuous change which is the basis of function must come before the structure which brings function into shape?

" Or, again, since, throughout all phases of life up to the

highest, every advance is the effecting of some better adjustment of inner to outer actions, and since the accompanying
new complexity of structure is simply a means of making
possible this better adjustment, it follows that function
is from beginning to end the determining cause of structure."
("Principles of Biology," vol. 1, p. 167.)

It seems to me that these extracts ought to carry conviction ; but I will quote once more, and this time from the
Duke of Argyll. He says : —

"The deeper we go into science the more certain it
becomes that all the realities of nature are in the region of
the invisible ; so that the saying is literally and not merely
figuratively true, that the things which are seen are tem-
poral, and it is only the things which are not seen that are
eternal. For example, we never see the phenomena of life
dissociated from organization ; yet the profoundest physiologists have come to the conclusion that organization is not the
cause of life, but, on the contrary, that life is the cause of
organization, life being something — a force of some kind,
by whatever name we may call it — which precedes organization, and fashions it, and builds it up. This is the conclusion come to by the great anatomist Hunter, and it is the
conclusion indorsed in our own day by such men as Dr.
Carpenter and Prof. Huxley, men neither of whom have
exhibited in their philosophy any undue bias towards either
theological or metaphysical explanations." ("Reign of
Law," p. 118.)

Many are now looking for the beginning of life among
very minute animals which are as little as possible removed
from inorganic matter, and if they could only once see inorganic matter changing into organic, and observe in what
this change consists, and how it is accomplished, then a

starting-point might be found. Some are still sanguine that this process will be discovered. I do not belong to this hopeful class.

It seems to me to be quite as profitable to scrutinize with more care the origin of animals higher in the scale of life. The inductive method can just as well be applied here, and apparently with quite as much profit. But most of this kind of investigation seems to have fallen into the hands of those who are inclined to believe that all the forces which make these wondrous changes inhere in matter itself.

Many of them are careful not to express their opinions, as to how or by whom this power became fixed in nature, though some are ready enough to state that, in their opinion, this power was never *placed* in nature, but that it has existed there eternally.

Since writing this last paragraph I see that Prof. Birks takes a similar view as to the proper place to begin investigations, when speaking of individuality (p. 279, " Modern Physical Fatalism "), as follows : —

" The objections which have been raised to the essential individuality of life are drawn entirely from its lowest and most obscure forms, or microscopic animalcules, invisible to the naked eye. These are exceedingly minute in size, their number immense, their modes of reproduction very similar, and the laws of their reproduction very difficult to trace. But it surely reverses the first lesson of genuine philosophy to have recourse to the most obscure corner of a wide and important science for its definitions. This is to interpret day by night, and clear sunshine by mist or darkness. In all the higher forms of life, with which mankind has been familiar for long ages, the marks of individuality are clear, decisive, and irresistible."

It may be asked, What good can come from inquiry into
such hidden mysteries? In turn, I ask, What harm can come
from it? The truth can stand the most searching inquiry;
and any theory which cannot abide the most searching investigation had better be surrendered.   I have no fears for the
safety of eternal truth.

Materialists contend that there is no such thing as "vital
force " separate from matter.

Monists assert that there can be only one original force in
the universe.

Dr. Hæckel, the greatest living exponent of monism, or
the unity of force and matter, writes (p. 456, vol. 2, "Evolution of Man ") : "Goethe says, matter can never exist
and act without spirit, neither can spirit without matter.
The real materialistic philosophy asserts that the vital phenomena of motion, like all other phenomena of motion, are
effects or products of matter."   That is, that all active forces
in living animals are the product of matter.

"The other opposite extreme, spiritualistic philosophy, asserts, on the contrary, that matter is the product of a motive
force, and that all material forms are produced by free
forces entirely independent of the matter itself.   Thus, according to the materialistic conception of the universe,
matter, or substance, precedes motion, or active force.   According to the spiritualistic conception of the universe, on
the contrary, active force, or motion, precedes matter."   That
is, the spiritualistic view is that there must have been an
active spiritual force to organize matter into worlds as well
as into living animals, or else they could not have existed.
Dr. Hæckel adds, in regard to both the materialistic and
spiritualistic views, as follows : "Both views are dualistic,
and we hold them both to be equally false.   A contrast to

both views is presented in the monistic philosophy, which can as little believe in force without matter as in matter without force." Also, " The spirit and mind of man are but forces which are inseparably connected with the material substance of our bodies."

Again (on p. 457) : " The magnet attracting iron filings, powder exploding, steam driving the locomotive, are active inorganic substances. They work by active force, just as does the sensitive mimosa when it folds its leaves at a touch, as does the amphioxus when it buries itself in the sand, as does man when he thinks."

" Only in these latter cases the combination of the different forces appearing as phenomena of motion is much more complex and much less easily recognized than in the former cases."

Although Hæckel does not say in so many words that the active inorganic and organic forces are just the same in kind, or that the living forces in men are of the same quality as the explosive qualities in gunpowder, yet, by all fair rules of reasoning, he leaves us to infer that all the difference he believes to be in these forces is in their complexity, and not in their kind ; that is, they appear to be different merely because one is more pronounced. But in the quality of the acts there is no difference : both proceed from the same forces in nature ; and these are one and indivisible in their real nature.

On p. 17, vol. 1, Dr. Hæckel says of the doctrine of evolution, "it has enabled us to substitute everywhere unconscious causes acting from necessity for conscious purposive causes." He adds that the monistic philosophy " must ultimately prevail through philosophy."

It is easy to make the statement that there is no need of

any spiritual being to organize matter into worlds, or to put life into living animals, if we are able to " substitute unconscious causes everywhere for the conscious causes," which people have thought must have existed, and thus dispense with the necessity of any intelligent planning and organizing of the universe, because the causes of all these things have acted from necessity.

But how does this account for the origin of things? How could this necessity of which he speaks exist unless some power behind or antecedent to this necessity ordered that things should of necessity take place? To attempt to account for the origin of things in this way is simply to plunge into greater darkness; for it accounts for nothing till he informs us how this necessity came to exist.

Prof. Birks says : " The attempt to get rid of purpose or design, so as to refer all the acts of living creatures to mechanical laws and processes alone, is revolting to the common-sense of mankind. Under learned phrases it strives vainly to conceal an unusual amount of self-contradiction and logical absurdity. The hive bee aims at constructing its cell, and then storing it with honey; the bird uses much skill in building its nest and preparing it for the future process of incubation. The mason does not seem more truly to follow the design of the architect than insects of various kinds satisfy the outlines of some plan or type in forming their habitations, which has been appointed to them from the beginning."

Now if nature alone (without any intelligence controlling the laws of nature) teaches the bees to build their combs, and the birds to build their nests, we may be unreasonable to require an answer as to how this supposed necessity happened to exist. But, in regard to the supposed innate powers of nature, or the power of originating life, which monists contend inheres in matter, it may be remarked that if the Deity, in pursuance of his plan, chose to endow matter with life-originating powers, without doubt he had the power to do so. But the simple question now to be answered is, has he done so?

All persons who believe that the body and the soul are separate and different qualities or entities are called dualists; and those who believe that the soul may exist prior to, or separate from, or independent of the physical organization are called spiritualists. But these last are also dualists. Under this classification all who believe the teachings of Socrates and Plato are spiritualists, though of necessity they are dualists.

We have stated our belief that "Life is the cause of organization;" and thus you will see that we must also believe in a principle of life existing antecedent to any outward manifestations of life either in men or animals, and in fact · that this indispensable force underlies all physical life.

On the other hand, materialists and monists deny that there is any living or life-giving force separate from or disconnected with matter; and the reason they can maintain what seems fallacious is because we cannot see any manifestations of force or being unless that force is connected with or acts on matter. Even an emotion of the soul, though doubtless immaterial, cannot be perceived by us except through the action of the brain, a physical organ, and thus it is impossible to demonstrate the existence of soul, mind, or feelings separate from our bodies; and this is why monists have the courage to challenge men to confute their statements.

It has been asserted that since the brain is the organ of the mind, mind cannot exist except in connection with the brain.

While conceding that man can see no manifestations of mind except through its physical organ, the brain, no one is justified in asserting that mind may not precede the very organization of the brain, and have existed prior to and hence separate from it.

For anything that man knows to the contrary preëxisting mind not perceptible by man may have been the cause which gave to the brain its particular shape, and then took the brain as its organ of communication with other intelligent creatures. For all that we know mind may be coexistent with life, and doubtless was in the beginning, if there ever was a beginning. So it may be coexistent with life in the ovum, at the very commencement, when the first combined cells begin to throw off other cells, and thus commence the development of the embryo.

When men assert that soul cannot exist separate from matter they state what they do not know; and thus we are again thrown back upon first principles, and obliged to reason not from what we can see with our eyes but upon general manifestations of existence as displayed all around us.

Much has been written upon this subject. I will now give some extracts from leading thinkers, that we may see the grounds of difference between them. There are different grades of each of the classes enumerated above, but when I refer to either of them it is as scientists, not as religionists. Thus, among spiritual scientists there are two essentially different classes. Some are of the Berkeley stamp, who do not believe in the existence of matter, and think " All being may be reduced to mind, or ideas in a mind."

J. G. Fichte says : "One of the two, spirit or matter, we
must let drop : the actually true and real being is spiritual;
and there is no other being."

Czolbe says (See "Voc. Phil. Sci.," by Krauth, p. 908) :
"The power of organisms cannot be explained by the plan-
less and formless chemical and physical activities. Nothing
is left us but to throw ourselves into the arms of mysti-
cism by accepting a supersensuous vital force, or in acknowledging the eternity of matter to acknowledge also the
eternity of form."

On the other hand, Moleschott "opposes the doctrine of
vital force, as he defines it, — a force without substratum,
and yet endowed with personal quality."

Schopenhauer says (Krauth, p. 909) : "The polemic
against the supposition of a vital force is stupid." "The
denial of the vital force is absurd. Were there not a
peculiar force of nature, to which it is as essential to act
in conformity with aim as it is essential to gravity to
draw bodies towards each other; did it not move, guide,
regulate the whole complicated mechanism of organism,
life would be an illusion, an imposition, and we should have
a mere automaton, a plaything of mechanical, physical, and
chemical forces. It is not disputed that physical and chemical forces are at work in organisms, but that which holds
them together and guides them, so that an organism con-
forms to its purpose, comes to being and subsists, — that is
vital force." "The vital force certainly uses and brings into
its employ the forces of inorganic nature, but by no means
consists of them ; just as little as a blacksmith consists of his
hammer and anvil." "Hence, not the very simplest plant life
can be explained by those forces, as, for example, by capillary
attraction, or by endosmosis, to say nothing of animal life,"

"A fundamental distinction between the vital force and all other forces of nature has been in the fact that when the vital force once forsakes a body it never takes it into possession again."

How radically different this from the action of natural, chemical, and mechanical forces, as electricity, magnetism, etc. ! The same body may be magnetized and demagnetized, or electrified and relieved of its electricity, many times, without change in the appearance of the body. So simple chemical elements may be compounded, decomposed, and recompounded, almost to any extent. Why? Because such action is mechanical instead of vital.

It seems to me that nearly every one who comes with unprejudiced mind to a careful study of the vital forces or principle must reach the conclusion that something besides mere mechanical and chemical forces is required to originate, build up, and preserve living, thinking, and reasonable men.

This question concerning an original living force is intimately connected with the origin of our conscious existence, and with the question, how can mental and spiritual existences be connected with physical systems? Here is a region in which reason and philosophy must take the place of physical demonstrations ; for, notwithstanding all claims to the contrary, there are no physical demonstrations on this point.

The Duke of Argyll well says ("Reign of Law," p. 271) : " Science should be allowed without suspicion or remonstrance to pursue her proper object, which is to detect, if she can, what the method of this work has been. There is no point short of the last and the highest at which science can be satisfied. Her curiosity is insatiable. It is a curiosity representing man's desire for knowledge. But that desire ex-

tends into regions where the means of investigation cease
and in which the processes of verification are of no avail.
Above and behind every detected method in nature there lies
the same ultimate question as before, — what is it by which
this is done? It is the great mystery of our being that we
have powers impelling us to ask such questions on the history of creation, when we have no powers enabling us to
solve them." "The faculties of both reason and imagination
fall back with a sense of impotence upon some favorite phrase,
some form of words built up out of the materials of analogy, and out of the experience of a mind, which, being finite,
is not creative. We beat against the bars in vain. The
only real rest is in the confession of ignorance, and the confession, too, that all ultimate physical truth is beyond the
reach of science."

This again brings us face to face with the question,
" Whence is life? " The Duke further says (p. 273) : Creation by law, evolution by law, development by law, or,
as including all those kindred ideas, the reign of law, is
nothing but the reign of creative force directed by creative
knowledge, worked under the control of creative power, and
in fulfilment of creative purpose." And after all our inquiries concerning the origin of life, and under what law it
came into existence, the reflecting mind cannot help going
further, and asking, " whither? "

With those who contend that life, soul, and matter are
inseparable, we cannot hold much argument on the direct
question of the origin of life ; for if life and intelligence are
of necessity coupled with matter, or sprung from matter,
there is nothing to argue about. But until monists and
materialists can bring something beyond mere assertion, I
shall proceed on the theory that a vital principle, or living

force, underlies all physical life, and that all living beings now on the earth received their life from antecedent life just as certainly as they have received their physical systems from beings with physical organs. And further, that all life now on the earth had its origin in the first self-existent being. But why assume the existence of a self-existent being? How can we comprehend this?

We comprehend this just as well as men do the assertion that matter must have existed eternally. There is quite as direct evidence of a self-existent, Almighty intelligence, as there is that matter, even in its *simple elements*, is eternal. If matter is eternal, it seems evident that its eternal qualities must inhere in its simple elements, or in cosmic vapor, and not in compound bodies, as matter now generally exists.

However, before proceeding further in the direct line of argument, let us consider some preliminary speculations and facts concerning the first origin of things. Every event which now occurs has some antecedent, and every effect has a cause; but, if the same laws of cause and effect always existed, how could we get to the first cause, or a cause which was not caused? Is there an infinitely-extended chain of causes without a beginning? We have two alternatives, viz., either to suppose that during past time or eternity the same relations of cause and effect which now act by or through invariable antecedents and sequence did not then exist as they do now, and hence that parts of what we now recognize as the laws of nature have not been eternally in existence, or we may assume that all natural laws have eternally existed.

But if we assume that something is self-existent, or always existed, what is that something? Mind certainly exists, and matter certainly appears to exist. Did mind precede the existence of matter? Or have both mind and matter existed eternally? Or has matter alone existed from all eternity, while mind has not so existed? And has mind been evolved from matter, as some suppose? If so, by what process was this evolution accomplished? Or, on the other hand, did mind, through its act or acts, cause matter to be spoken into existence? Our minds are so constituted that it is easier to conceive that both mind and matter existed eternally than to suppose that something material was created out of nothing. But we are necessarily driven to one of three conclusions : first, either the supposed existence of matter is a delusion ; or, secondly, something has been created out of nothing ; or, thirdly, that matter existed eternally. Can we believe that mind is the product of matter? How can we account for its existence? Can we conceive it as self-existent? If only one principle or entity can be self-existent, is that entity mind or matter, material or immaterial?

The same difficulties arise in regard to the origin of life as in regard to the origin of intelligence and of conscious existence ; and the question naturally arises, How did life first happen to exist? Can it be that life, by its very nature, was self-existent? Or was there an original self-existent being, who, from his very nature, is the father of all succeeding life, or, figuratively speaking, the fountain from which all succeeding streams of life have flowed?

Speculate as we may, there must be solid truth which would answer all these questions if we are able to discover it. But the difficulty which stares us in the face is the question, How can we discover the foundation truths in regard to these questions? Two thoughts readily arise : First, we may never be able to know these facts ; and, second, it may not be necessary that we should ever know. Another

question is this : if it is beyond the capacity of the human
mind to discover all the facts pertaining to the origin of life
through investigation and study, would a self-existent intelligence be likely to reveal to men the foundation facts in
regard to life's origin? Is it really necessary that man
should know this? If it is, does it not seem likely that a
being who nearly all thoughtful men believe existed eternally
might reveal the most important facts concerning this origin
to man? Men claiming to be inspired and instructed by a
self-existent intelligence have written what they assert to be
a divine revelation in regard to life's origin. Is it improbable that these men have had revealed to them the real
truth? Is it reasonable to believe that all life has been received from a self-existent life?

Can we think of a more probable origin, or name one
easier to be understood? Surely, if it is necessary for us to
know the fundamental truths concerning this question,
should we not reasonably expect that this knowledge would
be revealed to us?

It is easier to ask than to answer these questions ; but our
subject leads us to consider these questions and inquire how
near we may approximate to the proper answers. Following
out these lines of thought, we may assume that everything
compounded from simple substances must have been in
simple elements before it could be compounded; and if
so, the compound body must have come into existence as
such later than these simple elements, and hence, from its
very nature (if the above supposition is correct), the compound cannot be eternal.[1]

---

[1] While discussing questions concerning the origin of things, it is well to remember that we do not for a certainty know what either spirit or matter is; but
we must use these words according to their commonly accepted meanings.

Take, for instance, one of the most common elements in
nature, water : is it not philosophic to suppose that oxygen
and hydrogen existed in immense quantities within the
region occupied by the solar system before these gases
united in the proportion of eight to one in weight and two
to one in volume to form water, under the laws of nature?
Then what power first set the chemical, attractive, or other
forces at work to make the compound? Was it not the
same invisible and eternal power which, under natural laws,
said, let intelligence and brains be united? As the oxygen
might have existed separate from and independent of the
hydrogen, so mind, or intelligence, might have existed prior
to the existence of any physical organs. Who knows to the
contrary?

We must keep in mind that life and intelligence are
essentially different things ; and, although we are accustomed
to group them together, we do not know how intelligence
can exist separate from some kind of life. We suppose that
life may exist without intelligence ; but we believe that intelligence cannot exist without accompanying life. Yet intelligence may linger in a man even when we can detect no
signs of mind remaining. For instance, a pressure upon the
brain may destroy all appearance of intelligence, and the
removal of that pressure restore the power of action to the
brain, and with it the power of memory and reason. This
could not have been the case if the intelligence did not
really exist somewhere (though to our senses in an imperceptible degree), while the pressure continued upon the
brain.

But life exists in a tree without any accompanying manifestations of intelligence which we can see ; and yet we do
not know that trees may not have dim outlines of intelligence ;

but we take it for granted that they have no intelligence. But we have no tangible evidence that any intelligence now exists upon the earth without physical life, as we can perceive no intelligence except in living animals. We infer then that some kind of life must be coexistent with all intelligent action, as intelligence can be manifested only by living beings. But if, on the other hand, the visible manifestations of being in the world imply intelligent organization, then some intelligent power or force must have been coexistent with, if not existent prior to, the first physical organization.

It seems evident that the compound bodies which we now see, cannot, in the very nature of things, have been eternally in existence as such.

Well, then, did these simple elements, or cosmic vapors, rush blindly and by chance into the orderly combinations and exquisitely beautiful arrangements of worlds and systems of worlds as they are now, with all their surprising harmonies, and that without intelligent guidance?

If we can show that at the outset there must have been intelligent guidance, of course intelligence must have been coexistent with the first atom, or at least must have existed before the first ultimate atoms began to be attracted together, or rushed together, as believers in a chance world express it.

If our conceptions concerning the necessary connection of life with intelligence are correct, then a life not connected with a physical organization must have existed in the very beginning (if there ever was a beginning), or at least before the first original atoms of matter began to be attracted together, life being coexistent with the first intelligence. It then appears that life and intelligence would naturally be coexistent, and that each existed antecedent to the very first movements of matter even if they did not precede the very existence of matter. And if life was coexistent with the simple elements of matter, and these elements have existed eternally, it follows that life, or a living principle, must also have existed eternally. But it is as easy for me to conceive that intelligence and some kind of life may have existed prior to the primary elements of matter as to believe that both life and matter are eternal.

Certain men tell us that the human mind cannot conceive of such a thing as self-existent life or intelligence ; but I beg to dissent from that statement, which is simply an assumption, and also to say that, if parties making that statement cannot conceive of self-existent intelligence, it by no means follows that others may not be able to conceive of something pertaining to it, and they have no right to assert that others cannot justly reason about it.

The king of Siam could not understand how water, through the action of cold, could become solid, — for he had never seen ice, — and hence he rejected the statement that water could be made solid as absolutely absurd, because inconceivable to him.

I do not claim that the human mind can fully comprehend the idea of self-existence, or that it can comprehend the idea of the creation of something out of nothing, supposing such a thing ever could have happened ; but we know that something does exist, and the question is how that something came to exist, provided it did not exist eternally.

The creation of something out of nothing seems unthinkable ; and yet the fact of its being unthinkable by no means proves that it could not have been done, although I cannot comprehend any process through which it could have been done.

The mind is a mysterious thing, and no one has any right to assume that others may not understand or comprehend certain things because he cannot comprehend them. So with infinity and space. I have no doubt that some men have a kind of dim comprehension of what has generally been considered incomprehensible. I am not alone in this opinion, for such thinkers as R. W. Emerson and Theodore Parker have plainly intimated as much on this point; and I do not think they can be classed with those who believe too readily in the supernatural, or that they were unduly credulous.

I intend to examine the theory of spontaneous generation, but can now only glance at it, and the examination must be postponed for subsequent treatment.

Dr. Hæckel believes that men and animals have descended from minute living organisms called monera, and that these original organisms came from matter by "spontaneous generation" in the "Laurentian period." This is the way he accounts for the first origin of life upon the earth, rather than admit that it received its existence from a self-existent creator; but I cannot see how it is easier, or indeed how it is as easy, to imagine that matter, without preëxisting intelligence, could originate intelligence through chemical action, as it is to conceive that life and intelligence were originally self-existent. He simply substitutes matter, as the originating power, for living intelligence. Hence his theory of "spontaneous generation" does not help us one particle towards the solution of the question, whence is life? All the evidence in favor of his theory is entirely assumed, for no man ever saw "spontaneous generation," or anything like it. Besides, the investigations of M. Pasteur, the distinguished French chemist and physiologist, during the past fifteen years, aided by the able scientist Prof. Tyndall, and also by the exhaustive experiments of other competent chemists, have apparently exploded the evidence which certain chemists and naturalists had previously adduced in favor of the theory of " spontaneous generation," and proved that facts which they supposed indicated spontaneous generation did not indicate its existence, and that neither in the present nor past history of the world has positive evidence been produced which shows that such a thing as spontaneous generation ever existed.

The germ theory, which shows the fallacy of spontaneous generation theories, of itself does not state how, in the first place, these life-germs came to have existence ; but experiments tend to show that no living creatures now come into existence except through life-germs. As such a thing as spontaneous generation cannot be shown to exist now, is there any good reason to think it ever existed on the earth? The forces of nature (according to all we know, or as far as we can produce any evidence) are not now less than formerly. The doctrine of the conservation of energy, generally accepted by our scientific friends, forbids the idea that any particle of force is ever lost. Every cause now must have its full effect, and that effect must be properly related to and equal to its cause, and *vice versa*.

And until some one can show that in some past time present laws of cause and effect did not exist we must believe that they have existed substantially the same as now ever since, and probably before, this earth was condensed into its present nearly globular shape.

So now, as man begets man, life begets and has begotten life, and there can be no new life except from antecedent life. We could never have had life, according to the present laws of nature, unless there was antecedent life.   But there must have been an original life ; and that original, or first life could not have been begotten, from the want of any pre-existing life to beget it ; and hence we are forced to the conclusion that this original life was self-existent.

Advocates of the spontaneous generation theory, however, try to avoid this last conclusion by assuming that " spontaneous generation " existed in the early ages of the earth ; and they assume this without definite evidence that such a thing ever existed, and against what appears to be almost conclusive evidence that it has no present existence.

Now let some one show that, from the nature of the case, there could not be an original, self-existent, living, intelligent being, and then I will confess the reasonableness of the wildest scepticism concerning a belief in an original self-existent creator.   But in default of this, I must insist that it is reasonable to believe that all the life of which we see the manifestations is derived from a self-existent fountain of life, and is produced through infinite creative power.

How life comes into existence through secondary causes and is developed through the laws of nature will be considered in other chapters.

CHAPTER IV.

DEVELOPMENT THEORIES.

IN a previous chapter I inquired respecting the origin of life, and it is now proper to examine various theories concerning development of life ; for some biologists assert that all present living beings have descended from one common ancestor.

One of these theories is known as the hypothesis of Lamarck ; another, the Darwinian, — a great advance and improvement upon Lamarck's. Some who advocate these or like theories think they see a complete chain of life from the lowest to the highest types.

There is a common tendency among many who advocate radical development theories to accuse such as cannot see the consistency of extreme theories of lacking intelligence, or in effect saying that the reason why some men do not understand and fully accept these theories is because of their ignorance, or want of logical power.

It is well known that Sir Charles Lyell, the eminent geologist, came reluctantly to agree to a part of Darwin's theories. In commenting upon this reluctance, Prof. Allen, in his biographical sketch of Lyell in "Popular Science Monthly," March, 1882, writes : "I have illustrated this matter thus fully because it is one which very clearly shows the weak side of Lyell's intellect. With all his breadth of mind and freedom from prejudice, he was not ever one of those who really get to the deepest bottom of things. His tendencies were all in the right direction, and his instinct always inclined him to the true solution ; but he did not build himself up a set of first principles to start with, firmly based upon a philosophical foundation, and make these the fixed criteria of his judgments throughout." [1]

In Mr. Allen's article I find no other facts stated which indicate any lack of deep reasoning, except this one, viz., that it did not comport with Lyell's judgment to readily and fully embrace the popular development theories, including the supposed descent of man from ape-like mammals.

I mention this instance — by no means an uncommon one — from the fact that I have been particularly struck with the number of statements which occur in the writings of certain authors charging a lack of intelligence against those who do not accept doctrines of radical evolutionists.

That all life on the earth is modified by, or made to conform to, external as well as internal conditions is so perfectly natural that it was impressed upon the writer's mind before he has any recollection of learning that it was taught by men of science. If we vary the conditions surrounding us, whether in regard to climate, light, heat, or moisture, those very changed conditions must modify the physical systems of men, and with these physical modifications will come somewhat analogous mental changes. For instance, the reason that most of the inhabitants of Africa are negroes is not necessarily because they originally sprung from black progenitors, but rather because of the physical character-

---

[1] David Hume would hardly agree with Mr. Allen in regard to making a set of "first principles" "fixed criteria of judgments throughout." He says (Essays, p. 93), "When a philosopher has once laid hold of a favorite principle which perhaps accounts for many natural effects, he extends the same principle over the whole creation, and reduces to it every phenomenon, though by the most violent and absurd reasoning."

istics of that continent taken in connection with habits of living through many generations. These peculiar characteristics, however, originated anterior to any historical records. When European nations have colonized tropical countries, the descendants of these colonists have not taken on the peculiar characteristics of negroes, but generally, after a few generations, these descendants have ceased to produce offspring, and hence the races have run out. This fact strikingly shows how necessary certain environments are to the very existence of any race. Had these descendants been able to continue through many generations, perhaps some traits of negroes might have appeared in them.

Different races of animals and men live on the earth because the earth is fitted to be their place of residence, and not because they were first made to live whether their physical surroundings were suitable or not. Make the physical changes in the character of the earth great enough, and not a human inhabitant could exist upon it. Doubtless evolution through natural selection has had an immense influence in shaping the character and kinds of life, but it is doubtful whether it has done all that the ardent advocates of the doctrine believe it has.

Guyot teaches that even the mountains and the sound of the winds of a country will cause harshness or melody in the sounds of human language. To a certain extent man must be dependent upon physical environments; and whatever doctrines we may advocate concerning the origin and descent of species, and however great or however little stress we may lay upon the laws of heredity, natural selection, or any other theory of evolution, we must admit that the operations of laws of evolution go far beyond mere animals and plants. They probably extend even to the formation of worlds; and yet no man ever saw any one race of beings transformed into another distinct race.

The general positions of evolutionists are probably correct, yet it does not necessarily follow that all their assumptions are correct. Among those which may be fairly considered of doubtful character may be mentioned that of the supposed development of the human race from a catarrhine species of apes.

It may be asked, why, if the writer is inclined to think that the theory of the descent of men from animals somewhat resembling apes may be shown to be probably true, he does not say so, and let the matter rest there?

He does not desire to express any decided opinion concerning the actual scientific value of this hypothesis; but the conviction is forced on his mind that, whether the hypothesis is correct or incorrect, it is put forth by radical evolutionists with a greater degree of positiveness than our present knowledge on the subject justifies. But this theory now seems to be making strong headway, and carries before it most of those who do not stop to question the validity of widely prevalent ideas, and it has all the advocates it needs. The danger now is that important facts which appear to point in another direction may be overlooked.

If, however, the writer must choose between the old belief in several universal cataclysms, by which all the animals which have inhabited the earth at certain geological periods have been suddenly swept entirely off and a new set of animals suddenly created by successive almighty fiats, and the doctrine that the various species of animals which now inhabit the earth have been developed by infinitesimal and almost imperceptible accretions through immense ages from previously existing varieties, and these from one or more

original germs, he thinks there is no doubt that the latter
theory agrees better with what we know of the workings of
nature's laws, and thus it may seem probable that man is
really of animal extraction ; but, if so, it is likely that the race
branched off long before the state of apehood was reached,
and some reasons for this opinion can be given.   My efforts
will be directed toward showing that this descent might not
be through apes, and facts will be produced which throw
doubt upon his animal extraction.

The writer takes ground in common with evolutionists on
certain points as stated by Prof. Edward S. Morse in
" Popular Science Monthly," December, 1876, p. 189, viz. :
" If man has really been derived from an ancestor in common
with the ape, we must expect to show, first, that in his
earlier stages he recalls certain persistent characters in the
apes ; second, that the more ancient man will reveal more
ape-like features than the present existing man ; and, third,
that certain characteristics pertaining to early men still per-
sist in the inferior races of men."   Prof. Morse then devotes
several pages attempting to prove that such characteristics
do pertain to the earliest races of men.   He cites measurements and descriptions by Prof. Wyman of certain skulls
and bones found in the United States, and microcephalic
skulls from other places, and also mentions the Neanderthal
and Engis skulls.   Why he does not quote from the Duke
of Argyll, who writes concerning an ancient skull, " This
most ancient of all known human skulls is so ample in its
dimensions that it might have contained the brains of a
philosopher," the writer does not know.

Suffice to say, however, that from the evidence which he
mentions, Prof. Morse draws the conclusion that, " To a
mind unbiassed by preconceived opinions, and frankly willing

to interpret the facts as they stand revealed by the study of these ancient remains the world over, the evidence of man's lowly origin seems, indeed, overwhelming."

Notwithstanding the apparent probability that Prof. Morse is correct in this conclusion, the evidence given does not appear to be "*overwhelming*." But, without taking exception to the excellent spirit in which the Professor writes, I cannot help remarking that here indeed trouble comes, perhaps from " preconceived opinions ; " but it is pertinent to ask whether it was on account of "preconceived opinions" that Virchow declared at Munich that " at this moment there are few naturalists who are not of opinion that man is allied to the rest of the animal world. Vogt is of opinion that a connection will be found, if not with apes, then, perhaps, in some other direction. I should not be alarmed if proof were found that the ancestors of man were vertebrated animals. I work by preference in the field of anthropology, yet I must declare that every step of positive progress which we have made in the domain of prehistoric anthropology has really moved farther away from the proof of this connection." He further states that, " only ten years ago, when a skull was found in peat, or in the lake dwellings, a wild and undeveloped state was seen in it. We were then scenting monkey air. But these old troglodytes turn out to be quite respectable society."

Some may try to evade the force of this by asserting that Virchow is not a consistent evolutionist. But on p. 840, " Popular Science Monthly," October, 1882, the following statement occurs concerning Virchow : " His attitude towards Darwinism has been likewise misapprehended. Far from being an opponent of Darwinism, he should be regarded as one of its forerunners."

Is it on account of "preconceived opinions" that Prof. Boyd Dawkins (who is styled by Grant Allen a "consistent and bold evolutionist") states that, in his opinion, the "cave" or "river-drift" men were fully equal to the modern Esquimaux?

Is it on account of "preconceived opinions" that Dr. Mitchell, of Edinburgh, gives his opinion that the "cave men" were fully equal to the present races of savages, if not equal to the present average Englishmen?

Now let us shift our question. Was it on account of "preconceived opinions" that a great many evolutionists ten years since were "scenting monkey air?" and so much so that questionable facts concerning certain peculiarities pertaining to fossil specimens of men and animals were colored to make them support the opinions of those who believe that man must of necessity have descended from ape-like ancestors? This disposition to grasp every fact which is doubtful in character, and claim that the very fact of its being doubtful argues in favor of the animal descent of man, appears to be *prima facie* evidence that such claimants are at least partially aware that no unequivocal evidence pointing directly to such animal origin has been discovered.

Some writers suppose that the fossil human skulls, concerning which so much has been written, may not have belonged to primitive men at all. These men might have lived upon the outskirts of a much higher civilization then existing, and at the same time in other parts of the earth much higher races of men may have lived.

The difference of the style of living and the culture may have been as great between men inhabiting Egypt and Europe in those remote times as the difference which now exists between the highest nations of Europe and the present Egyptians.

When the men who bore the Engis and Neanderthal skulls were living and acting their parts, races of much higher culture and mental ability may have lived in localities around Persia, China, or Babylonia. Who knows to the contrary?

The real value of any hypothesis may be approximately known by the number of facts which it fairly explains, or which are fairly explained by it. For instance, if out of ten well-known facts nine appear to perfectly agree with or be consistent with an hypothesis, and only one known fact is apparently inconsistent with the supposed hypothesis, then, generally speaking, we may say that there are nine chances in ten that the hypothesis is a correct one. If one fact appears utterly inconsistent with the hypothesis, then we may justly reject the hypothesis, or hold the theory provisionally, and look for further light.

Thus, with the general theory of evolution, so many facts appear to be perfectly consistent with it, and so few apparently inconsistent with it, it must be confessed that the probabilities of its general correctness greatly outweigh the probabilities that it is not correct.

But it is one thing for a general theory to be correct, and quite another to assert that all the apparent inferences from that theory must of necessity be correct.

Let us now briefly examine the common assertion that if the workings of nature are always consistent, man must of necessity have descended through the lower animals.

That a healthy reaction against inordinate haste to assume as proved the statement that man *must* have descended from ape-like animals has set in is one of the favorable signs of the times. If we are to proclaim such an origin, let it be from proper evidence, and not by jumping to a conclusion from a limited number of specimens. According to Virchow, as above quoted, the latest geological and paleontological evidence seems to point away from rather than towards proof of man's animal extraction.

Narrowed down, the question at issue is, Are the laws relating to the origin and development of man in any way different from those pertaining to the origin and development of the rest of the animal creation? or, Was the way or method of man's creation in any way different from that by which other animals were originally produced?

The writer does not presume to assert that man was produced by an exceptional method; but he does assert that the contrary has not been shown; and some facts would seem to indicate that the laws relating to the production of man may possibly have been different from those which were most active in the origin and development of other animals.

Huxley pertinently remarks in regard to his own opinions: "We scientific men get an awkward habit — no, I won't call it that, for it is a valuable habit — of reasoning, so that we believe nothing unless there is evidence for it; and we have a way of looking upon belief which is not based upon evidence not only as illogical but as immoral."

But the particular point to which attention will be first called is not so much the question of actual fact concerning the line of man's descent as the dogmatic style of argument favored by some radical advocates of the theory of man's descent from pithecoid ancestors. These dogmatic assertions are repeated, notwithstanding the fact that such a competent anthropologist as Quatrefages says that certain changes in the skulls of men and apes as they go from youth to adult life show that man could not have descended from a pithecoid ancestor.

In the "Contemporary Review" for March, 1883, Rev. George Edmundson writes as follows : "Popular scientific lecturers and writers have acquired in these days a very unpleasant habit of dogmatism. They assume an air of infallibility, and express in no measured language their mean opinion of those who do not swallow a new-fangled doctrine, however unpalatable or distasteful, without making one wry face. Science is declared to be the unerring guide to all truth and its teachings. Well, 'New professor is but old prophet writ large.' Not such is the spirit of truly great discoverers and thinkers, men of the stamp of Newton and of Darwin : such men are always modest and reserved in their assertions; but the mantle of the master does not always descend upon the disciple."

Dr. Lionel Beale, several years since also noticed the tendency to disparage the intelligence of disbelievers in certain theories, and writes (pp. 103, 104, "Matter of Life ") : " If a physical writer should be in any doubt about gaining the desired number of converts to his views, and should feel a little misgiving lest some of his readers might not be inclined to accept the conclusions upon which he desired they should rely, it would be easy for him to add to his arguments a little literary terrorism. He might remark with effect, that, ' an argument like the above must, indeed, be convincing to any one who possesses any mind at all. He who hesitated to accept such a demonstration would thereby prove himself to be foolish, or savage, or both ; ' and so forth, the metaphors being varied from time to time to suit the circumstances of each particular case."

Even so eminent a naturalist and scholar as Hæckel, a

man who ought to be above all attempts at intellectual or literary terrorism, is moved to say (p. 332, "History of Creation," vol. 2) : " The recognition of the theory of development and the monistic philosophy based upon it forms the best criterion for the degree of man's mental development." On the contrary, it may be confidently asserted that there is now a large proportion of partial students of natural history who accept so-called scientific statements which they cannot comprehend, in a way quite analogous to what obtained during the middle ages, when men accepted theological dogmas they could not comprehend; and their fears of the social consequences from rejection of scientific dogmas are as real though of a somewhat different kind. Hence you will frequently hear men who confess they never read a page from the writings of Darwin, Lamarck, or Hæckel say, "Well, it really seems that the evolutionists have proved their case; for nearly all intelligent scientific men have accepted the doctrines of evolution."

However, there are several rational examples of men in high position who indorse Darwin in the main, and honestly state their positions, and also as honestly state that part of Darwin's hypothesis has not been proved, and in fact may be incapable of proof in our present state of knowledge. Among such authors may be mentioned Darwin himself and Huxley. They certainly have done much to help men in important lines of investigation.

But we meet two classes of evolutionists : the one recognizes an intelligent power behind and directing all the phenomena of evolution; while the other can see only a blind and unintelligent force directing nature's laws, but concerning the nature of which force we are and must be in total ignorance. This last class is apt to be the most positive in their assertions that their propositions must inevitably prove correct.

But the constant repetition by the atheistic that certain supposed ways of working by the Creator are not scientific, and that those who do not assent to those assertions are either ignorant or illogical, is of questionable taste, to say the least.   Can such bind the Creator to work just in their own way or not at all?   Who is the author of the very laws of nature?

We grant that if the Deity in creating man has chosen to work upon the Darwinian or Lamarckian plan He has the power and right to do so, just as well as upon some other plan.

The simple question at issue is one of fact, viz., has He done so?

All statements that He must have done so, and that it would be unscientific to suppose He could do any other way, are the merest non-sequiturs, and the pretence that science has thrown any decisive light on the way life first came into existence is the boldest quackery, as all careful students of facts concerning life's origin well know.   If the rocks show that creation came about in a certain way, bring out the facts.   Facts, and not unsupported theories, are what we want.

Huxley has well described what should be understood by scientific reasoning ; and it is but just to say that, while all proper deference should be paid to scientific statements, there is as much real scientific cant as there is religious cant. On p. 57, " Origin of Species," Huxley writes as follows : "You have all heard it repeated, I dare say, that men of science work by means of induction and deduction, and that by the help of these operations, they, in a sort of sense, wring from nature certain other things, which are called natural laws, and causes, and that out of these, by some cunning skill of their own, they build up hypotheses and theories. And it is imagined by many that the operations of the common mind can be by no means compared with these processes, and that they have to be acquired by a sort of special apprenticeship to the craft. To hear all these large words, you would think that the mind of a man of science must be constituted differently from that of his fellow-men ; but if you will not be frightened by terms you will discover that you are quite wrong, and that all these terrible apparatus are being used by yourselves every day and every hour of your lives."

"Probably there is not one here to-night who has not in the course of the day had occasion to set in motion a complex train of reasoning, of the very same kind, though differing of course in degree, as that which a scientific man goes through in tracing the causes of natural phenomena." In another place he says (pp. 54, 55) : "I must dwell a little on this point, for I wish you to leave this room with a very clear conviction that scientific investigation is not, as many people seem to suppose, some kind of modern black-art. I say that you might easily gather this impression from the manner in which many persons speak of scientific inquiry, or talk about inductive and deductive philosophy, or the principles of the 'Baconian philosophy.' I do protest that, of the vast number of cants in this world, there are none, to my mind, so contemptible as the pseudo-scientific cant which is talked about the 'Baconian philosophy.'"

As Huxley further explains, if you buy an apple that is hard and green, and you find it sour, and then buy another hard and green, and find the same result, you suspect that

all hard and green apples may be sour. This is inductive
reasoning. Does not any farmer's boy know enough to reason
in this way? But suppose he should afterwards find apples
that were hard and green which were not sour, then he would
say that the conclusions he drew from the first two apples
were wrong in certain cases, and he would also see that his
first deduction was wrong, or at least that his rule was not
of universal application. The great trouble with present
scientific men is that they are inclined to go too fast, and
draw their conclusions from too few facts. And this is
especially true in regard to theories claimed to result from
the teachings of geology.

On p. 38, "Origin of Species," Huxley writes, concerning
the amount of our geological knowledge, as follows : " Under
these circumstances it follows that, even with reference to
that kind of imperfect information which we can possess, it
is only about the ten-thousandth part of the accessible parts
of the earth that has been examined properly. Therefore,
it is with justice that the most thoughtful of those who are
concerned in these inquiries insist continually upon the imperfection of the geological record ; for, I repeat, it is absolutely necessary, from the nature of things, that that record
should be of the most fragmentary and imperfect character.
Unfortunately this circumstance has been constantly forgotten. Men of science, like young colts in a fresh pasture,
are apt to be exhilarated on being turned into a new field of
inquiry, and to go off at a hand-gallop, in total disregard of
hedges and ditches, losing sight of the real limitation of their
inquiries, and to forget the extreme imperfection of what is
really known. Geologists have imagined that they could
tell us what was going on at all parts of the earth's surface
during a given epoch ; they have talked of this deposit

being contemporaneous with that deposit, until, from our little local histories of the changes at limited spots of the earth's surface, they have constructed a universal history of the globe as full of wonders and portents as any other story of antiquity."

This is the candid testimony of a strictly scientific man; for in his writings I have never seen any intimation that he . believes in any supernatural revelation. His book of revelation consists of science and its teachings.

The human intellect is a wondrously complicated piece of machinery, and men equally intelligent and equally learned differ in their conclusions when the same facts are placed before them. Especially is this true in matters where truth must be definite and cannot contradict itself. One would naturally suppose that scientific reasoning from the same data would invariably lead to the same conclusions; but the fact is quite the reverse. Especially is this so in regard to the matter of our previous inquiry, " Whence is life?" And like differences arise concerning the other question which we now have under consideration, viz., given life already originated, how has it been developed into the living creatures we now see around us?

When examining this question, certain evidence will weigh heavily in one mind, and the same evidence be considered very light by another mind.

When searching for scientific truth all agree that we ought to lay aside all prejudice, and come with the most sincere desire to ascertain just what the exact truth is; and it is of no consequence, so far as actual truth is concerned, whether one man believes a fact to be truth or not: truth is always truth; and no man's opinion can alter an actual fact.

But, when we try to philosophize about truths which are, in a measure, concealed, the opinions of intelligent men who have investigated these lines of truth should have due weight in shaping our opinions.

This is especially true respecting certain statements, which, from their very nature, must be hard to comprehend ; for we should bear in mind, in regard to many assertions concerning the origin and development of life, that, with our present knowledge, we cannot with certainty tell whether they are based on truth or not, though we well know that they must be either true or false.

I cannot better illustrate this than by comparing the opinions of two learned naturalists, Louis Agassiz and Ernst Hæckel, in regard to the origin of species. Agassiz came to the investigation of this question with a great reverence for the Creator of all things, whom he believed to be an Almighty Intelligence. Hæckel comes to the subject from an exactly opposite stand point.

However, when we attempt to compare the opposite positions taken in their published works in regard to the origin of species, we should bear in mind that the " Classification of Species," by Agassiz, was written before the publication of Darwin's "Origin of Species ; " and if Agassiz had had the benefit of Darwin's investigations previous to writing his " Classification " doubtless he would have written differently in several respects.

One test of the clearness with which any debater sees his conclusion may be observed in his manner of carrying on the discussion. The man (other things being equal) most cloudy in his appreciation of the exact truth is most likely to lose his temper in the discussion, and perhaps accuse his opponent with not properly treating the subject, or of being ignorant and lacking intelligence. Above all, when discussing a subject concerning which neither knows with certainty what the truth is, this bitterness is likely to be manifested. Cloudiness of perception has been the fruitful source of religious persecution. Because religious bigots could not demonstrate their statements to be true, and because their declarations were not received for truth without demonstration, the fagot and the Inquisition have been brought into requisition. Let us lay it down as a general rule in scientific as well as in religious discussions that the party who sees most clearly the truth will be most tolerant of the mistakes of opponents, especially when he has reason to believe these mistakes are honest ones. Because of his confidence in what he believes to be true he will have additional confidence that he can make others see the truth, and thus can afford to wait till time shall make the facts plain.

I propose to quote somewhat from the writings of various authors, that the reader may get a clear idea of the wide divergence of conclusions at which they arrive, while each has the same facts from which to draw his conclusions.

All scientific investigations, however, should be based on the rejection of all hypotheses that apparently contradict common-sense until such hypotheses are proved true beyond reasonable doubt.

Men naturally love new views, and if these views tend to undermine long-settled convictions, the charm is all the greater, with a large proportion of studious men. It must be admitted, however, that some (through previous habits of thought) hold on to antiquated ideas, when it would be much better if they would open their minds to receive new views of truth.

Dr. Hæckel states the radical evolutionary position as

follows (vol. 2, "History of Creation," p. 278) : "The most ancient ancestors of man, as of all other organisms, were living creatures of the simplest kind imaginable, organisms without organs, like the still living monera. They consisted of simple, homogeneous, structureless and formless little lumps of mucus, or albuminous matter (protoplasm), like the still living Protamœba primitiva." "The form value of these most ancient ancestors of man was not even equal to that of a cell, but merely that of a cytod, for, as in the case of all monera, the little lump of protoplasm did not as yet possess a cell-kernel. The first of these monera originated in the beginning of the Laurentian period, by spontaneous generation, or archigony, out of so-called 'inorganic combinations,' namely, out of simple combinations of carbon, oxygen, hydrogen, and nitrogen."

"The assumption of this spontaneous generation, that is, of a mechanical origin of the first organisms from inorganic matter, has been proved, in our thirteenth chapter, to be a necessary hypothesis."

The way Hæckel proves this is shown by the following extract from vol. 1, "History of Creation," pp. 347, 348 : —

"The origin of the first monera by spontaneous generation appears to us as a simple and necessary event in the process of the development of the earth. We admit that this process, as long as it is not directly observed or repeated by experiment, remains a pure hypothesis.

"But I must again say that this hypothesis is indispensable for the consistent completion of the non-miraculous history of the creation, that it has absolutely nothing forced or miraculous about it, and that certainly it can never be positively refuted."

But we are not yet through our difficulties. If we admit

that probably the origin of all life came through spontaneous generation of monera, how many of these monera were at first so generated? Did all life descend from one single original microscopic speck, that is from one single moner? To make Hæckel's theory consistent, it seems to me that we must presume that all living beings are either descended from one single original moner, or else suppose that monera may still be spontaneously generated.

The gist of his argument is this : that this spontaneous generation hypothesis " can never be positively refuted," and does not necessitate anything miraculous about creation, and, notwithstanding there never has been any proof of its existence either by experiment or observation, yet, as the hypothesis seems perfectly consistent, and cannot be " positively refuted," it should be received and considered to be true. Here the doctor completely begs the question when he assumes that the creation was non-miraculous ; for the question whether it was or was not miraculous contains the gist of the whole matter in dispute. If he was possessed of infinite knowledge, and was in every way infallible, his authority would constitute a final answer to the question. But, being of a sceptical turn of mind, I am led to ask, what does this announcement prove, according to his own statements? Is it not clearly this, viz. : that it is necessary to assume that life came through spontaneous generation, or his doctrine that life and its development can be accounted for through non-purposive causes cannot stand? " Spontaneous generation " is a thing that no man ever saw (as Hæckel himself admits), and, according to the most careful scientific tests, has no present existence, and, in so far as we know, the laws of nature have not changed since they were first instituted, and there seems to be no good reason to believe that " spontaneous generation " ever took place.   Then would not one naturally infer that he has built his mechanical or chemical theory of the origin of life upon a foundation which probably never had an existence ?

He seems to prophesy, as Huxley expresses it, " backwards," and somewhat as Moses did when he wrote, " In the beginning God created the heavens and the earth."

But his statement is varied to suit the advanced knowledge of present times.   Instead of being simply, " in the beginning," it is, " in the beginning of the Laurentian period " the ancestors of men were not created, but spontaneously generated.

He does not attempt to tell us how long ago this took place, but we infer from other statements that the Laurentian period must have been since the earth became cool enough to condense the hot mist, or steam that once enveloped the earth, into water.   We accept this supposition about the temperature of the earth before animal or plant life could exist, inasmuch as it was stated by Thales, six hundred years before Christ, that no animal life could exist without water, and that life came from water : and a statement which has gone so many years without being successfully contradicted must be supposed to be true.   But suppose it should be shown that it is highly probable that life existed on the earth long ages before the " beginning of the Laurentian period," how will that comport with the positive assertion that the " most ancient ancestors of man as of all other organisms " " originated in the beginning of the Laurentian period " ?

Prof. Fiske, in vol. 2, p. 39, " Cosmic Philosophy," says : " It is now generally admitted that even the Laurentian strata are modern compared with the beginnings of life upon our globe."

In reference to an address of Du Bois Reymond, at Leipzig, in 1873, Hæckel says, p. xx., "Evolution of Man": "This eloquent address, the source of such triumph to the opponents of the theory of evolution, the cause of such pain to all friends of intellectual advance, is essentially a great denial of the history of evolution." In that address Du Bois Reymond asserts, concerning the origin of sensation and consciousness, "We shall never know that 'Ignorabimus.'"

On p. xxi. he writes: "With this 'Ignorabimus' the Berlin School of Biology tries to stop science in its advance along the paths of evolution. This seemingly humble but really audacious 'Ignorabimus' is the 'Ignoratis' of the infallible Vatican and of the 'Black International' which it leads; that mischievous host against which the modern civilized state has now at last begun in earnest 'the struggle for culture.'"

It is difficult to see just what the infallible "Vatican" has to do with this fact in natural science. Either Hæckel is right, or he is wrong, in his assumptions concerning the origin and development of life and consciousness, and whether he is right or wrong must be decided by the teachings of natural science.

A scientific fact cannot be changed by scientists, or by statements of pope, cardinal, bishop, or any other ecclesiastic. Facts in natural history cannot be altered; but there evidently is a limit somewhere to our knowledge, and intelligent men differ as to where this line is to be drawn. If Du Bois Reymond thinks we shall never understand the origin of consciousness, and Mr. Hæckel thinks we shall understand this origin, let Hæckel show plainly the *how* of the existence of this origin, and we will believe in him. But running away from the question to anathematize pope, cardinals and churches cannot help us to the desired information. So, of the origin of life, if Hæckel can demonstrate that his order in creation is correct, or the fact that original " spontaneous generation " took place, let him do so, and then we must believe in him, *nolens volens.*

But if Du Bois Reymond differs from him in opinion respecting what are actual facts in natural history, or thinks we can never know for a certainty what are the actual facts in certain phases of the development of life and intelligence, why, on that account, should the Berlin physiologist and the Berlin School of Biology be accused of working to sustain, or in harmony with the " Black International," whatever that may mean?

Much has been written about man's place in nature, and the attempt has been made to show that man has had, and still continues to have, false opinions concerning the importance of the position he holds in nature, and the tendency of the writings of several of the most prominent naturalists has been to show that man has no right to believe he is a being " destined for eternity " or to an immortal existence. They further intimate that this supposition, or rather " delusion," about immortality, in which man indulges, warps his reasoning when considering facts concerning his origin. Also that his belief in immortality makes him think he occupies a radically different sphere from that occupied by other animals, and this gives him false and altogether too exalted ideas of his actual place in nature.

But, query : If a belief in immortality warps his reasoning powers in one way, will not the non-belief in immortality warp the reasoning powers in another way?   Is it possible that belief in one way will warp a sane man's mind in one direction, and that non-belief may not warp his mind in another direction?

On reading Hæckel further, we find another astonishing truth (provided it is truth) stated as follows: In vol. 2, "History of Creation," p. 264, he writes: "Just as the *geocentric* conception of the universe — namely, the false opinion that the earth was the centre of the universe, and that all its other portions revolved around the earth — was overthrown by the system of the universe established by Copernicus and his followers, so the *anthropocentric* conception of the universe — the vain delusion that man is the centre of terrestrial nature, and that its whole aim is merely to serve him — is overthrown by the application (attempted long since by Lamarck) of the theory of descent to man. As Copernicus' system of the universe was mechanically established by Newton's theory of gravitation, we see Lamarck's theory of descent attain its causal establishment by Darwin's theory of selection."

But if it shall be shown that Lamarck's theories are merely suppositions, and far from being demonstrated, and that some parts of Darwin's hypotheses are as yet far from receiving anything like proof; and if we shall find that in our present state of knowledge it is actually impossible to attain to proof of the correctness of these assumptions concerning the descent of man, will not this indicate that the assertions of the doctor are too positive?

Let us see what Huxley (who is one of the strongest supporters of Darwin's views) says of the principal part of Lamarck's hypothesis. In "Origin of Species" (p. 144), he says: " Take the Lamarckian hypothesis, for example. Lamarck was a great naturalist, and, to a certain extent, went the right way to work. He argued from what was undoubtedly a true cause of some of the phenomena of organic nature. He said it is a matter of experience that an animal may be modified more or less in consequence of its desires and consequent actions. Thus, if a man exercise himself as a blacksmith his arms will become strong and muscular; such organic modification is a result of this particular action and exercise. Lamarck thought that by a very simple supposition based on this truth he could explain the origin of the various animal species; he said, for example, that the short-legged birds, which live on fish, had been converted into the long-legged waders by desiring to get the fish without wetting their feet, and so stretching their legs more and more, through successive generations. If Lamarck could have shown experimentally that even races of animals could be produced in this way, there might have been some ground for his speculations. But he could show nothing of the kind, and his hypothesis has pretty well dropped into oblivion, as it deserved to do."

Now, if, on further investigation, it should appear that parts of Darwin's theory of the descent of man may possibly belong alongside of Lamarck's, which " dropped into oblivion, as it deserved to do," what will become of the doctor's *demonstration* founded upon Darwin's hypothesis?

Hæckel considers Lamarck to be the real founder of Darwin's theory, for (on p. 85, vol. 1, " Evolution of Man,") he says : " These are the principal outlines of the theory of Lamarck, now called the theory of descent or transmutation, and to which, fifty years later, attention was again called by Darwin, who firmly supported it with new proofs. Lamarck, therefore, is the real founder of this theory of descent or transmutation, and it is a mistake to attribute its origin to Darwin. Lamarck was the first to formulate the scientific theory of the natural origin of all organisms including man, and at the same time to draw the two ultimate inferences from this theory : firstly, the doctrine of the origin of the most ancient organisms through spontaneous generation ; and, secondly, the descent of man from the mammal most closely resembling man, — the ape."

But let us see how Mr. Huxley agrees with Hæckel upon this point. Huxley (in " Origin of Species," p. 144) says : "I said in an earlier lecture that there are hypotheses and hypotheses, and when people tell you that Mr. Darwin's strongly-based hypothesis is nothing but a mere modification of Lamarck's, you will know what to think of their capacity for forming a judgment on this subject."

I suppose that most men who give careful attention to this subject at once perceive that the moving forces in Lamarck's and Darwin's theories come from radically different points.

Lamarck's initiatory impulses towards development come from wants within the organism ; while the modifying powers, according to Darwin's theory, generally come from without, or through the environments.

But, in trying to fix the proper sphere of man in the animal creation, Hæckel looks at him as a mere animal, and would dissect him as he would a frog or a horse, simply to find out his physiological, morphological, and anatomical structure, regardless of any difference in mental structure between man and other animal existences. In so far as he confines himself to the mere physical structure to the exclusion of all mental characteristics, he may be fair if he states that that is all he is looking for, and providing he does not deny that he ought to take into consideration the mental characteristics when he attempts to fix man's full station.

But he cannot find man's full sphere without taking into consideration his peculiar mental qualities as distinguished from those of the brutes. Hæckel has told us that we must, for the time being, divest ourselves of all our "deep-rooted prejudices" which we have imbibed in our youth, and leave out of consideration all our notions respecting the "spiritual side" of our natures, if we would arrive at the genuine truth respecting our descent. But if we would arrive at the genuine truth of our inheritance, we must take into consideration *all* of the facts bearing on the case; — and we shall be more liable to arrive at false conclusions if we try to restrict the field of observation. Mental as well as physical characteristics are inherited; and my point is, that if there is an essential difference in the mental constitutions of men and the brutes, or a difference so great and marked as to make it appear evident that one mental constitution could not be inherited or developed from the preceding one, then this very fact would seem to show that the physical side, so intimately connected with the mental, could not be inherited from any ape-like animal.

A mere naturalist examining man in physical structure only, as he would a bug or a bee, does not take into consideration the whole man.

CHAPTER V.

MAN IN HIS COMPOUND NATURE.

MAN is a compound animal, having mind as well as body. If it is of no consequence whether there is a radical difference between men and brutes in their mental structures, then to compare them only anatomically or physiologically is fair. But there appears to be a radical mental difference, and hence it is not fair to compare men with mere animals by the physiological organization alone, and by such comparison attempt to fix man's real rank in nature, for nature comprises the mental as well as physical organization. It may be said that beasts have mental traits in many respects like men, — granted; but it is not granted in the highest and most important respect. True, the beasts have loves and hatreds, joys and sorrows, somewhat analogous to those of men; but their sorrows differ from men in this, that the very elements which add depth and intensity to the pangs of sorrow in men arise from their reflective faculties, and their feelings of joy are often most active in anticipation of some future good. There is, however, a disposition to be faithful in some beasts, and some will defend their acquired possessions like men. Dogs lament the loss of friends, as instances of watching the graves of their masters will show.

Animals have memory; and the growth and decay of their bodies are as regular as with men. We may be asked who knows that the lives of the brutes are not coexistent with those of men? If man has a soul, who knows that brutes

have no souls? In what does man differ from brutes except
in the degree of intelligence? This question is a fair one.
But we know what men desire and think about and talk
about. We know they have hopes and fears concerning a
future life, and these hopes and fears seem to be inborn;
but we have no evidence that brutes have the least idea of
any future or spiritual existence; and we have absolutely no
evidence that they have the least apprehension of anything
pertaining to a spiritual life. But we do know that in many
intelligent men one of the very strongest of all desires
centres in the hope of eternal life, or of a conscious existence
after death. Many have suffered death in its most repulsive
forms rather than speak one word indicating a doubt of the
realities of a spiritual existence.

If we call these hopes and fears superstitious, that
does not alter the fact of their existence, nor does it
explain how these hopes and fears came to exist. Notwithstanding the high authority claimed in favor of the ghost
theory, or that the belief in another or spiritual self originally
came from dreams, that does not satisfactorily explain how
men originally came to believe that they possess an *immortal*
self.

Peschel, in regard to another radical difference, says
(p. 5, " Races of Men ") : " We cannot conclude these observations without answering the accusation, which may perhaps be silently made, that we leave out of sight the intellectual functions of mankind. We at once repeat what
Darwin has already said, that the motions of conscience as
connected with repentance, and the feelings of duty, are the
most important differences which separate us from the animal; that in the latter there is no capability of solving a
mathematical problem, or of admiring a landscape painting,

or a manifestation of power. Neither can any reflection take place respecting the correllation of phenomena, and still less as to the hypothesis of a First Cause or a Divine Will."

Hear Mr. Wallace, a naturalist of no mean order, who was getting ready to publish his own theory of development when, in 1859, Darwin hurried up the publication of his book (quoted by Mivart, p. 301) : " Mr. Wallace observes, that on his view man is to be placed ' apart,' as not only the head and culminating point of the grand series of organic nature, but as in some degree a new and distinct order of being." Also, on p. 302, Mivart has the following : "At length, however, there came into existence a being in whom that subtle force we term mind became of greater importance than his mere bodily structure. Though with a naked and unprotected body, this gave him clothing against the varying inclemencies of the seasons. Though unable to compete with the deer in swiftness, or with the wild bull in strength, this gave him weapons with which to capture or overcome both. Though less capable than most other animals of living on the herbs and the fruits that unaided Nature supplies, this wonderful faculty taught him to govern and direct Nature to his own benefit, and make her produce food for him when and where he pleased. From the moment when the first skin was used as a covering; when the first rude spear was formed to assist in the chase ; when fire was first used to cook his food ; when the first seed was sown, or shoot planted, a grand revolution was effected in Nature, a revolution which in all the previous ages of the earth's history had had no parallel ; for a being had arisen who was no longer necessarily subject to change with the changing universe, a being who was in some degree superior to Nature, inasmuch as he knew how to control and regulate her action, and could keep himself in harmony with her, not by a change in body but by an advance in mind."

Physical science probably can never prove or disprove (in a sense of actual demonstration) the reality or non-reality of the existence of a soul either in or separate from the body. What our consciousness witnesses, reason and analogy must be brought into requisition if we would balance these probabilities.

But the objection is urged that speculations concerning our spiritual natures cannot be considered scientific, because neither the positive nor the negative side of the question can be demonstrable; yet these same objectors may speculate concerning the character or nature of the inhabitants of the planets, or concerning the nebular hypothesis, and call such speculations scientific.

Hæckel (in chap. 22, "Hist. of Creation") gives descriptions of manlike apes, and shows how similar they are to men in several respects. But what does this amount to upon the point under consideration until he can show psychological as well as physical similarities? While he tries to show that man holds a certain relationship to the apes he as clearly states that man could not possibly have descended from any of the present races of apes, and that even the fossil remains of the immediate ancestors of man have not yet been discovered.

He says (p. 277, vol. 2, "Hist. of Creation") : "I must here also point out what in fact is self-evident, that not one of all the still living apes, and consequently not one of the so-called Manlike Apes, can be the progenitor of the Human Race. This opinion, in fact, has never been maintained by thoughtful adherents of the Theory of Descent, but it has been assigned to them by their thoughtless opponents. The Ape-

like progenitors of the Human Race are long since extinct.
We may possibly still find their fossil bones in the tertiary
rocks of southern Asia or Africa. In any case, they will,
in the zoölogical system, have to be classed in the group of
tail-less narrow-nosed Apes."

Even the very bones of the supposed ancestors, which
might show the connecting link between man and the supposed ancestral race have never been found, and this is the
very thing needed to furnish anything like *proof* of the
correctness of his supposed line of descent. There is no
geological evidence to show that any ape-like race of animals
from which man could have descended existed prior to or
since man's first existence. There is evidence of man's
very early existence, but no definite evidence has been produced that any ape-men, from which man might have descended, have existed during the whole records of time.
How then can any one positively assert that man has descended from apes when it cannot be shown that ape-men
existed before or since the earliest men? If such ape-men
existed earlier than or even during the earliest periods of
man's existence, why should we not be able to find such a
fossil-monkey or ape-man skull as well as fossil men's
skulls?

Some kinds of apes, or ape-like animals, existed very far
back in the history of the earth. A. R. Wallace, who in general supports Darwin's Theory of Descent, writes ("Popular Science Monthly" for Nov., 1876, p. 64) : "But so far
back as the miocene deposits of Europe, we find the remains
of apes allied to these various forms, and especially the gib-
bons ; so that in all probability the special line of variation
which led up to men branched off at a still earlier period."
This agrees with the statement of Darwin ; but neither

Wallace nor Darwin intimates that he thinks man could possibly have descended from any of the ape-like animals which existed in the miocene periods.

Peschel (pp. 4, 5, "Races of Man") says : "It is only a popular misapprehension, that, by the theory of transmutation of species, man is supposed to be descended from one of the four highest species of apes. Neither Darwin nor any of his adherents ever asserted anything of the sort, but, on the contrary, they maintain that the ancestors of mankind branched off, in the first or earliest part of the tertiary period, from species of the Catarrhine group long since extinct."

But that the reader may see what Darwin says concerning the origin of man, I will quote extracts from Darwin, pp. 155–157, "Descent of Man."

On the birthplace and antiquity of man : " We are naturally led to inquire, where was the birthplace of man at that stage of descent when our progenitors diverged from the Catarrhine stock? The fact that they belonged to this stock clearly shows that they inhabited the Old World, but not Australia nor any oceanic island, as we may infer from the laws of geographical distribution. In each great region of the world the living mammals are closely related to the extinct species of the same region. It is therefore probable that Africa was formerly inhabited by extinct apes closely allied to the gorilla and chimpanzee; and as these two species are now man's nearest allies, it is somewhat more probable that our early progenitors lived on the African continent than elsewhere. But it is useless to speculate on this subject; for two or three anthropomorphous apes, one the Dryopithecus of Lartet, nearly as large as a man, and closely allied to Hylobates, existed in Europe during the

Miocene age; and since so remote a period the earth has certainly undergone many great revolutions, and there has been ample time for migration on the largest scale."

" At the period and place, whenever and wherever it was, when man first lost his hairy covering, he probably inhabited a hot country; a circumstance favorable for the frugiferous diet on which, judging from analogy, he subsisted. We are far from knowing how long ago it was when man first diverged from the Catarrhine stock, but it may have occurred at an epoch as remote as the Eocene period; for that the higher apes had diverged from the lower apes as early as the Upper Miocene period is shown by the existence of the Dryopithecus."

" The great break in the organic chain between man and his nearest allies, which cannot be bridged over by any extinct or living species, has often been advanced as a grave objection to the belief that man is descended from some lower form; but this objection will not appear of much weight to those who, from general reasons, believe in the general principle of evolution. Breaks often occur in all parts of the series, some being wide, sharp and defined, others less so in various degrees; as between the orang and its nearest allies, — between the Tarsius and the other Lemuridæ, — between the elephant, and in a more striking manner between the Ornithorhynchus or Echidna, and all other mammals. But these breaks depend merely on the number of related forms which have become extinct. At some future period, not very distant as measured by centuries, the civilized races of man will almost certainly exterminate, and replace, the savage races throughout the world. At the same time the anthropomorphous apes, as Prof. Schaaffhausen has remarked, will no doubt be exterminated. The break between man and his nearest allies will then be wider, for it will intervene between man in a more civilized state, as we may hope, even than the Caucasian, and some ape as low as a baboon, instead of as now between the negro or Australian and the gorilla."

"With respect to the absence of fossil remains, serving to connect man with his ape-like progenitors, no one will lay much stress on this fact who reads Sir C. Lyell's discussion, where he shows that in all the vertebrate classes the discovery of fossil remains has been a very slow and fortuitous process. Nor should it be forgotten that those regions which are the most likely to afford remains connecting man with some extinct ape-like creature, have not as yet been searched by geologists."

Two remarks of Mr. Darwin in the above are especially worthy of attention. The first refers to the fact that serious breaks in the chain of evidence occur, and he says: "This objection will not appear of much weight to those who, from general reasons, believe in the general principle of evolution."

Very true, for, when one becomes a strong believer in the general principles of any theory, it is not difficult for his imagination to supply all the necessary connections so as to make the whole system entirely consistent. If this imagination could be considered in the light of evidence, then almost any popular theory or system might be rounded out into beautiful and symmetrical proportions.

The second assertion is as follows: "With respect to the absence of fossil remains, serving to connect man with his ape-like progenitors, no one will lay much stress on this fact who reads Sir C. Lyell's discussion, where he shows that in all the vertebrate classes the discovery of fossil remains has been a very slow and fortuitous process." Surely so; but why, in effect, assume that the evidence which is lacking would, if it could be discovered, be favorable to one theory, when perhaps by further searching for these missing links something might be discovered which would be the very reverse of favorable to the theory?

It is very strange that while man-like apes nearly as large as a man existed in Europe during the Miocene age, and geological evidence should fully attest that fact, yet we do not find evidence that these apes were developed upward or became of a higher order during the immense time intervening between the Miocene and Pliocene ages. We may talk about the "imperfection of the geological record" with much truth; and the very fact that it is imperfect should make us modest in our assumptions concerning the full purport of its teachings. But, if man has been developed from an ape-like race, why should we not expect to find some direct evidence of the former existence of a race from which man might have descended as well as find the remains of man-like apes which lived long ages before we have any evidence that man existed?

Or, in other words, why should we not find some definite geological evidence of the existence of ape-men before we assume as an undoubted fact that such a race ever existed?

It is also worthy of note that there is a difference of opinion between Darwin and Hæckel in regard to the birthplace of man. In his map Hæckel places the supposed "Paradise?" in Lemuria, a locality now under the waters of the Indian Ocean. Darwin did not think the birthplace of men could have been on any "oceanic island," but that "it is more probable that our progenitors lived on the African continent than elsewhere." Darwin also thought that "when man first lost his hairy covering he probably inhabited a hot country."

Several questions naturally arise from this last idea. First, how does any one know that man ever had a "hairy covering" to lose? Those who believe in Hæckel's law of biogeny may conclude, from the fact that the human embryo for three or four months previous to birth is covered with woolly hair, that this is evidence that man's ancestors once had a "hairy covering." Hæckel says (vol. 2, pp. 206, 207, "Evolution of Man") : "During the last three or four months before birth the human embryo is usually covered by a thick coating of delicate woolly hairs. This embryonic wool-covering is often lost during the last weeks of embryonic life, and, at any rate, soon after birth, when it is replaced by the thinner permanent hair covering."

"Occasionally the dark hair is retained for several weeks, or even months, after birth. This remarkable woolly covering can only be explained as an inheritance from our primordial long-haired ancestors, the Apes."

Surely this is a very clear explanation ; but it lacks one important element, viz., proof of the truth of its inference, viz., that because the human embryo has a hairy covering which it generally loses before birth, therefore its primordial ancestors must have had a hairy covering, which their human descendants have lost.

We must infer from the theory of natural selection that this loss of the original "hairy covering" (if it ever occurred) was of special advantage, for "the survival of the fittest," or the most useful, is its motto. Possibly, in a very hot climate, loss of hair might be an advantage. But how about such advantage to those who inhabit a very cold climate? Would not this "hairy covering" (which it is supposed they lost) be of immense advantage to men who inhabit a cold climate? According to the foundation principles of "natural selection," why should not a "hairy" or fur-like covering now grow to protect men who need such a covering?

Is "Nature blundering," as Lewes expresses it?

It is said that at the time of birth the young of apes are hairless, and that hair is an after-growth. Does not this very fact seem to indicate that the development of men and apes is in this respect in entirely different directions? And may not this also indicate that this supposed hairy covering never existed on the ancestors of men?

But we will further consider the probability of the truth of this descent theory from diverse points of view. There are many things involved, and circumstances to be considered, besides those which relate to mere anatomy, morphology, or physiology. Before we assume that man is a mere animal, and nothing more, it will be well to explain how the belief that man has a spiritual nature has become so nearly universal. Are these hundreds of millions of intelligent men who believe in a spiritual existence all deluded? Certainly they must be, if there is no spiritual existence. But before we assert dogmatically that all these millions are deluded would it not be well to exhibit something in the nature of proof that such is the case, rather than depend upon mere assertions?

Because a thousand men deny that there is any such thing as spiritual existence, when, from the very nature of the case, they cannot know whether it exists or not, these denials, no matter how positively made, are no evidence that spiritual existences may not be real entities. We must make certain allowances for almost universal convictions when reasoning concerning matters, which, from their very nature, must be uncertain, or our doctrines will rest upon very insecure foundations. It is useless to repeat as applicable to this case the fact that the ancients were deceived when thinking that the earth stood still, and that the sun revolved around it. Conceptions and convictions of a spiritual nature are of a very different kind.

Desires and aspirations after continued existence are in the very constitutions of our natures. How came these, and how were these desires implanted? Desires for long life are one means of securing the continuance of life. When a healthy man craves food we naturally infer that such food is needed, and also that such craving is one means used by nature to indicate what is necessary for continued corporeal existence. When we assert the universal and harmonious application of nature's laws shall we overlook these mental laws, and say that all mental desires are mere shadows, and without any reality behind them? Is life really a complete mockery?

The apparently inborn conceptions and convictions concerning man's spiritual nature are not things which can be measured by a mathematical rule, or discovered by microscope or telescope, for spirit (if it exists) is invisible. Rules of reasoning which properly apply to purely material substances may not be at all applicable to spiritual matters. The materialist denies that spiritual existences are real. How does he know this? To assume that such is the fact is begging the question; for he knows not whether spiritual existences are real or unreal.

I place the almost universal convictions of mankind (however these convictions may have originated) against any dogmatic assertions that these convictions are all delusions; and, if they are not delusions, then materialistic doctrines cannot be true, and man is a compound of physical and spiritual existence.

Certain doctrines concerning man's descent take for granted the assumption that man, outside of his physical organization, can have no spiritual nature, and that intelligence and life cannot exist separate from a physical system ; but until some different kind of evidence is produced to show that man may not have a spiritual as well as a physical nature, any theory built upon such a negative assumption must, of necessity, rest upon uncertain foundations.

One strange characteristic of many professedly scientific reasonings is, that while their authors treat those arguments which tend to induce a belief in man's spiritual nature as entirely unscientific unless they are based upon clearly demonstrable facts, yet, when they argue for their own favorite theories from positions which they have never shown to rest upon the rock-bed of truth, they proclaim themselves to be the champions of purely scientific methods.

The theory that man descended from certain man-like apes is founded almost entirely upon analogies drawn from the production of plants and animals ; and so long as no bones of any race from which man could have sprung by direct descent have been found, why should we (upon the evidence offered) receive the theory as anything beyond an hypothesis which future investigation may or may not show to have truth for its foundation ?

This theory of descent appears plausible, and also seems to accord with much which we know of the operations of nature's laws. The chief objection which I now raise is against the *positiveness* with which the truth of the theory is asserted. There can be no doubt as to how the laws of evolution apply in the development of each human being from a single cell; nor that the intellectual and moral faculties which so distinguish the man from the brute are, in some sense, the result of progressive development; and surely this line of development *may* be typical of man's line of descent from an original one-celled ancestor, but the burden of proof is on the other side.

Such bones as evolutionists state should belong to the immediate ancestors of man may yet be found; but when a theory so different from what has generally been supposed to be true is proposed, something besides analogies should be adduced before it should be placed in the region of proved facts.

I am aware that the answer will be that nature always acts in a uniform way, and that, if the doctrine of evolution in regard to the lower animals is correct, it is only reasonable to conclude that the same laws must also apply to the development of man; and if a lower order of animals can be developed into a higher order, then man has probably been developed from a lower order. But if, while man is an animal he is also something more than animal, then, as before intimated, another factor comes in to modify our reasonings and analogies. But nature does not always work in the same direction of development. If she worked universally from the lower to a higher state of development, we might assume that there could not be any exceptions to the direction of developments. But there are very notable exceptions.

The author of "Cosmic Philosophy," himself a strong evolutionist, states, in a note to pp. 450, 451, vol. 1 : —

"Kowalewsky has discovered some wonderful likenesses between the embryonic development of the ascidian and that of the amphioxus, or lowest known vertebrate. Of all the 'missing links,' the assumed absence of which is so persistently cited by the adherents of the dogma of fixity of species, the most important one would here appear to have been found; for it is a link which connects the complex and highly-evolved vertebrate with a very lowly form which passes its natural existence rooted plant-like to the soil, or rather to the sea-bottom. The ascidian cannot, indeed, be regarded as typifying the direct ancestors of the vertebrata. It is a curiously aberrant and degraded form, and its own progenitors had doubtless once 'seen better days.' In its embryonic state it possesses a well-marked vertebral column, and it behaves in general very much as if it were going to grow to something like the amphioxus. But it afterwards falls considerably short of this mark. Already in early life its vertebræ begin to become 'rudimentary' or evanescent; and when fully matured it stops swimming about after its prey, and, striking root in the submarine soil, remains thereafter standing, with its broad pitcher-like mouth ever in readiness to suck down such organisms floating by as may serve for its nutriment. That vertebræ should be found in the embryo of such an animal is a most interesting and striking fact. It would seem to mark the ascidian as a retrograded off-shoot of those primitive forms on the way toward assuming the vertebrate structure, of which the more fortunate ones succeeded in leaving as their representative the amphioxus."

This case shows a decided break in the general lines of development; and how many more as striking anomalies may exist we have not yet the means of knowing.

The case of the ascidians used as a " missing link " seems to point in an exactly opposite direction from the general line of evolution.

It much better accords with Plato's theory of degenerations running downward than with the theory that development is always upward. Its manner of development also seems inconsistent with the quite generally proclaimed theory that every vertebrate in its immature condition passes through conditions which pertain to all orders of the animal creation which are below it.

Reasoning from analogy, may we not as justly assume (for all that has been shown to the contrary) that man may have a line of development from ancestral races as different from the general line as that which we find in the ascidians?

So long as the brain is the organ of the mind, man's real position in nature and the probabilities relating to his line of descent cannot be fully and fairly balanced without keeping prominently in mind his mental structure and the testimony of his consciousness in regard to his position as a moral agent.

But, we may be asked, if ideas of God, immortality, and moral responsibility are innate in man, why not class as beasts certain races of men which seem to have no ideas of a moral nature or a future life?

Upon the question whether such ignorant and degraded races do exist, authorities are divided. Some assert positively that such races do exist; while others as positively assert, that, upon a better or more intimate acquaintance with such races, ideas of God and a future life are found to exist, and that the reason why certain travellers were unable to discover indications of such conception was a want of confidence of these savages in these travellers, but that when one becomes sufficiently intimate with them to acquire their confidence he plainly recognizes evidences of a belief in a Supreme Being or beings. But upon the supposition that races as degraded as above supposed do really exist, I

can't say to what depth of degradation certain races may
have descended, nor from what height of former intellectual
and spiritual development they may have fallen ; but surely
the idea of immortality is implanted in the minds of a majority of the people comprising the most intellectual races,
and if we deny that this idea of immortality is a rational one,
we must admit that these cultivated and fairly educated
people have in some way imbibed more irrational notions
concerning the origin and destiny of our being than such
most ignorant and degraded races have ; for, generally
speaking, the most enlightened races do believe in man's
spiritual nature.

While reflecting upon the strange positions taken by
certain men of acknowledged scientific attainments, it has
seemed to me that the majority of common-sense men, though
less learned, are more likely to be right on the question of
man's destiny than the most learned speculators in the
physical sciences can be, while leaving out of view the spiritual side of man's nature.

Either we must admit that the prevailing belief of the
most intelligent and cultivated races concerning God and
immortality is in its general features probably true, rather
than the negations or absence of belief of the most ignorant races ; or we must admit that such study of things
pertaining to the unknown conditions of existence as the
most intelligent and enlightened races have been accustomed
to give serves to mislead rather than give correct ideas of
the real facts of the case.

It is really curious to observe how extremes meet, — as exemplified in the case of men supposed to be so ignorant and
degraded that they have no ideas of God or of immortal
existence, and hence do not apprehend anything relating to

immortality, and certain learned men who reject doctrines implying the existence of God and the immortality of the human soul. Whether one believes that these lowest races of men are right or wrong concerning a conscious immortal existence, in so far as they have any opinions upon the subject, the strange coincidence still exists between those supposed to be so ignorant as to have no conceptions of a Supreme Intelligence, and atheistic writers, who conceive that an Omniscient and Supreme Intelligence cannot be in existence.

It would appear to be strange if the most degraded and ignorant races and a few of the learned men should be right, while the majority of learned men and the great body of men comprising the fairly intelligent common people should be in the wrong on this question. But it cannot be true that study tends to mislead and draw away from rational truth, if the student gives proper consideration to *all* facts which ought to be considered. The reason why many become atheistic through study is doubtless because they entirely disregard facts pertaining to the "spiritual side of man's nature," and hence while looking at one side they take only partial views of the whole field. What then can we expect, but that they should have one-sided and contracted views? This, it seems to me is just what we do find.

Upon this point the sceptic Hume (whom I suppose, no one will accuse of lack of intelligence) says in his "Essays," p. 551: "Though the stupidity of men, barbarous and uninstructed, be so great that they may not see a Sovereign Author in the more obvious works of nature to which they are so much familiarized; yet it scarcely seems possible that any one of good understanding should reject that idea, when once it is suggested to him."

Again, he says, p. 552, *ibid.* : " The universal propensity
to believe in invisible, intelligent power, if not an original
instinct, being at least a general attendant of human nature,
may be considered as a kind of mark or stamp, which the
Divine Workman has set upon his work ; and nothing surely
can more dignify mankind than to be thus selected from all
other parts of the creation, and to bear the image or impression of the Creator."

" What a noble privilege is it of human reason to attain
the knowledge of the Supreme Being, and, from the visible
works of nature, be enabled to infer so sublime a principle
as its Supreme Creator ! "   " Look out for a people entirely
destitute of religion ; if you find them at all, be assured that
they are but few degrees removed from brutes."

Darwin takes a somewhat different view, as follows,
p. 126, " Descent of Man " : " The ennobling belief in God
is not universal with man ; and the belief in spiritual agencies
naturally follows from other mental powers.   The moral
sense perhaps affords the best and highest distinction between
man and the lower animals."

I will now introduce a witness whom even Hæckel will
not try to discredit, viz., Mr. T. H. Huxley.   Mr. Huxley
has with great ability discussed questions pertaining to the
origin of species, and candidly states that positive proof that
one species of animals has changed into another has not yet
been adduced.

On p. 141, " Origin of Species," writing of changes of
species ; Mr. Huxley says : " For you see, if you have not done
that you have not strictly fulfilled all the conditions of the
problem ; you have not shown that you can produce by the
cause assumed all the phenomena which you have in nature.
Here are the phenomena of hybridism staring you in the

face, and you cannot say, 'I can, by selective modification, produce these same results.' Now it is admitted on all hands that, at present, so far as experiments have gone, it has not been found possible to produce this complete physiological divergence by selective breeding. I stated this very clearly before, and I now refer to the point, because, if it could be proved not only that this *has* not been done, but that it *cannot* be done, if it could be demonstrated that it is impossible to breed selectively, from any stock, a form which shall not breed with another produced from the same stock ; and if we were shown that this must be the necessary and inevitable result of all experiments, I hold that Mr. Darwin's hypothesis would be utterly shattered. But has this been done? Or what is really the state of the case? It is simply that, so far as we have gone yet with our breeding, we have not produced from a common stock two breeds which are not more or less fertile with one another."

Also Huxley writes ("Man's Place in Nature," p. 127) : " But, for all this, our acceptance of the Darwinian hypothesis must be provisional so long as one link in the chain of evidence is wanting ; and so long as all the animals and plants certainly produced by selective breeding from a common stock are fertile, and their progeny are fertile with one another, that link will be wanting ; for, so long, selective breeding will not be proved to be competent to do all that is required of it to produce natural species."

If all the difficulties which Huxley here states have so far prevented the truth of the Darwinian theory concerning changes of species from being demonstrated were removed, even then more evidence would be required before the Darwinian hypothesis of the descent of man could be considered proved. For if, by selective breeding from a common stock, races should be produced so different that they are not fertile between themselves, that would simply show that natural selection *may* account for differences of races of animals ; but that would not show that it can account for the difference between men and animals.

If we could by extra care in selective breeding produce such a race as Mr. Huxley supposes might be produced, it would simply show what could be done under the intelligent guidance of man among animals ; but it would by no means show that such a race ever did or probably ever would be produced through the guidance of mere instinct, or through the dim intelligence of the brutes.   We have no reason for supposing that the general species of animals have had any- thing more than brute intelligence or instinct to guide them towards the almost numberless variations of development which we find.

But if it has not been shown that by the greatest care in selective breeding among animals, under the intelligent guidance of men, the required differences or transmutations of species can be obtained, how long would it take to pro- duce such results by chance-breeding alone, or by natural selection, without intelligent guidance?   And if, among animals quite similar in their general structure and habits, men have not been able to produce new species by careful selected breeding, how long would it take, through blind chance, to develop men from apes?

We must, however, confess that the statement of Agassiz, that each separate existing species represents a separate creative thought of God, does not now find a favorable re- sponse from a majority of naturalists.

If Agassiz were still living, and were again to write upon the same subject, he probably would considerably modify some of his former statements. But we must not be hasty in concluding that he was greatly in error in his statement above quoted ; for the history of past scientific theories in relation to evolution, and creation, including the origin of life, is sufficient evidence of the utter unreliability of theories which may carry all before them in the scientific world for even a century.

Take, for instance, the case of the evolution theory, based upon the idea that every human being that ever lived or ever will live was in the germ in the ovary of Mother Eve, and also the other contrary theory, that all life comes from the male or sperm cell, and that the germs of all subsequent human life were in the loins of Adam. The first theory held its ground against all scientific comers for about a century ; and the second had powerful defenders for about another century. These two theories were disputed about by most intelligent and most learned men, who were pitted against each other in argument for nearly a century, and why ?

Because there were no naturalists or biologists of sufficient learning and ability to convince the world that either of these theories was incorrect, and remove the weight of error that inhered in both. I will now give a short history of these theories, partly taken from the more extended history by Hæckel.

The theory of encasement, or that of the ovulists, viz., that the germs of all subsequent human existences were in the ovaries of Eve, held its ground and was generally accepted till 1690. Then the theory of the animalculists, or that all came from the loins of Adam, took its turn, and the two entered into a contest for supremacy.

Leeuwenhoek, in 1690, started the spermatozoid theory.

And from that came the doctrine that the germs of every human being whieh has ever existed or ever will exist to the very latest time were in the loins of Adam, and that each spermatozoon had in its microscopic proportions en-wrapped the germs of an almost infinite number of human beings who were to sueeeed in all generations. From Hebrews, 7 : 10, it is evident that a similar belief obtained in the time of St. Paul, for he there represents Levi, the great-grandson of Abraham, as paying tithes to Melchisedec while he was in the loins of Abraham.

Abraham's meeting with Melchisedee was several hundred years before the Levitieal priesthood was established. These two theories of evolution, the one of the male running baek to Adam, and the other of the female running back to Eve, had vigorous defenders, and these discussions were continued through the period allotted to several generations.

Among the eelebrated defenders of the ovulist theory were Leibnitz, Bonnet, and Haller.

On the other side were Leeuwenhoek, the originator, and afterwards Spalanzani and other very learned men. Haller eontended that there was no sueh thing as any new creation, and that the germs not only of life but the germs of every member of the body existed from the beginning, and that every form of life is but the unfolding of what existed from the very first creation. This is evolution in earnest; and I may say that Haller's disciples still survive, for I have heard the same, or nearly the same, statement made by a well-edueated gentleman within a short time.

Haller went so far as to ealculate the number of human beings in the ovaries of Mother Eve, and (aeeording to Hæekel's statement) this number was " 200,000,000,000," supposing that the world would stand six thousand years.

What was to become of the world after that time we are not
informed.   The celebrated Leibnitz went so far as to claim
that the souls of men were in monads or the primary elements of matter.   According to him the monads were
"without extent, incorruptible, and so constituted that their
whole future is contained in their beginning."   "In every
monad might be read the world's history from beginning to
end; each of them being a kind of Deity."   "God is the
absolute, original monad, from which all the rest are generated; the primitive and necessary substance, in which the
detail of changes exists emanantly."   ("Am. Cyc.," p. 325,
vol. 10.)

Either the ovulist or the animalculist theory held sway
with the majority of men, both learned and unlearned,
until after the beginning of the nineteenth century.   From
1690 to 1812 one or the other theory held the uppermost
position among scientific men; and for about two hundred
years one or the other of these theories held especial prominence in scientific discussions.

The supporters of present evolutionary theories are not
superior in intellectual vigor to Leibnitz, Haller, and others,
who, a hundred or more years ago, were fully satisfied that
they were correct in the views which they promulgated concerning the origin and development of life.   So also the
doctrine of cataclysms, which Cuvier believed, and which
hosts of other great men believed, held almost universal
acceptance until Lyell showed that the building of the earth's
different strata might have been accomplished through
long ages, quietly, and under the regular operations of
nature.

The fact that a theory may apparently explain certain
heretofore unexplained phenomena by no means shows that

some other theory may not explain these phenomena much better.

While it is true that men and apes are wonderfully similar in their affectionate attachments, and the grief of the ape mother on being deprived of her children by death is much like that of the human mother, and the disposition to curiously examine and investigate concerning all objects within their reach is much alike in men and apes, yet something more than proof of similarities of disposition and physical structure is needed to show that one of these species could ever have descended from the other.

The assent of a majority of the most learned naturalists and biologists for a whole generation is not enough, in a matter like the origin of the human race (concerning which unimpeachable evidence has not been obtained from science), to reasonably induce a fully settled belief in theories which have not, and probably cannot, at present, be demonstrated. In "Popular Science Monthly" for June, 1885, there is a very able article on "The Ways of Monkeys," from the pen of the noted German naturalist, Alfred E. Brehm. Brehm had extensive and uncommon opportunities for studying the nature and habits of the apes, both in captivity and in the wilds where they live, and he closes his article as follows : —

"Was the ancestor of the human race a monkey? That is the vexed question which still raises so much dust.

"There is no doubt that man is not more and not less than the chief creature in the animal kingdom, and that the monkeys are his immediate neighbors ; but I cannot see why this fact should logically involve the assumption that our great-great-uncles were gambolling in Paradise in the shape of apes. The doctrine of gradual evolution may seem trustworthy in the highest degree, and beautiful from the scientific

stand-point, but it is based upon a simple hypothesis ; and a
hypothesis is not a proof; and here I wish not to be misun-
derstood.   Even if the physical and intellectual development
and perfection of humanity throughout the succession of thousands of centuries is a fact, there is no authority for the inference that, *eo ipso*, a monkey-nest was the cradle of mankind.

"Darwin's treatise on the variation of species gave rise to
the ardent controversy of our days.   Darwin used the wrong
word.   It is not 'species' he ought to have said, but
'varieties ; ' for species never interbreed with each other.
Man and monkey, though belonging to the same group,
represent two distinct species.   There is, consequently, a
simple and irrefragable natural law refuting peremptorily the
thesis of the enthusiastic propugnators of the pedigree root-
ing somewhere amid a grinning tribe gambolling in the wild
forests of Asia or Africa.   The criterion that the human race
has large, round hands, and blunt, canine teeth would be
sufficient of itself to establish the truth that no monkey-blood
is pulsating in our veins.   But there are more distinctive
features.   Men have strong, well-shaped legs, walk constantly in an erect posture, and enjoy the faculty of speech.

"The monkeys rank near humanity in the general organization of the world ; they show in many instances much likeness with mankind, physically as well as intellectually.   But
a further concession would be a denial of positive natural
laws.   Nay ; old Adam was not a monkey, not a baboon,
not even a chimpanzee ! "

This declaration of Dr. Brehm will be considered scientific
scepticism.   But do we not sadly need more of this kind of
scepticism ?   It is curious to observe, however, that those
most impatient with this kind of scepticism are accustomed

to compliment other kinds of scepticism with the name of philosophical inquiry.

In one respect Hæckel differs widely from Mr. Huxley. With Huxley scientific scepticism is a duty. He says, in substance, "compel assent if you can," or compel me to receive the proposed hypothesis if you can, and I will receive it. But Hæckel says of Darwin's Theory of Descent ("Hist. of Creation," p. 28) : "In any case we are in duty bound to accept this theory till a better one be found which will undertake to explain the same amount of facts in an equally simple manner. Until now we have been in utter want of such a theory." And, further, when he wishes to show that there is no necessity for supposing that there was an original Creator, he says : "It cannot fail to appear, in the light of the Doctrine of Descent, no longer as the ingeniously designed work of a Creator building up according to a definite purpose, but as the necessary consequence of active causes which are inherent in the chemical combination of matter itself, and in its physical properties." (p. 27, "Hist. of Creation.")

How has the doctor or any one else learned that these " active causes which are inherent in the chemical combination of matter itself" are naturally "inherent?" How does he know that these "inherent" qualities are not the agencies of the very Creator he would so summarily dispense with? It is easy for most men to believe what they really wish to believe.

CHAPTER VI.

THE DEVELOPMENT OF LIFE.

THE question whether there is a designing intelligence behind the phenomena which we observe in nature will continually meet us.

Does the material universe (as well as the entire list of animals) exhibit itself so unskilfully and clumsily constituted that its construction is disgraceful to or unworthy of a designing intelligence? Is it because all nature is so poorly arranged for intended purposes that a certain class of writers must attribute its existence to blind, unconscious, purposeless forces, or to necessity? Because we can see no evidence of design in certain things which exist, shall we assume that the many apparent evidences of design are all deceptive?

This raises questions concerning the connection between mind and matter, and concerning their dependence on or independence of each other : whether mind is dependent upon matter for its existence, or whether mind existed prior to or can exist independent of matter.

Is it reasonable to suppose that the mind, which moulds matter according to its purposes, which uses matter as it wills, to which all matter is subject, can be itself subject to material laws, and itself the child of matter?

Like begets like : can intelligence spring from a source which is not itself intelligent, or from something having a less intellectual nature than an intelligent being? Can in-

telligence be evolved from mere matter, which it is supposed
has no intelligence? What is the real origin of thought?
How did it first have an existence? Whence came the
consciousness of our own existence? Is the idea that thought
can have been evolved or derived from an unthinking source
a thinkable one?

Must we not conclude that there is a self-existent intelligent source of thought, unless we are prepared to confess
that an effect has been produced without any adequate
cause?

Can the mind, through which matter is made subservient
to the desires of man, be itself derived from matter? Is a
machine the producer of the mind which first conceives the
idea of its construction? Which precedes in the order of time,
the machine, or the plan of the machine, in the mind of its
inventor? Carry this idea through the whole realm of
nature, even to the construction of the worlds which constitute the universe, and you will find that the analogy holds
good.

Sidney Billing says (p. 8, "Scientific Materialism"):
" When the symbol photographed in the eye receives transla-
tion it becomes our reality. How then can it be said the
major (mind) has its origin in the minor? (matter); logically we know all majors are composed of minors, but this
can be said only of related things; pile as we may atom
on atom we should never elicit mind; pile idea on idea and
a wisdom would be attainable approaching the precincts of
infinitude. Perceptive knowledge is built up of the symbols
of things, not of things. How then can we say that the
symbolical expression of that we term matter, objective
forms, creates the subjecting intellect?"

But I hear it repeated, that living and active forces inhere in the very atoms of which the universe itself consists. Well, how did these active forces get into these atoms? Who placed them there? Did these forces make themselves? Were they self-originating? Were they self-existent? If we predicate self-existence of matter, by what just reasoning can we deny self-existence to intelligence?

Agassiz went to the very bottom of this subject, and acknowledged a first and ultimate cause; but Hæckel says, " All our knowledge is limited, and we can never apprehend the first causes of any phenomena."

While it is not likely that we shall ever "apprehend" or comprehend "first causes," we know that there must have been a first cause, or "cause of causes," or else an endless chain of causes. Agassiz refers all to a great first cause. Hæckel does not inquire about the first cause, but only in regard to the action of secondary causes. He does not seem to consider that these secondary causes must be dependent for their action on a great first cause. I do not think Darwin ever denied the creative acts of a great first cause. Darwin started in his calculation and theories with life already in existence, and reasoned from what has succeeded the first creation. Darwin closed his enlarged and corrected sixth edition of the " Origin of Species " with these words : " There is grandeur in this view of life, with its several powers, having been originally breathed by the Creator into a few forms or into one, and that, whilst this planet has gone cycling on according to the fixed law of gravity, from so simple a beginning endless forms most beautiful and most wonderful have been, and are being evolved." Here Darwin acknowledges that the Creator originally breathed life into " a few forms or into one."

But if you ask the atheistic class how life or living beings came to exist on the earth, when it is evident from the teachings of geology that there was once a time when no life existed on the earth, the answer readily comes, "By spontaneous generation."

But if this "spontaneous" theory is true, what has been spontaneously generated? Bits or particles of protoplasm? How large were these particles of the first living matter? If molecules of living matter can be spontaneously generated, why may not larger living particles also be generated spontaneously?

How do we know that what we call "spontaneous" is not something ordered by a divine creative power? And if this "spontaneous" or creative power could bring into being from non-being molecules of living matter, why could not this force or power also bring into being larger masses of protoplasm, or even living animals? And if animals of the very simplest structure, why not those of more complex structure, or even animals of the higher orders? Where shall we stop the possibilities of this power, whether we call it creator, living force, or by any other name? Some power has brought the living from the non-living. Then by what philosophical consistency can we ridicule the idea of special creations, even if we cannot prove that there ever has been any special creation?

We have been accustomed to see nature work in certain ways, and we have never observed it to work in any different way, and hence we infer that it cannot work in any other way. But this is by no means the necessary conclusion; and yet from the very constitution of our minds we are inclined to draw such an inference. If we had never seen anything spring up and grow as certain kinds of vegetation do, and one should attempt to explain how such a thing might exist, we might doubt its existence. His statement might seem to us as wonderful and inexplicable as some other events which have been deemed miraculous, and this simply because it was so different from anything we had ever seen or contemplated. So we see living things produced in certain ways. We know that animals and plants come into existence in certain ways, and we infer that they have always come into existence in the same way, and we also infer that they cannot be brought into existence in any other way; but this last inference is by no means a necessary one.

The fact that we have never known a certain thing to exist furnishes no proof that such a thing has not existed, or may not exist. Thus both spontaneous generation and the " Immaculate Conception " have been supposed to exist, and probably as many believe that the " Immaculate Conception" actually took place as believe that " spontaneous generation " ever took place; and the believers in the " Immaculate Conception " are not inferior intellectually to the believers in " spontaneous generation ; " yet nearly all believers in spontaneous generation ridicule the doctrine of the " Immaculate Conception." But whether either spontaneous generation or the " Immaculate Conception " ever existed may be incapable of proof or disproof through any scientific demonstrations.

Because there is a general similarity of plan in the building up of all animals, trees, and vegetables, and all other living things, the inference is drawn that all these forms have descended from some common ancestor. It is just here that the development and the former creative theories branch off from each other. Their point of contact is like the entering part of a wedge, and from that point they diverge. Evolutionists contend that it is easier and more philosophical to believe that this striking resemblance in all animal existences is caused by development through the laws of descent from a common ancestor than to believe it comes from separate creative acts.

But this similarity does not stop on the earth, or with life on the earth either in the animal or vegetable forms; but the same proportions and similarities run through the planetary systems; and we might ask, From what ancestors did the planetary system descend? How about the solar system? How comes it that there are such striking proportions between the planetary distances and the groups of leaves on the trees and the flowers in the garden or on the hill-side? (See Agassiz on "Classification," p. 193.) Why should proportional numbers of the various orders of plants so correspond to the distances of the planets?

This question, if answered, might carry out the development hypothesis to its philosophical or logical conclusions. But, further, how comes it that the solar system appears to be but a picture, or type of the universe, which certain astronomers have supposed revolves around a great central sun at a period numbering millions of years? It can easily be conceived how the moon may, in a figurative manner, be called a child of the earth, for perhaps fifty millions of years ago (more or less) the moon may have been thrown off from the surface of the earth when the earth's revolutions were so rapid as to overcome the attractive forces.

It is not probable that in like manner the planets can be called children of the sun, for it appears probable that the earth became consolidated from cosmic vapor earlier in time than the sun.

Doubtless all suns, stars, and planets are governed by

fixed and immutable laws, and their shapes, being nearly globular, are substantially alike. And further, perhaps their material substances or chemical combinations may be substantially alike. This is all within the range of probability. By "immutable laws" I mean the observed antecedence and sequence of events, and their connection with and dependence upon each other. When we assume this immutability we do not know that there may not be thousands of antecedents and consequents, the nature of which we cannot comprehend.

But what reflective and unbiassed man can see all this immense system, commencing at the smallest particle which can be seen with the microscope, and trace it up through all sizes and types, and find the same beautiful order running from the smallest animalcule to the largest planets and suns, and then see no Supreme Architect for all these infinite variations?

I am aware that those who do not believe that mind or spirit can have a real existence separate from matter, but who assume that mind is a mere process or a variation of some form of life, will not consider this mode of treatment scientific. But before such become too positive in their statements concerning the nature of the original mind, intelligence, or spiritual existence, it will be well for them to give us something besides speculative assumptions upon which they build their theories.

Which is the more dignified and the more reasonable? to believe in the existence of an Almighty Intelligent Power, who created, and still sustains the universe by his constant care, or to believe that dead, soulless, mindless matter, without any purpose, and through "unconscious causes," brought into existence the sun, planets, and stars through space illimitable, together with all the intelligence of rational creatures?

In regard to the beautiful and perfect arrangement of the heavenly bodies, Robert Chambers, the author of "Vestiges of the Creation," says (pp. 17, 18, Harper's edition) : " Proportions of numbers and geometrical figures rest at the bottom of the whole. These considerations, when the mind is thoroughly prepared for them, tend to raise our ideas with respect to the character of physical laws, even though we do not go a single step further in the investigation ; but it is impossible for an intelligent mind to stop there. We advance from law to law, and ask, What is that? Whence have come all these beautiful regulations? Here science leaves us, but only to conclude, from other grounds, that there is a first cause, to which all others are secondary and ministrative, a primitive, almighty will, of which these laws are merely the mandates. That great Being, — who shall say where is his dwelling-place, or what his history? Man pauses breathless at the contemplation of a subject so much above his finite faculties, and can only wonder and adore."

Opinions of scientific men on these points are no better than those of so many farmers. Reason and common-sense must be our guide here (if we reject the idea of revelation), for all know that certain facts exist which man has never explained. The lines that somebody once wrote about two kinds of fools are applicable here, viz. : " The simple fool is he who knows that he does not know ; the compound fool is he who does not know that he does not know."

Possibly, if the advocates of various conflicting theories concerning the origin of things could better understand the positions of their opponents, there might not appear to be a very wide divergence at the real foundations of their beliefs; but these differences of opinion now seem to be radical at the very foundation. But I may remark that all men believe there is an invisible force or power acting through nature; and the very germ of the whole inquiry on this point lies in this, viz. : is this invisible power an intelligent one? Does this intelligent power (if it exists) exist separate from and independent of matter? or, if it exists and inheres in matter now, did it exist prior to matter, and organize matter into bodies as they now exist? or, if matter in its elements is eternal, and spirit eternal also, did this intelligence or power create the forces that drew these elements of matter together into worlds and systems of worlds? Are what we call the laws of nature simply unconscious forces? or are they manifestations of an intelligent being by whose power these forces were created, and by whose will they are kept in unerring operation? If one admits that these forces are under intelligent or purposive direction, he admits the most essential part of the theistic argument; for if this intelligent power exists and acts, it matters little (from a scientific stand-point) by what name we call it, whether we call it God, Allah, Jehovah, or by some other name.

But in a religious sense it makes a vast difference, for no one would consider a simple power of nature worthy of adoration and worship. But if this power is like or akin to what we term personal, and of the highest intelligence, it is in the highest degree proper that he should be revered and worshipped; for by this power all life, all good must be held. All our well-being, not only now but for the whole of our existence (be that longer or shorter), and whether the soul survives the body or not, is in his keeping. If the soul does not survive the dissolution of the body, then all the happiness we can ever experience will be in this world,

and even that is of the greatest moment ; for it is the greatest
boon we can have.   If this intelligence exists and is, or is
like a personal being, it is certainly reasonable to hope that
he may have sympathies and affections.

Every intelligent creature of which we have any knowledge
has sympathy ; and why should we imagine that the very
highest intelligence should be devoid of sympathy? and if
not devoid of sympathy, why, in a scientific sense, is it not
reasonable to strive to be worthy of this sympathy, and why
should we not also hope that we may do something towards
deepening this sympathy in our behalf?   If we believe as
the major part of the greatest thinkers in the most enlightened
nations of the earth have believed in regard to the soul's immortality, or as Socrates and his illustrious disciple Plato
taught, or as, later, Jesus taught, "That man is a being destined for eternity," then this question concerning immortal
existence must be a very important one ; and if the belief in
its reality is founded on fact then this idea deepens into one
of supreme importance.   In the presence of this question all
others dwindle into comparative insignificance.

But if we conclude that we cannot demonstrate the correctness or incorrectness of the existence of an almighty and
benevolent Intelligence, and a conscious immortal existence,
still this is no trifling question, for it lies at the very root of
our most important interests.   It would seem as if all might
be agreed here.   I am aware that it is impossible for human
thought to grasp the terms Infinity, Omnipotence, Omniscience, and the like, and that in attempting to apply human
words to describe The Ineffable, or one infinitely above all
our conceptions, we can make but a sorry approach towards
such expressions as we would like to make.   Being ourselves
of limited intellectual powers, we cannot fathom the myste-

rious essence of a power infinitely above our highest intellectual conceptions; but in speaking of Him we are obliged to use human language, and are also confined within the limits of human thought; hence all our descriptions and conceptions of the Divine One must of necessity be very imperfect. But though we cannot comprehend the idea of infinity or eternity, we are not debarred from reasoning concerning them.

Considerable misunderstanding has arisen concerning what is meant by the term "creative theory." Many understand by this something like Milton's poetical descriptions, or that each separate species of animals was originally created with characteristics essentially like those they now possess. But it by no means follows that another theory may not properly claim the name creative. Any theory which necessitates the existence of an original creator is a creative theory.

The theory which is distinctively in opposition to the "spontaneous generation" theory of life is properly called creative. The doctrines of evolution as taught by Darwin necessitate the existence of creative intelligence to start life into being, — as Darwin himself intimates in the closing paragraph of his "Origin of Species," — and any theory which calls for this creative beginning is properly styled a creative one. It is true that Huxley demolished a certain theory which he called creative, viz., "The Miltonic Theory;" but even Huxley was obliged to admit that some time during past ages the present laws of nature might not have acted in the invariable order in which they now act. Even if only one form or type of life was originally created, and all succeeding types or forms however varied have been evolved from that original form, creative intelligence is none the less needed to start that original form of life. The intelligent being or power who set in motion causes which would result in such a surprising variety of living creatures through descent from one single form (if life has thus been evolved) must be indeed of the very highest order of intelligence. If this being set in order laws through which the world both animate and inanimate would run on without any disturbance of its natural relations for millions of years without intelligent supervision, that being must, if possible, be of even a higher order of intelligence than one that should originate a system that would run regularly with intelligent supervision.

What I claim, however, is that this immense machinery of life, as well as of inorganic nature, which, we say, is governed by the laws of nature, could not originate itself; but it must have been originated or set in motion by a power, force, or being having an infinitely high order of intelligence. Nothing less than this could plan and execute all that is involved in the continued preservation of life, as well as keep in regular orbits the planetary worlds.

If the Darwinian theory is correct, and all animals and plants have been, through countless ages, developed from a "few original forms," then this very system of development, so constant and regular in its operations, necessitates the existence of an Omnipotent and Omniscient Power to ordain, guide, regulate and execute these complicated natural laws so that, ever acting, they never clash or fail in their unvarying regularity.

Much ingenuity and a considerable amount of learning have been employed to show that the all-pervading power, which every reflecting person must see exists, and which governs all the operations of nature, is not an intelligent being, but only a blind force, or simple necessity, operating in a manner purely mechanical. While others admit that there must have been an intelligent power to originate natural laws, they contend that, when once instituted, these laws run on without need of any intelligent supervision.

Dr. Hitchcock, on pp. 294, 295, "Religion and Geology," writes concerning the position of the advocates of this last theory as follows : —

"I know, indeed, that La Place, and some other advocates of this latter hypothesis, do not admit any necessity for a Deity even to originate matter or its laws ; and to prove this was the object of the nebular hypothesis. But how evident that in this he signally failed! For even though he could show how nebulous matter, placed in a certain position, and having a revolution, might be separated into sun and planets by merely mechanical laws, yet where, save in an infinite Deity, lie the power and the wisdom to originate that matter, and to bring it into such a condition, that, by blind laws alone, it would produce such a universe — so harmonious, so varied, so nicely adjusted in its parts and relations, as the one we inhabit? Especially, how does this hypothesis show in what manner these worlds could be peopled by countless myriads of organic natures, most exquisitely contrived, and fitted to their condition? The atheist may say that matter is eternal. But if so, what but an infinite mind could in time begin the work of organic creation? If the matter existed for eternal ages without being brought into order, and into organic structure, why did it not continue in the same state forever? Does the atheist say, All is the result of laws inherent in matter? But how could those laws remain dormant through all past eternity, — that is, through a period literally infinite, — and then at length be aroused into intense action? Besides, to impute the present wise arrangements and organic creations of the world to law is to endow that law with all the attributes with which the theist invests the Deity. Nothing short of intelligence, and wisdom, and benevolence, and power, infinitely above what man possesses will account for the present world. If there is, then, a power inherent in matter adequate to the production of such effects, that power must be the same as the Deity; and, therefore, it is truly the Deity, by whatever name we call it."

The idea that blind, unconscious forces are the ruling powers of the world well agrees with the leading tenets of Buddhism. The Buddhist religion does not mention any God as the creator and ruler of the world. Neither do they have any idea of the moral quality of any act being at all changed or modified because it is according to the will of any God. All the idea of morality they have is simply a fitness of things, and the consequences of acts follow not as we should suppose, with invariable sequence, but often by a sort of fitful irregularity. But their doctrine of transmigration of souls gives them the chance to account for all the evils which befall any one here; for the sufferings which one has here are the result of acts which he may have committed in a previous state of existence when he might have been an elephant, or, perhaps, a tiger. This well accords with the evolutionary theory of inherited tendencies, characters, or traits.

Arnold, in "Light of Asia," p. 96, writes : —

> " That — once and wheresoe'er, and whence begun —
> Life runs its rounds of living, climbing up
> From mote, and gnat, and worm, reptile and fish,
> Bird and shagged beast, man, demon, deva, God,
> To clod and mote again; so are we kin
> To all that is."

Of course, with the absence of a belief in an eternal self-existent Deity, the idea of immortality must, of necessity, be absent. But according to Buddhist teachings, the least time which the bad will have to stay in one of their one hundred and thirty-six hells is ten millions of years, and the least time in their heaven is ten billions of years; yet this is not immortality, for at the end of these immense cycles death comes, and then the unfortunate must be born again, into what shape, whether animal, vegetable, or human, no one previously knows. Buddha arrived at such a state of knowledge that he could remember what he did when he was in the shape of several different animals before he was born a man, — so the sacred books inform us, — and that, to him, must amount to a demonstration of his line of descent.

Speculations concerning the origin of the universe, as well as of organic life, are no new thing.

Plato noticed the arrangements and motions of the planets and those of animated nature; for, according to Bain, he considered the Cosmos, "in its totality a vast and comprehensive animated being; the model for it is the Idea of Animal — the Self-Animal. As created, the Kosmos is a scheme of rotatory spheres, and has both a Soul and a Body. The Soul, rooted at the centre, and pervading the whole, is *self-moving*, and the cause of movement in the Kosmical body." ("Mind and Body," p. 147.) This universal Soul typified the laws of attraction or gravitation. Plato likewise believed in degrees of intelligence and station, and in a line of reasoning like that of the present evolutionists, only he starts from a different stand-point. He starts with the gods as the highest intelligence, and then runs down in a series of degeneracies through men to the animals. He makes the seat of the immortal soul in the brain; but this soul has to contend with two other principles which sadly hamper it in its harmonious acts and desires. He also believed in self-existent ideas, or intelligence anterior to the formation of the world ; but it would seem that Plato believed in the eternal existence of matter in its simple constituents, — a scientific idea which many modern philosophers still cling to.

It is evident, however, that Plato believed in one original great First Cause, or one eternal, intelligent, self-existing Being, who was the organizer of all things ; but that, subsequently, other inferior deities presided over the destinies of the Cosmos.

These inferior deities may well represent the secondary causes, or natural laws.

In regard to the creation, or, rather, formation of worlds, the theory of La Place has been widely received, and may be as philosophical as any other which has been proposed. Summarized by Dr. Hitchcock, it is as follows, p. 287 : —

" He (La Place) supposes that, originally, the whole solar system constituted only one vast mass of nebulous matter, being expanded into the thinnest vapor and gas by heat, and more than filling the space at present occupied by the planets. This vapor he still further supposes had a revolution from west to east on an axis. As the heat diminished by radiation, the nebulous matter must condense, and consequently the velocity of rotation must increase, and an exterior zone of vapor might be detached, since the central attraction might not be able to overcome the increased centrifugal force. This ring of vapor might sometimes retain its original form, as in the case of Saturn's ring ; but the tendency would be, in general, to divide into several masses, which, by coalescing again, would form a single mass, having a revolution about the sun, and on its axis. This would constitute a planet in a state of vapor; and by the detachment of successive rings might all the planets be produced. As they went on contracting, by the same law, satellites might be formed to each; and the ultimate result would be solid planets and satellites, revolving around the sun in nearly the same plane, and in the same direction, and also on their axes."

The above statement applies to the formation of the solar system; but it is only a part of the nebular hypothesis; and why should the solar system be created, or formed in a manner different from the formation of other worlds comprising the universe? And if this thin cosmic vapor originally filled the whole space, and even beyond that now occupied by the solar system, why should not a like cosmic vapor from which the entire universe has been formed exist and also fill all space?

This still leaves us in the dark as to how this cosmic vapor happened to be in existence before this motion commenced.

La Place thought he could dispense with the necessity of a creator, and substitute natural causes or laws in his place; but he only pushed the inquiry one degree further back, and the question still recurs, what less than infinite intelligence and power could have instituted these laws of nature?

The monists contend that there is really but one original force in the universe, and that what we call living and dead matter are one and the same, as to their ultimate vital condition and forces. Hæckel says (in vol. 1, "History of Creation," p. 23, as quoted in another place) : " We thus arrive at the extremely important conviction that all natural bodies which are known to us are equally animated, that the

distinction which has been made between animate and inanimate bodies does not exist."

However, he is not the first to discover, even among
moderns, that all things are "equally animated;" for, according to Henslow, Robinet wrote, more than a hundred years
ago, that all things alike have sentient perceptions; all grow,
desire, and propagate. Thus he says, fire is hungry and
voracious; it feeds on air, and if air be wanting, it expires.
So, too, air feeds on water, while water feeds on other substances. And thus he accounts for such minerals as salt,
iron, etc., being found in mineral springs. The following
quotation will illustrate his style of reasoning: —

"I have sought for the germs of stones and the vessels
which contain them; nor have my researches been fruitless.
I have even discovered how stones and minerals eject their
germs. If I have been unable to detect their sexes, how
many animals and plants are in the same condition! Finally
we have seen an infinity of fœtal stones and metals in their
wombs, with their envelops and placentas; we have seen
them growing and nourishing them like animals. There
may be stones which multiply by budding, as is the case
with trees and some animals. But observations are wanting
to confirm this conjecture." ("Evolution of Living Things,"
pp. 16, 17.)

The words, "Observations are wanting to confirm," in
this last sentence, are well introduced by Robinet; and I
think that "observations" to prove that all things are
"equally animated" will be "wanting to confirm that conjecture" for a long time to come.

Monists contend that the forces which build the crystals
are living as well as those which build the bodies of living
animals, but the difference between the living and the dead,

or between the organic and inorganic matter, is radical. The crystal is built from the outside by natural forces, and when its particles or molecules are once placed in their natural positions, by inherent natural forces, they may remain æons of time without the least change, unless taken away by absorption or by being dissolved or ground away.

To change a crystal in the least degree without mechanical violence, the very force which caused it to be built up must be reversed, and stronger forces must operate in a different direction.   When the crystal is once built it is built to last forever, or till other forces in nature commence to take the molecules of which it is composed from the outside, one by one, by forces just the opposite from that through which they were placed in position.   But in all living animal organisms there is continuous motion through growth and decay.   The living animal organism never remains stationary for a single second of time.   In fact, the instant vital motion stops death takes place, or, more properly speaking, this vital motion or action always continues until death occurs.   Ceasing of vital motion is death.

It is true a living structure (a plant, for instance) may perish slowly, by almost imperceptible degrees ; but this decay is none the less sure because slow.

It is useless to assert that the ultimate atoms of which inorganic matter is composed must of necessity in all cases be in constant motion, while we can produce no tangible evidence that such supposed condition of things really exists. Living motion is continuous in the very lowest animals ; but it is more easily perceived in the higher organisms.

The forces which act to build the crystals come from without, while the active forces in living organisms come from within.   How can we reasonably confound the two?

Quatrefages ("Human Species," pp. 4, 5) says:
"The reason is that, in the organized being, the repose of
the crystal is replaced by an incessant movement; that,
instead of remaining immovable and unalterable, the molecules are unceasingly undergoing transformation, changing
their composition, producing fresh substances, retaining
some and rejecting others. Far from resembling a pile
of shot, the organized being may much rather be compared
to the combination of a number of physico-chemical apparatus, constantly in action to burn or reduce materials
borrowed from without, and ever making use of their own
substance for its incessant renewal."

"In other words, in the crystal once formed the forces
remain in a state of *stable equilibrium*, which is only inter-
rupted by the influence of exterior causes. Hence the possibility of its indefinite continuance without any change either
of its forms or of its properties. In the organized being the
equilibrium is *unstable*, or, rather, there is no equilibrium,
properly so called. Every moment the organized being
expends as much *force* as *matter*, and owes its continuance
solely to the *balance of the gain and loss.* Hence the
possibility of a modification of its properties and form without its ceasing to exist. Such are the bare facts, which rest
upon no hypothesis whatever; and how can we, in the
presence of these facts, compare the crystal which grows in a
saline solution to the germ which becomes in succession
embryo, fœtus, and finally a complete animal? How can
we confuse the *inanimate body* with the *organized being?*"

"But organized beings have also their special phenomena
radically distinct from, or even opposed to, the former. Is
it possible to refer all of them to one, or to several, identical
causes? I think not. For this reason, I admit with a

great number of eminent men of every age and country, —
and, I believe, with the majority of those that respect modern
science, that organized beings owe their distinctive characteristics to a *Special Cause*, to a *Special Force*, to *Life*,
which, in them, is associated with the inorganic forces.
For this reason I consider it legitimate to call them *Living
Beings*."

At the first development or unfolding of life the living
action in the vegetable is essentially like that in the animal.
While the seed is germinating there is a constant molecular
action, and this motion being continuous is like that in the
lowest forms of animal life; and in most cases it is not till the
plant has risen above the surface of the ground and is acted
upon by the sunlight, and chlorophil is absorbed by the
plant, that what is generally considered distinctive vegetable
life appears. All the protoplasm necessary to the growth of
either plants or animals must be taken in a comparatively
fluid state, and the particles placed where they belong, after
which the water that has held these particles in solution is
absorbed or evaporated. Vegetables take their nourishment
from the outside through their rootlets or through their
leaves. They also convert inorganic substances into organic,
— a thing which, generally speaking, animals cannot do.
Animals generally take food through mouths into a stomach,
and can be nourished by organic matter only. But some
animals do not seem to have any stomach.

The ultimate principle of life in the animal and the vegetable seems to be one and the same; but a very noticeable
difference is, that, when the living particles are once firmly
placed in a tree, they appear to be stationary, and not to
change, as in the case of animals. Every part of animals, —
bones, muscles, and tissues, — is in a state of constant change.

It is believed that not a single particle of matter which is in he child remains in his body till adult life is reached. But he wonderful fact remains that the individuality or personal identity continues though every particle of the matter of the body has been changed. What is this wonderful entity which preserves personal identity, and makes one still the same person though all else has been changed? Can it be other than a living force?

CHAPTER VII.

THE DEVELOPMENT OF LIFE.

This chapter is chiefly devoted to further examination of various theories of the development of life.

An actual fact is not changed, whether it is stated by one who is learned or by one who is comparatively ignorant, — the fact still remains eternal truth.

Agassiz believed that an almighty creative intelligence established the very laws of nature themselves. Had Agassiz yielded to the demands of that class who do not believe that a being of infinite intelligence was the originator of earthly existence, and taught that species came to exist through the laws of nature without the intervention of a creator, might he not have passed with them for a distributor of opinions of the highest scientific value? But every person who was fortunate enough to be acquainted with that gifted naturalist is convinced that he taught only what he believed to be true.

Hæckel writes, p. 117 : " When, in 1873, the grave closed over Louis Agassiz, the last great upholder of the constancy of species and of miraculous creation, the dogma of the constancy of species came to an end, and the contrary assumption — the assertion that all the various species descend from common ancestral forms — now no longer encounters serious difficulties."

Suppose " that the assumption that all the various species descended from common ancestral forms now encounters no serious difficulties " in consequence of the death of Agassiz, does not that very statement seem to imply that the validity of that doctrine might be in some measure dependent upon the teachings of men? What difference could the living or dying of any man make as to the truth or falsity of actual facts?

By constancy of species Agassiz meant that there has been no change of one species into another. Thus, he taught that lions are descendants of lions, or some ancestor of the cat family; and sheep of sheep from their first creation, and that the descendants of lions will be lions, and the descendants of sheep, sheep, etc., and that these animals will never in the future change into any other race of animals essentially different from the present races.

He taught that the ancestors of men were men from their earliest creation, and their descendants, to their latest posterity, will also be men with mental and physical characteristics essentially like those now living.

Most of those who indorse the theory of man's descent from an original one-celled ancestor contend that there is a continuous line of development by the laws of nature.

It should be borne in mind, however, that there are many firm believers in the doctrines of evolution who also firmly believe that an almighty creative intelligence established the laws of development, and that what we call the laws of nature are only the manifestations of his manner of working.

Concerning Lamarck's theory, Hæckel writes, vol. 1, "Evolution of Man," p. 85: "Lamarck was the first to formulate the scientific theory of the natural origin of all organisms, including man, and at the same time to draw the two ultimate inferences from this theory; firstly, the doctrine of the origin of the most ancient organisms through spontaneous generation ; and, secondly, the descent of Man from the Mammal most closely resembling Man, — the Ape."

In attempting to explain how this came about, " he considered that, on the one hand, practice and habit (adaptation), and, on the other, heredity, are the most important of these causes."

On page 86 he adduces examples as follows : " To mention examples, the Woodpecker and the Humming-bird owe their peculiarly long tongue to their habit of using these organs to take their food out of narrow and deep crevices ; the Frog acquired a web between its toes from the motions of swimming ; the Giraffe gained its long neck by stretching it up to the branches of trees." " Lamarck fully perceived that Heredity must necessarily coöperate with Adaptation."

To sum up, he contends that the first step made by apes towards becoming men, was when they gave up the habit of climbing trees, and " accustomed themselves to an upright gait." This exercise developed the spine and the pelvis ; and the fore-legs, instead of being used for climbing, developed into arms and hands for the " purpose of grasping and touching," while the hind pair were used for walking, and their extremities were developed into true feet. " In consequence of the totally changed mode of life," there came a change of jaws and teeth, and, consequently, of the whole shape of the face. The tail, no longer needed, disappeared. Then, as the apes began to live in communities, social instincts developed, and family relations began to subsist, and the apes' language of sounds developed into the language of men, etc. Then the brain changed its shape, and grew larger by its more constant use, etc.

9

"These important ideas of Lamarck contain the first and oldest germs of a real history of the human tribe."

To give the reader, as clear an idea as possible of the theories of Lamarck and others of his school in a small compass, I will quote a summary from Dr. Edward Hitchcock ("Religion of Geology," pp. 289, 290) : "The French zoölogist, Lamarck, first drew out and formally defended this hypothesis, aided by others, as Geoffroy St. Hilaire and Bory St. Vincent. Their supposition was that there is a power in nature, which they sometimes denominated the Deity, yet did not allow it to be intelligent and independent, but a mere blind, instrumental force. This power, they supposed, was able to produce what they called monads, or rough draughts of animals and plants. These monads were the simplest of all organic beings, mere aggregations of matter, some of them supposed to be inherently vital. And such monads are the only things ever produced directly by this blind Deity. But in these monads there was supposed to reside an inherent tendency to progressive improvement. The wants of this living mass of jelly were supposed to produce such effects as would gradually form new organs, as the hands, the feet, and the mouth. These changes would be aided by another principle, which they called the *force of external circumstances*, by which they meant the influence upon its development of its peculiar condition ; as, for instance, a conatus for flying, produced by the internal principle, would form wings in birds ; a conatus for swimming in water would form the fins and tails of fishes ; and a conatus for walking would form the feet and legs of quadrupeds. Thus the organs were not formed to meet the wants, but by the wants of the animal and plant. Of course, new wants would produce new organs ; and thus have animals been growing more and more complicated and perfect from the earliest periods of geological history. Man began his course as a monad ; but, by the force of Lamarck's two principles, has reached the most elevated rank on the scale of animals. His last condition before his present was that of the monkey tribe, especially that of the orang-outang."

Lamarck has much more of similar import, carrying out and developing ideas of which these are the bases ; but what wants first inclined these apes to give up " the habit of climbing trees," and adopt " an upright gait," so that their fore-legs became " developed into hands and arms," and their " extremities were developed into true feet " ?

Also, how did these monads become possessed of an " inherent tendency to progressive improvement"? And what first caused those wants which led to the formation of new organs? Supposing this theory is substantially correct, does any one know that these so-called new organs did not exist in a rudimentary state before there was any known tendency to develop new organs? Who knows that some which are now called useless rudimentary organs may not yet become developed into active and useful organs ?

Did the trees cease to give the apes food, and were they thus obliged to resort to the ground to find food ? And is this the reason why they gave up their arboreal habits ? And if they went upon the ground for food, why should they walk upright, instead of upon four feet as before?

Again, it should be borne in mind that Lamarck completely begs the question, for he does not show that any race of apes from which man might have been developed, existed on the earth prior to the existence of men. He seems to take it for granted that development is upward ; but if it should be shown that there has also been a degeneration in some races as well as an upward development in other races, his principles might not apply here.

Plato accounted for the degradation of the quadrupeds and creeping animals by the fact that their lower propensities naturally drew them nearer the earth.

To show that there has been a degradation in some races, I will quote from Dr. Hitchcock, pp. 313, 314 : —

"'The lower Silurian,' says Sir Roderick Murchison, in 1847, ' is no longer to be viewed as an invertebrate period ; for the onchus (a genus of fish) has been found in the Llandeilo Flags, and in the lower Silurian rocks of Bala.

"'It is also a most important fact, that this fish of the oldest rock was not, as the development scheme would require, of a low organization, but quite high on the scale of fishes. The same is true of all the earliest species of this class.' ' All our most ancient fossil fishes,' says Professor Sedwick, 'belong to a high organic type ; and the very oldest species that are well determined fall naturally into an order of fishes which Owen and Müller place, not at the bottom, but at the top of the whole class.'

"This point has been fully and ably discussed by Hugh Miller, Esq., in his late work, ' The Footprints of the Creator, or the Asterolepis of Stromness.' The asterolepis was one of these fishes found in the old red sandstone, sometimes over twenty feet long ; yet, says Mr. Miller, ' instead of being, as the development hypothesis would require, a fish low in its organization, it seems to have ranged on the level of the highest ichthyic-reptilian families ever called into existence.'

"Another point which Mr. Miller has labored hard to establish, and of which there seems to be no reasonable

doubt, is, that in many families of animals, not only were
the first species that appeared of high organization, but
there was a gradual degradation among those that were
created afterwards. Of the fishes, generally, he says that
'The progress of the race, as a whole, though it still retains
not a few of the higher forms, has been a progress, not of
development from the low to the high, but of degradation
from the high to the low.' .Again, he says, ' We know, as
geologists, that the dynasty of the fish was succeeded by that
of the reptile ; that the dynasty of the reptile was succeeded
by that of the mammiferous quadruped ; and that the
dynasty of the mammiferous quadruped was succeeded by
that of man, as man now exists — a creature of a mixed
character, and subject, in all conditions, to wide alternations
of enjoyment and suffering. We know further, — so far,
at least, as we have succeeded in deciphering the record, —
that the several dynasties were introduced, not in their
lower, but in their higher forms ; that, in short, in the
imposing programme of creation, it was arranged as a
general rule, that in each of the great divisions of the pro-
cession the magnates should walk first.' "

Upon the testimony of men like the Duke of Argyll, and
Virchow we learn that the oldest fossil human skulls yet
discovered are of a high rather than a low order.   Looking
from this stand-point, why, in absence of proof to the contrary, may we not infer that the early races of men may
have been of a high rather than of a low order, as well as
to receive as proved, what the rocks testify, viz., that certain very early classes of fishes were of a high order?

All pertinent testimony should be carefully and dispas-
sionately weighed, and all germane facts receive due consideration, and the strongest, most direct, and weighty

evidence should prevail. But here is a balancing of probabilities rather than an actual weighing of positive evidence; for much of what some consider positive evidence may be of a doubtful character. What one considers positive evidence another may consider hypothetical.

The evidence in favor of the general principles of evolution appears satisfactory to a majority of the students of natural history, and hence the probability that these general principles are correct; but certain radical evolutionists assert that arguments nearly equivalent to a demonstration have already been presented, and intimate that those who cannot see this are lacking either in learning or intellectual ability. But accusations of ignorance and want of logical power should have no place here; for a correct decision must rest upon actual facts.

If we assert that woodpeckers' tongues are now longer than they were five thousand years ago (of which assumption no proof has been given), then, who gave these woodpeckers a disposition to stick their comparatively short tongues into deep and narrow crevices to get their food? Why, if their tongues were originally short, should they commence putting them into such narrow and deep crevices, rather than take such food as other birds sought? So with the humming birds, and the giraffe. Who gave the giraffe a disposition to reach high for its food, and thus develop such a long neck?

If it is asserted that the giraffes were obliged to reach high among the trees for food on account of the failure of lower vegetation, we want evidence that such was the case. What evidence have we that animals with short necks and which feed off the ground have not lived and their descendants been preserved in localities inhabited by these giraffes?

Unless some such evidence can be presented, such suppositions of development are unsatisfactory because of the absence of facts in their support.

I have given you an epitome of these theories; the one supposes that the woodpecker, and the humming-bird and the giraffe, were, from the commencement of their existence, as distinct species, peculiarly fitted for obtaining their food as they now do; and being thus formed is why they now, as always before, obtain their food each in his own peculiar manner.

The other theory supposes that the giraffes' necks and the woodpeckers' tongues were originally short, but have been developed to much greater length by their peculiar modes of getting food.

Mivart ("Genesis of Species," pp. 36, 37, 38) on this theory remarks: "But some of the cases which have been brought forward, and which have met with very general acceptance, seem less satisfactory when carefully analyzed, than they at first appear to be. Among these we may mention 'the neck of the giraffe.'

"At first sight it would seem as though a better example in support of 'Natural Selection' could hardly have been chosen. Let the fact of the occurrence of occasional severe droughts in the country which that animal has inhabited be granted. In that case, when the ground vegetation has been consumed, and the trees alone remain, it is plain that at such times only those individuals (of what we assume to be the nascent giraffe species) which were able to reach high up would be preserved, and would become the parents of the following generation, some individuals of which would, of course, inherit that high-reaching power which alone preserved their parents. Only the high-reaching issue of these high-reaching individuals would again, *cæteris paribus,* be preserved at the next drought, and would again transmit to their off-spring their still loftier stature ; and so on, from period to period through æons of time, all the individuals tending to revert to the ancient shorter type of body, being ruthlessly destroyed at the occurrence of each drought.

" But against this it may be said, in the first place, that the argument proves too much ; for, on this supposition, many species must have tended to undergo a similar modification, and we ought to have at least several forms similar to the giraffe developed from different Ungulata. A careful observer of animal life, who has long resided in South Africa, explored the interior, and lived in the giraffe country, has assured the author that the giraffe has powers of locomotion and endurance fully equal to those possessed by any of the other Ungulata of that continent. It would seem, therefore, that some of these other Ungulates ought to have developed in a similar manner as to the neck, under pain of being starved, when the long neck of the giraffe was in its incipient stage.

" To this criticism it has been objected that different kinds of animals are preserved, in the struggle for life, in very different ways, and even that ' high reaching ' may be attained in more modes than one, — as, for example, by the trunk of the elephant. This is, indeed, true, but then none of the African Ungulata have, nor do they appear ever to have had, any proboscis whatsoever ; nor have they acquired such a development as to allow them to rise on their hind limbs and graze on trees in a kangaroo attitude, nor a power of climb-ing, nor, as far as known, any other modification tending to compensate for the comparative shortness of the neck. Again, it may perhaps be said that leaf-eating forms are ex-ceptional, and that, therefore, the struggle to attain high branches would not affect many Ungulates. But surely, when these severe droughts necessary for the theory occur, the ground vegetation is supposed to be exhausted, and indeed the giraffe is quite capable of feeding from off the ground. So that, in these cases, the other Ungulata must have taken to leaf-eating or have starved, and thus must have had any accidental long-necked varieties favored and preserved exactly as the long-necked varieties of the giraffe are supposed to have been favored and preserved."

But I am told that short-necked vegetable-eating animals live in the same localities as the long-necked giraffes. Why have not these short-necked races become long-necked, or died out during the protracted droughts, if long necks were necessary to the preservation of existence? Put these statements side by side.

But we know that animals, under the guidance of men, have been developed into very strong and excellent specimens of their races ; but there is no definite evidence that different breeds of domestic animals have developed themselves into particularly strong races without intelligent guidance outside of themselves ; though diversities of climate, kinds of food, laws of heredity, "natural selection," and other outward circumstances, doubtless greatly tend to modify the character and strength of races of animals as well as of men.

There is no doubt that the descendants of weak and barbarous races, through the influence of food, climate, education, habits of living, etc., have become developed into strong and civilized races, nor that the descendants of strong and vigorous races, through bad habits of living, improper food, etc., may degenerate into much lower types of humanity. And it is probable that many of what are classed as different species (more properly varieties) may, during the ages past, have descended from some common ancestor. But it should be kept in mind that it is one thing to believe that animals and plants now classed as different species have descended from some common ancestor; and it is quite another to unhesitatingly accept the statement that men have been developed from an ape-like mammal. Until one is prepared to accept this last dogma he will by some be considered illogical to stop half-way on the evolutionary road.

The Duke of Argyll, in "Primeval Man" (p. 39, 40), says: "But no such experience ever comes to us casting any light on the Origin of our own Race, or of any other. Some varieties of form are effected, in the case of a few animals, by domestication, and by constant care in the selection of peculiarities transmissible to the young. But these variations are all within certain limits; and, wherever human care relaxes or is abandoned, the old forms return, and the selected characters disappear. The founding of new forms by the union of different species, even when standing in close natural relation to each other, is absolutely forbidden by the sentence of sterility which Nature pronounces and enforces upon all hybrid offspring. And so it results that man has never seen the origin of any species. Creation by birth is the only kind of creation he has ever seen; and from this kind of creation he has never seen a new species come."

The world is full of analogies, and we can learn much from these if we rightly interpret them. A tree, for instance, in physical construction, is, in a general way, a type of the physical construction of many species of animals. Even a leaf is a type of the tree and of a vertebrate animal. Most leaves have a vertebral column, ribs, etc., and a breathing apparatus.

How similar the construction of a pod of the common pea to the body of a man! It has a vertebral column and ribs, and the peas themselves are located in a manner similar to the viscera and reproductive organs of vertebrate animals.

How strangely like living actions are the operations of frost in making the appearance of leaves upon the window-glass! Can that which forms these frost-leaves be the same force as that which forms the leaves upon the trees, which they so much resemble?

When we say a tree is a physical type of animated nature, we refer to its structure, growth, and vital properties; for trees and animals are developed from germs in a precisely similar manner, and in their secretion and exhalations they are wonderfully similar.

But, if animals and men have been developed from an original one-celled ancestor, it seems to me that there must have been a preëxisting vital principle to give life to the monera, or they would have never existed as living organisms. We can easily understand what is generally meant by the term "spontaneous generation."

I might rest here with a flat denial of this foundation principle till some one could show us that "spontaneous generation" now takes place. But many are accustomed to connect a theory and its starting-point together, not perceiving that it is possible for a theory to be correct after it has left its starting-point, while the very foundation on which the starting-point rests may be perfectly unreliable.

The starting-point, "spontaneous generation," appears to have no actual basis, as the experiments of M. Pasteur, Tyndall and others have proved.

But if we recognize the existence of an almighty creative intelligence, and allow that this creative power was the cause of life, all seems to follow naturally and logically to the final conclusion.

All animated forms indeed bear a resemblance in certain particulars. Thus when we are told that the chick in the egg, from the commencement of incubation to the time it breaks its shell and runs free, is a type of the development of the embryo in all the higher forms of animal life, we hear what is doubtless true.

Notwithstanding the fact that the theory is very plausible, it by no means follows that, because during the forty weeks preceding the birth of a human child stages typical of or similar to certain different races that have existed or now exist among the lower orders of creation are passed through, therefore man is descended through races of animals, of which these changes in the embryo are a type.

It by no means follows that, because oxen and horses are quite similar in their general physical structure and dispositions, therefore, they must have descended from some common ancestor.

If we are to deal in assumptions or presumptions, why may we not as well assume, as our fathers did, that the Creator originally designed all animal life on one general plan, but with almost infinite variations?

It should be borne in mind, however, in regard to the *origin* of life, that Darwin disagrees with Hæckel; for Darwin did not intimate that he believed in " spontaneous generation," but acknowledged that the Creator originally breathed the breath of life into the " original forms or form of life."

By the term " bona species " Agassiz meant absolutely different races which do not interbreed, and not those which are similar, like the wolf and the dog, which do interbreed and produce a progeny of wolf-dogs.

Dr. Hæckel charges (p. 116), that "The divine Creator, as represented by Agassiz, is but an idealized man, a highly imaginative architect, who is always preparing new building plans and elaborating new species."

If the Creator, or this underlying invisible Power, is in His nature incomprehensible (as I believe He is), how does any one know that the much-ridiculed " anthropomorphic conceptions " are entirely incorrect? Why assume that particular " conceptions " of Him are essentially wrong, while we cannot tell whether such conceptions are correct or incorrect? When one assumes that he knows that the Creator cannot exist and act in certain ways, does he not, by that very assumption, virtually claim that he can tell how He may exist and act? Does not such an assumption virtually set a limit to the powers of the Creator?

Why may not the Creator (if He chooses), work on new creations now as well as in the beginning? New varieties of living creatures are being discovered. Who knows that some of these are not new creations? Who knows that new worlds are not now in process of construction? Who knows that comets are not the nuclei around which, æons hence, new worlds may be in process of construction? If the solar system was evolved from cosmic vapor, and was æons in being consolidated, why may not cosmic vapor still exist which is not yet consolidated, from which other worlds may yet be constructed? Possibly the earth may have been constructed or consolidated millions of ages subsequent to the construction of the great suns which we call the fixed stars. Does any man know to the contrary? Has the Creator become so tired that He must rest, and let all the mighty

powers and forces of nature run without His personal supervision? Why should those who deny the existence of a
personal almighty intelligence, claim exclusive knowledge of
the mysteries of our existence?

Again, on these questions of our descent, when reasoning
from peculiarities of our physical organism, we may well
suppose that physiologists know something. Yet Hæckel
says (p. 20, vol. 1, "Evolution of Man ") : " Physiology,
however, has, especially during the last twenty years, been
far more one-sided in its progress than Morphology. Not
only has it entirely neglected to apply the comparative
method, by which Morphology has gained its greatest results,
but it has altogether disregarded the History of Evolution."
Also (on p. 21), he says : "Indeed the direction at present
taken by Physiology is so one-sided that it has even
neglected the recognition of the most important functions of
Evolution, namely, Heredity and Adaptation, and has left
this entirely physiological task to morphologists."

This is a virtual confession that physiologists have not
generally received to their full extent the doctrines of evolution.

Many have adopted these doctrines in their general application ; but not so many as radical evolutionists claim have
adopted them in their full extent. Physiologists are slow to
do so. But the general principles which underlie the popular
development theory are very ingeniously explained, and the
"spontaneous generation " part of the theory is peculiarly
palatable to such as would vote the Creator out of existence.
And yet, if the Creator has chosen to create and develop men
according to the theory of Darwin or Hæckel, or even
according to the theories of their most radical disciples, who
shall question His right or power to do so ?

Another reason why some receive the radical development theories may be seen by looking at the history of scientific theories for the past two thousand years. When new and startling theories have been broached, they have created a sort of philosophic craze, and the vagaries have their run, like a fever, till burned out, or till some succeeding theory swallows up the preceding.

It is now in some respects as it was in the days of Paul, many want "to hear or tell some new thing," and if enough that is new cannot be found in the real, then something new must be invented. Or, as Huxley said, when referring to the ingenuity displayed by Hæckel in his "History of the Creation," "Whether one agrees or disagrees with him, one feels that he has forced the mind into new lines of thought in which it is more profitable to go wrong than to stand still." So a great many now are better pleased to receive unproved theories than to stand still.

It has often been asked, if species do interchange, or so develop as to become radically different races, why have we not some evidence during the past four thousand years that some one species has changed into or towards some other specific species? Why, since evolutionists are so particular about facts from experience, or experimental knowledge, do they not show facts to prove their theory, instead of pointing to so many analogies, and asserting that these establish their theory?

It is true that during thousands of ages, in geologic time, by an almost infinite number of accretions of infinitesimal differences, animals may, and probably have, essentially changed in construction and appearance, when so short a time as four thousand years might make no appreciable difference. But, admitting that this may be probable, the burden of proof still rests upon the evolutionists.

One strong point of Dr. Hæckel's theory, and one which he repeats over and over again, is what he calls, "the fundamental law of organic evolution, or the first principle of biogeny" (pp. 6, 7), and it is thus expressed : "The series of forms through which the individual organism passes during its progress from the egg-cell to its fully-developed state, is a brief, compressed reproduction of the long series of forms through which the animal ancestors of that organism (or the ancestral forms of its species) have passed from the earliest periods of so called organic creation down to the present time."

This is his law, and it is clearly enough expressed, and it is the very corner-stone of his fabric. And it must be confessed that he has made this theory appear very plausible ; but if he could prove that the changes which the chick in the shell goes through are an exact type of all the changes which the chick's mature ancestors have gone through during the millions of years since it came (through the process of development) from an original one-celled ancestor, then his whole case would be proved, and it would be useless to combat it. But he assumes the very fact that needs to be proved. How does he know that these changes in the chick are a type of its previous ancestors through the many stages of development? He mentions certain facts that seem to point in that direction. But is that *proof*? No. The whole theory rests upon assumption ; but no man can tell for a certainty whether it is a true or a false assumption.

The point under consideration is important, for it is fundamental. One school asserts that the changes in the human embryo are a type of the mature animals of the

ancestral races through which, by the process of development, men have descended.

One can readily see, by following out analogies which we
find in nature, from the smallest particles of matter which
we can discover with the microscope to the planets themselves, that there are striking resemblances, and that there
are certain general laws applicable to all. All nature in
its action seems like a wheel within a wheel; but I do not see
why we should assume that the development of the chick in
its shell and the development of the human embryo should
be like the progressive stages of development which the
mature ancestors of the embryo or chick have passed through
in each succeeding generation from their original ancestors,
any more than the development of the chick in the shell
should be typical of the growth of the chick from the time
of hatching through the whole of its remaining physical
existence, or from its birth to its death.

I would not raise objections against the *plausibility* of
this "Law of Biogeny;" but it is the positiveness with which
its truth is asserted which troubles me. I simply protest
against drawing positive and sweeping conclusions too
hastily from insufficient data.

But, if it be shown that the human embryo is never like
any mature animal, but is simply like another embryo,
then the doctrine of this equivalence, or general agreement
with other races, is greatly weakened.

Now let us see what competent naturalists assert. According to K. E. von Baer, as quoted by Agassiz
("Classification," pp. 351, 352), "the results at which
K. E. von Baer had arrived by his embryological investigations respecting the fundamental relations existing
among animals, differed considerably from the ideas then

prevailing. In order, therefore, to be correctly understood, he begins, with his accustomed accuracy and clearness, to present a condensed account of those opinions with which he disagreed, in these words : 'Few views of the relations existing in the organic world have received so much approbation as this : that the higher animal forms in the several stages of the development of the individual, from the beginning of its existence to its complete formation, correspond to the permanent forms in the animal series, and that the development of the several animals follows the same laws as those of the entire animal series ; that, consequently, the most highly organized animal, in its individual development, passes, in all that is essential, through the stages that are permanent below it, so that the periodical differences of the individual may be reduced to the differences of the permanent animal forms.' "

Now let us see what von Baer did find from his investigations (p. 357, Agassiz). He says, "Comparing these four types with the embryonic development, von Baer shows that there is only a general similarity between the lower animals and the embryonic stages of the higher ones, arising mainly from the absence of differentiation in the body, and not from a typical resemblance. The embryo does not pass from one type to the other ; on the contrary, the type of each animal is defined from the beginning, and controls the whole development. The embryo of the Vertebrate is a Vertebrate from the beginning, and does not exhibit at any time a correspondence with the Invertebrate. The embryos of Vertebrates do not pass, in their development, through other permanent types of animals. The fundamental type is first developed, and afterwards more and more subordinate characters appear. From a more general type the more special is manifested; and the more two forms of animals differ, the earlier must their development be traced back to discern an agreement between them. It is barely possible that, in their first beginning, all animals are alike, and present only hollow spheres; but the individual development of the higher animals certainly does not pass through the permanent forms of lower ones. What is common in a higher group of animals is always sooner developed in their embryos than what is special; out of that which is most general arises that which is less general, until that which is most special appears. Each embryo of a given type of animals, instead of passing through other definite types, becomes, on the contrary, more and more unlike them. An embryo of a higher type is, therefore, never identical with another animal type, but only with an embryo."

If von Baer was correct in this statement then those who have stated that the human embryos pass through all the essential distinctive characteristics which remain permanent in the species which are below it must be in error; and thus, this would seem to be in opposition to Hæckel's " Law of Biogeny." Other learned naturalists besides Agassiz agree with von Baer. Prof. Orton (p. 201, "Comp. Zoölogy") says : " At the outset, all animals, from the sponge to man, are indistinguishable from one another. They are mainly drops of fluid, a little more transparent on one side than the other ; and, in all cases, this almost homogeneous globule must develop three well-defined parts, — a germinal dot, germinal vesicle, and yolk. But while vertebrates and invertebrates can travel together on the same road up to this point, here they diverge, never to meet again. For, every grand group early shows that it has a peculiar type of construction. Every egg is from the first impressed with the power of developing in one direction only, and never does it lose its fundamental characters."

Let us, however, not forget what has been before stated, that, on account of the general peculiarities which, with numerous variations, run through the whole universality of living things, it may not be unreasonable to suppose that the law of organic evolution may embody types of all living beings which have ever existed or ever will exist; and that the development of an acorn into an oak, or a chick into a fowl may in some respects be typical of the development of all animated nature ever since animated nature existed.

That resemblances should run through nature in all its forms is indeed wonderful; but, the more wonderful this is, the greater the necessity for the existence of an intelligent worker to make all things in such similar correspondence, even to the certainty of the shape of the various crystals formed by the evaporation of solutions. The perfectly unvarying laws that govern all things appear to be the work of some infinitely high intelligence.

But, if the changes passed through during the forty weeks necessary for the development of the human embryo to a perfect infant, or the three weeks for the development of the chick in the shell, or the uncertain or indefinite time during which an acorn develops into an oak, are partial types of the arrangements of all animated nature, that does not by any means prove that present species of animals have been developed out of radically different species of animals; nor does it by any means show that the human race must have passed through a line of ancestral forms similar to all the changes which take place in the embryo before the perfect human physical system is developed.

There are several stubborn facts which seem to indicate

that the theory of the descent of man through apes is not correct. De Quatrefages states that the angle of the sphenoid bone, or the bone upon which the brain rests, constantly grows less as the human approaches manhood; while in the apes, the angle of this bone grows larger, averaging about twenty-seven degrees greater in mature apes than in infant apes. And he adds ("Human Species," p. 380) : "I have already insisted that facts of this nature are irreconcilable with those theories which attribute a more or less pithecoid ancestor to man."

Peschel says (p. 4 "Races of Man ") : "Finally, the early disappearance of the intermaxillary bone in the human infant may be cited as a distinction from the apes.

"These last facts oblige us to glance at the evolutionary history of man, which has gained great importance since Johann Friedrich Meckel, of Halle, asserted, in 1812, that every animal in its immature condition (and this lasts from the fecundation of the egg to the first sexual functions) passes through all the forms which occur during the entire life of the animals of every grade beneath it.

"At the time of birth the gap between the child and the young of the ape is as yet very narrow. The brains of children and young apes approach very closely in size, but of all parts of the body the brain of the ape grows the least. Thus, although the brain of the anthropomorphous ape contains all the main parts of the human skull, its development, nevertheless, assumes quite another direction." . . . . "Before the change of teeth has begun, the brain of the ape has usually attained its completion, whereas, in the child its proper development is just then actively beginning.

"In the apes, on the contrary, the facial bones grow in an animal direction, so that finally the largest ape has the brain of a child and the jaws of an ox. Thence it follows that a man would never originate from the progressive evolution of the apes, for their development is directed to different ends, and the longer they advance towards these ends the greater are the contrasts."

Prof. Virchow, in an address at Munich, before quoted from (according to Billing, p. 79, "Scientific Materialism"), said : " I should not be alarmed if proof were found that the ancestors of man were vertebrated animals. I work by preference in the field of anthropology ; yet I must declare that every step of positive progress which we have made in the domain of prehistoric anthropology has really moved further away from the proof of this connection. Cuvier maintained in the quaternary period man did not exist; but now quaternary man is a real doctrine, tertiary man a problem, and yet there are questions in discussion for the existence of man during the tertiary period. Even ecclesiastics admit, as Bourgeois, that man existed in the tertiary period. Quaternary fossil man we find just the same as ourselves. Only ten years ago, when a skull was found in peat, or in the lake dwellings, a wild and undeveloped state was seen in it. We were *then scenting monkey air*, but these old troglodytes turn out to be quite respectable society. Our French neighbors warn us not to count too much on these big heads ; it may be possible the old brains had more intermediary tissue than those of the now day, and that their nerve substance, notwithstanding the size of the receptacle, remained at a low state of development. Comparing the total of fossil men found with the existing types, *we find that, in the present, there is relatively a much larger number of lower types than there were in that period.*

" In the fossil types the lower developments are absolutely wanting. That only the higher geniuses of the quaternary period were preserved I dare not suppose, but this can be said, that one fossil monkey skull or ape-man has never been found. It is possible in some special spot on earth tertiary man lived, for the remarkable discovery of the fossil ancestors of the horse in America, from which the horse had entirely disappeared, gives countenance to the idea. It may be that tertiary man has existed in Greenland or Lemuria and will be brought to light somewhere or other. *We cannot teach, we cannot designate it as a revelation of science, that man descends from the ape or any other animal.* Bacon said, with perfect truth, '*scientia est potentia*' (knowledge is power) ; but the knowledge he meant was not specu- lative, not the knowledge of problems, but the objective knowledge of facts. We should abuse and endanger our power if, in our teaching, *we do not* fall back upon this perfectly justified, perfectly safe, and impregnable domain."

There is no reliable evidence that apes from which men could be developed lived before man existed. If they did not so exist, how can man be descended from them? If they did so exist, why has not a fossil monkey or ape-man's skull ever been found? Such remains may yet be found ; but until they are found, the acceptance of the above theory of descent must be received as provisional only.

What is stated to be fact in the above can be safely con- sidered fact, and one fact is worth more than a score of scientific suppositions. Another stubborn fact that seems to go against the Darwinian theory of human descent is, that man, in the very earliest stages of his existence, even to the

oldest skeleton ever discovered, shows no greater resemblance
to the apes than present races of men do. The Duke of
Argyll, as previously quoted, says (p. 73, "Primeval
Man") : "The other skeleton, respecting which the evidence
of extreme antiquity is the strongest, is not only perfectly
human in all its proportions, but its skull has a cranial
capacity not inferior to that of many modern Europeans.
This most ancient of all known human skulls is so ample in
its dimensions that it might have contained the brains of a
philosopher."

The point mentioned by Virchow concerning man in the
tertiary period is of importance ; but, even supposing that
man dates back no farther than the quarternary period, one is
naturally inclined to ask a mathematical question, viz., if
we go back 30,000 to 50,000 years, and find that at that
time there was a smaller proportion of individual men of a
low type than there is at the present time, how far back must
we go to make a connection between men and apes ? It is
one thing to be possible, and quite another to be probable ;
and even probability falls very far short of proof. Is it fair
and philosophical to claim that a mere hypothesis is already
equivalent to a fact, because no one has yet been able to
show that the hypothesis is not founded in fact ? It is
common for parties to make rash statements, and then,
if no one can show that these statements are actually
untrue, to claim that they have shown them to be true.
Thus a thousand statements may be made concerning which
no demonstrations exist either for or against ; but what do
such statements amount to ? Is it not unphilosophical to
claim all things which are uncertain to be on our side of the
argument ? Suppose one should lay claim to all property,
real and personal, concerning which there is uncertainty of

ownership, — how would that work? Thus, in arguments, the class of uncertain claims should have its due weight; but its due weight, in many cases, amounts to about zero. Some one has said that it will not do to tell school-boys that some things are certain and others uncertain; for they will get things mixed, and believe the facts to be the uncertain things, and some of the uncertain things to be facts; but when we are talking to educated men, or to philosophers, it will do to confess that there are many things which we do not know for a certainty. I trust my readers will be so much like philosophers that they will not mistake the uncertain things for the certain, or reject positive facts, and receive as facts things which are uncertain. Certain writers have accused the believers in a creative theory with accepting absurd notions. Can there be greater folly, while the atheistic are themselves ignorant of the character or mode of existence of that almighty force or power which underlies all the manifestations and phenomena of life? Man has the highest intelligence of any being concerning whom they have positive knowledge. How can they, in their own minds, form a conception of an intelligent being, acting from reason, who does not reason in a manner somewhat similar to the reasonings of the most intelligent men? They extol reason, and call it the only unerring guide. Why then, should not the highest intelligence we can conceive of work also in accordance with some unerring guide?

I am aware that Omniscience may have no need of any process of reasoning; for, knowing all things, He must be without the necessity for any course of reasoning; yet I cannot understand how Omniscience and Omnipotence combined should have ordained and established the immutable laws of nature without some reasons for so doing.

Could we conceive of a man with infinite intelligence, would he not be likely to reason in some respects as a finite being does? How do we know that finite reason may not be in some respects typical of infinite reason? Let the wisest show us the actual truth concerning infinite wisdom and intelligence, if he can.

CHAPTER VIII.

DOES LIFE INHERE IN MATTER ITSELF?

It would seem to ordinary observers that there must be a distinct line between the dead and the living. Hæckel denies that such a line exists in such a sense as is generally supposed. Others have, in substance, stated that organic and inorganic matter shade into, or so intermingle with each other that no distinct line between the dead and the living can be drawn.

If asked to state upon what facts they base the opinion that there is no absolute vital difference between dead and living matter, they may cite the ultimate atoms, and assume that they are endowed with the principle of life, providing there be such a thing as a life principle. They might also mention the theory of Leibnitz in relation to monads. Leibnitz believed monads to be mathematical points, — " the simple active elements of things, the veritable, living atoms of nature, the immaterial, indivisible and final forces of the universe."

He held that both mind and matter are composed of monads, but that mind is represented by conscious monads, and matter by unconscious monads. "But these two classes of monads are wholly unlike, and exert no influence on each other," — a conclusion to which materialists will hardly assent.

If all the original and ultimate atoms are alike, and endowed with the same properties, then the living and the dead are composed of these atoms.

Materialists do not acknowledge a vital principle separate

from matter, but consider life merely a result of the action
of matter ; or that life is a mere condition or process depend-
ing entirely upon the action of matter. Following out this
idea, some consider death to be simply a molecular change.
A similar idea of death is mentioned by Huxley in connection
with the opinions of Needham and Buffon. Needham, however, believed in indestructible living particles of matter,
as distinguished from non-living particles. Huxley (pp.
355, 356, "Lay Sermons") states Needham's opinions as
follows : "Life is the indefeasible property of certain indestructible molecules of matter, which exist in all living things,
and have inherent activities by which they are distinguished
from not living matter. Each individual living organism is
formed by their temporary combination. They stand to it
in the relation of the particles of water to a cascade or a
whirlpool ; or to a mould into which the water is poured.

"The form of the organism is thus determined by the reaction between external conditions and the inherent activities of the organic molecules of which it is composed ; and,
as the stoppage of a whirlpool destroys nothing but a form,
and leaves the molecules of the water, with all their inherent
activities intact, so what we call the death and putrefaction
of an animal, or of a plant, is merely the breaking up of the
form, or manner of association, of its constituent organic
molecules, which are then set free as infusorial animalcules.

"It will be perceived that this doctrine is by no means
identical with *Abiogenesis*, with which it is often confounded.
On this hypothesis, a piece of beef, or a handful of hay, is
dead only in a limited sense. The beef is dead ox, and the
hay is dead grass ; but the "organic molecules" of the beef
or the hay are not dead, but are ready to manifest their
vitality as soon as the bovine or herbaceous shroud in which

they are imprisoned are rent by the macerating action of water."

Various other like theories seem to be intertangled to a great extent, and may live to be discussed ages hence; but the science of modern chemistry has dispelled these illusions of Needham and Buffon, and probably further investigation will demonstrate the untenableness of many other opinions on this point.

In some cases it is extremely difficult to tell just where this line between life and death is drawn. In certain cases, it may be impossible to distinguish between organic and inorganic matter, even with the most powerful microscopes; for the organic matter may have lines of structure so fine that we cannot discover them, and living organisms may be so minute that we cannot discover them. Organic matter may be structureless.

It may be impossible in some cases to tell whether organic matter is dead or alive. But because not obvious no one has a right to assume that this distinction does not exist.

If we break a piece from a block of marble the piece we take off remains of the same quality as it originally was. The separation does not change the quality or manner of its existence; but if we break a branch from a living plant or tree how soon this branch changes, and the difference between the living and the dead branch appears. The marble statue is largely composed of the remains of once living beings. But when one states that organic and inorganic matter are equally living, if the organic matter is in living animals, we see the inaccuracy of the statement. But when the statement is made concerning what we cannot readily class, though the dividing line may be absolute, it makes a vast difference with many as to the truth or falsity of the statement. The following passage, taken from Leo H. Grindon, gives his idea of life as manifested in inorganic nature ("Life, Its Nature, etc." pp. 23, 24) : —

"That life does not necessarily imply organization or reproduction is shown in what may without impropriety be called the Life of the World. Doubtless, there is an impassable chasm between the mineral and the vegetable, as between the vegetable and the animal, and between the animal and man. But this inorganic nature, which is represented as 'dead,' because it has not the same life with the animal or plant, is it then, to quote Guyot, destitute of all life? It has all the *signs* of life, we cannot but confess. Has it not motion in the water which streams and murmurs on the surface of the continents, and which tosses in the waves of the sea? Has it not sympathies and antipathies in those mysterious elective affinities of the molecules of matter which chemistry investigates? Has it not the powerful attractions of bodies to each other which govern the motions of the stars scattered in the immensity of space, and keep them in an admirable harmony? Do we not see, and always with a secret astonishment, the magnetic needle agitated at the approach of a particle of iron, and leaping under the fire of the Northern Light? Place any material body whatever by the side of another, do they not immediately enter into relations of interchange, of molecular attraction, of electricity, of magnetism? In the inorganic part of matter, as in the organic, all is acting, all is promoting change, all is itself undergoing transformation. And thus, though this life of the globe, this physiology of our planet, is not the life of the tree or the bird, is it not *also* a life? Assuredly it is. We cannot refuse so to call those lively actions and reactions, that perpetual play of the

THE DEVELOPMENT OF LIFE.

forces of matter, of which we are every day the witnesses. The thousand voices of nature which make themselves heard around us, and in so many ways betoken incessant and prodigious activity, proclaim it so loudly that we cannot shut our ears to their language."

Though the above extracts indicate that Grindon and Guyot believed, in certain respects, that there are manifestations like those called living in inorganic matter, yet they by no means intend to imply that the life of men, plants and minerals is the same; for Grindon further says, p. 24: "Indeed the life of the soul, or that which is played forth as the activity of the intellect and the affections, is the highest expression of all. Compared with *this* life, the life of animals and plants, and the life of the globe, are but mimicries and shadows."

Grindon calls what is usually termed *Life*, "physiological life;" but when he attempts to account for the *origin* of life he says (p. 29): "God is the only independent existence, and He is the cause of all causes. He alone has life in himself."

And on p. 40 he further says: "Inorganic life, the first named of these three great varieties or manifestations of the vitalizing principle, has been illustrated in the preceding chapters. It will suffice to add here that it has nothing *in common* with organic or physiological life, much less with the spiritual; nothing, that is to say, except the Divine origin and sustentation."

We shall soon see to what errors the following out an assumed theory may lead us. As before quoted, Hæckel says (p. 23, vol. 1, "History of Creation"): "When in a solution of salt a crystal is formed, the phenomenon is neither more nor less a mechanical manifestation of life than the growth and flowering of plants, than the propagation of animals or the activity of their senses, than the perception or the formation of thought in man."

Though this extract does not, in so many words, state that the *quality* of life in minerals, plants and animals is *the same*, yet the idea seems to be that as the mechanical actions in minerals and plants are alike, or very similar, the vital properties are also alike.

In this view of life Hæekel's philosophy is strikingly similar to that of various savage tribes. For instance, the Zuñi Indians are said to believe that all motion reveals a sign of life; hence, behind the swaying branches of trees and the rolling of waves on the waters, they recognize a living personality, or life, as the cause of these motions. I have before stated that in animals and plants the nutriment goes from outside to inside by a motion peculiar to life, and entirely dissimilar to the formation of erystals; and, when this nutriment has been used, the waste in animals goes, by a peculiar motion, from inside to outside, and this action is continuous. Crystals grow by the aggregation of crystalline particles lodging on the outside, which forms them into particular shapes, and so long as the erystals do not dissolve or decompose, no action or change of place oceurs in these particles. The growth is so unlike living growth that for a sane man to assert that they are governed by the same prineiples seems very strange. The act of crystallization cannot justly be called a living aetion. There are some, however, who clutch at a statement like the above, viz., that organic and inorganic matter are equally living, and receive it as profound truth. This class of philosophers, or rather speculators in science, has existed since early historie times. Some have done much to stimulate inquiry, and thus sharpen the intellect through its effort to separate truth from error and fact from fiction.

Briefly stated this philosophy amounts to this : That life is merely an adjustment of relations, and that the difference between the living and non-living is one of degree, but not of kind ; that life, to some extent, inheres in everything, or in every material substance ; and that the action of the heart as well as the circulation of the blood is only an exhibition of mechanical force just as really as the operations of a steam-engine ; and that the original driving forces are one and the same. But such do not seem to consider that the steam-engine may be stopped, and take a lengthened rest, and then be started up again without any detriment to its powers. Not so with the action of the heart. When that has once fairly ceased its action that action is never resumed ; when it has once really ceased to beat for five consecutive minutes its action has forever ceased. We know that there is a mechanical action of the heart ; but there is a vital principle behind its normal action. Materialists may deny the existence of this vital principle ; but mere denial has no real force. Radcliffe (as quoted by S. Billing, " Scientific Materialism," p. 13) says, "We can only suppose that the vital fact exemplifies its energy by physical means in its application to the animal economy. Whatever be the physics of the mechanism, they can but be conducted by waste. The vital energy using them as its methods *repairs the waste, and thus excludes all idea of physical force (per se) being the initiatory impulse.*

" If vital action resulted alone in mechanical motion it might be said that muscular force was physical force ; but no physical force reproduces itself."

If physical force could reproduce itself, we might easily solve the problem of perpetual motion.

From a great multitude of facts gathered, and inferences deduced from investigation, Hæckel weaves what to him and many others seems a beautiful web of truth. But he has taken premises in the unknown, and hence is likely to err, because he does not know whether or not the principles on which he has built his foundations are resting upon absolute truth. His followers (and they are legion) contend that there was originally in matter itself the power to originate life.

This theory dispenses with the necessity of a Creator; for, if matter is eternal, and has in itself the power to originate life, then there would not appear to be any necessity for a self-existent life (which was originally independent of matter) to cause the manifestations of life which we see in matter.

Geologists state that the earth, during its early existence, was so hot that no life could exist on it. It was then simply dead matter, though later on plant life existed when no animal could live. But life, both plant and animal, now exists. Whence did this life come? How did it spring into existence? Did the dead matter of the earth, in itself, have power to originate life? In other words, did that which was dead have power to bring into existence what it did not itself possess, viz., life? If it did, did it not create something out of nothing? But the philosophic maxim is, "From nothing, nothing comes."

There seems no way to obviate this difficulty, without acknowledging a Creator, except to assume that all natural bodies are equally living; and thus at the time when we suppose the earth was simply dead matter it was not so, but that the life-giving power was already there. What warrant is there for such an assumption? On the contrary, did not a vital principle move on this dead matter, and transform inorganic matter into organic, or living matter?

It has been stated that Liebig assumed that dead matter can produce fermentation ; but, as Tyndall well says : " With Liebig, fermentation was by no means synonymous with *life*. It meant, according to him, the shaking asunder by chemical disturbance of unstable molecules. Does the life of our flasks, then, proceed from *dead* particles? If my co-inquirer should reply ' Yes,' then I would ask him, ' What warrant does Nature offer for such an assumption? Where, amid the multitude of vital phenomena in which her operations have been clearly traced, is the slightest countenance given to the notion that the sowing of dead particles can produce a living crop? ' " (p. 296, " Floating Matter.")

No one has yet clearly described the line that separates life from death ; hence, in this case, even with the most learned, analogy and common-sense must be strong witnesses. When we take into consideration the facts which we have before stated, and which seem to show that life is the cause of organization, we must conclude that life had its original beginning in some power outside of and above mere matter. To say that life was originally evolved by chemical processes which occurred during the long ages while the earth was cooling is a mere supposition, for there are no known facts to substantiate that statement.

Light, heat, electricity and moisture are mighty instrumentalities, and, operating on organic matter, produce great and beneficent changes, and also great modifications of the forms of life. But to produce modifications is one thing, and to produce a new creation is quite another. There must have been a beginning somewhere or somehow, and the reasoning mind wants more than guesswork to satisfy it in its inquiries.

The germs of life are everywhere ; in the air we breathe, in the dust beneath our feet, and in the depths of the sea. Where did these germs of life come from?

Living animals only one ninety-thousandth of an inch in diameter can be seen ; but who can tell how much smaller living creatures there may be which cannot be seen with the microscope? As Nature is infinite in extension, so she may also be in minuteness.

Infusions of hay, and of turnip, and of a score of other articles, have been boiled, with the intent of destroying all life contained in them. These infusions were put in glass bottles, and hermetically sealed ; but in a few days they were found teeming with living organisms. Where did these organisms come from?

From a great number of like experiments, made on both sides of the Atlantic, some learned men came to the conclusion that these living beings came by " spontaneous genera- tion," or (perhaps more properly expressed) that this new life was evolved from dead matter, and that new life is being now constantly evolved by the power of nature alone. So extensive and various have these experiments been that it is not safe to turn these trials, tests, and conclusions off without consideration.

It is with pleasure, however, that I can say that the labors of M. Pasteur, a French chemist, and of Prof. Tyndall, aided by experiments of other able and careful scientists dur- ing the past fifteen years, have almost entirely revolutionized what was the commonly received scientific opinion twenty years since in regard to this theory of "spontaneous genera- tion ;" and the germ theory of life, which was once opposed

by nearly the whole force of chemical authority, is now as
generally accepted as it was formerly rejected ; or, according
to Dr. Carpenter, it is now accepted by all, "except a few
irreconcilables."

We have not been informed where these life-germs originally came from, or how they were originated. The germ
theory destroys the doctrine of "spontaneous generation,"
but it does not tell us how or when the floating germs in the
air were placed there, or how life happens to be in the germs.
This simply places the originating power one step farther
back.

But let us see whether our germ theory will help us get
life into hermetically sealed bottles after all previous life
has been destroyed by boiling. If life cannot be spontaneously generated, can it be that all life above a certain
stage of development may be destroyed by boiling, while
the original invisible germs of life are not destroyed?
Can these germs, still retaining their vitality through the
boiling, afterwards become developed into visible living
organisms? Germs of life are indeed wonderful things ;
they consist of many varieties, for each kind is believed
to start a life of its particular kind only. I cannot think
these germs start one kind or species of life, and then evolve
themselves into another species. Not only germs for propagation of healthy animal life exist, but disease-germs, which,
though living, tend to destroy animal, and even plant life ;
and each kind of these germs is distinctly different from
every other kind.

Different kinds of disease-germs never intermingle, but
always breed diseases of their own peculiar kind, typhoid-
fever germs do not breed small-pox, nor small-pox breed
measles, nor measles, diphtheria.

Prof. Tyndall says (p. 41, "Floating Matter") : "From their respective viruses, you may plant typhoid-fever, scarlatina, or small-pox. What is the crop which arises from this husbandry? As surely as a thistle rises from a thistle seed, as surely as the fig comes from the fig, the grape from the grape, the thorn from the thorn, so surely does the typhoid virus increase and multiply into typhoid-fever, the scarlatina virus into scarlatina, the small-pox virus into small-pox. What is the conclusion that suggests itself here? It is this : That the thing which we vaguely call a virus is, to all intents and purposes, a *seed*. Excluding the notion of vitality, in the whole range of chemical science you cannot point to an action which illustrates this perfect parallelism with the phenomena of life, — this demonstrated power of self-multiplication and reproduction. The germ theory alone accounts for the phenomena."

As germs in grain always develop into stock and grain of their own peculiar kind, so all germs, whether good or evil, develop into their own kinds. But another question now arises. Can germs of living animals or plants pass through materials through which disease germs cannot pass?

Disease-germs may be destroyed by carbolic acid and other disinfectants ; but can the original, invisible germs of life (if such exist) be thus destroyed? I now propose, in the next few pages, to go outside of the proper domains of scientific demonstrations.

If the following brief suggestions seem puerile, let the wisest answer the questions if he can. These suppositions are not introduced because it is necessary to resort to such hypotheses to dispose of the doctrine of " spontaneous generation," but they show that, even if we could not filter out all the life-germs (which, luckily, we can), the doctrine of "spontaneous generation," with all the evidence which has been produced in its favor, would fail of anything like demonstration.

Is there an original and invisible principle of life which is indestructible? Are immaterial essences connected with the minute material germs? and, if so, how large are they? If the original germs are wholly material, are they larger than what are supposed to be the ultimate and indivisible atoms of matter? Of course, what can be filtered out may be a thousand times larger.

Do invisible vivifying influences, or vital forces, which are immaterial, or spiritual, exist prior to the material germs or substances from which animals or vegetables are generated or developed, and cause the animal or vegetable life to spring into existence? And if so, can any material substance interfere to hinder the free passage of the spiritual or vital forces to any place where suitable conditions for development exist? Is not Evolution itself dependent upon the action of immaterial forces? Of course, a thing immaterial (if such exists) must become connected with a material substance before we can have any knowledge of it through our senses.

A pain or emotion may be immaterial; but we can have no knowledge of it, except through our physical system.

It is probable that pains, thoughts and emotions (though in themselves immaterial) are accompanied by molecular action upon or within the nervous system, and that this very action results in the consciousness of pain, joy, or sorrow and other emotions, and yet there is doubtless something antecedent to these molecular actions; and the agitation of these molecules may be simply an accompaniment of some mysterious and invisible agency which causes mental states of fear, joy, hope, etc., and also bodily feelings of pain, etc.

There may be a vital principle of which we can have no knowledge before it becomes connected with the living organisms ; but lack of definite knowledge on this point does not indicate that such a vital principle does not preëxist. There are phenomena connected with animal life that I cannot account for except upon the supposition that a vital principle is preëxistent.

Sidney Billing says (p. 16, " Scientific Materialism ") : " If we collate the facts, what do we find ? Vital force as the inherent fact of all things ; physical or material force but a consequence of the organization. Vital force originates, physical force acts only through an impulsion. Vital force congregates, disintegrates, and multiplies itself; physical force acts only in masses through gravitation. Vital force cannot be originated, nor its issues directed ; but physical force may be directed and called into action at will, and may be made the plaything of the hour, as the incitation of muscular elasticity after death."

Now about the generation of life in hermetically sealed vessels. From all the evidence *pro* and *con*, it seems clear that no life appears in any solution where life germs have been fully destroyed, unless the solution in some way comes in contact with the air, through some want of care in making the experiment, or by some defect in the testing apparatus, or unless it comes in contact with some other substance containing the life-germs ; for the thousand experiments made by Prof. Tyndall with various solutions in moteless air, and no life appearing, would seem to settle the question against " spontaneous generation " in such solutions. But even if his experiments had turned out otherwise, and life had appeared in hermetically sealed vessels after all proper precautions had been taken, that would not

necessarily prove the doctrine of "spontaneous generation."

Suppose the original atoms touch each other in glass, or
in dense metals, and that, according to the general forms of
matter as found in drops of water and the planets, these
atoms are globular, interstices between the atoms must still
exist, as in a case of shot, however fine. How then do we
know, even in this case, that the interstices between ultimate atoms are not large enough to allow the essential or
vital principle of life to pass through?

It has been stated that by the action of electricity particles
of gold have been driven into plates of glass, which (if true)
seems to indicate that what we call solid glass is, in reality,
porous, — and this would seem to agree with the atomic
theory ; and further, that the atoms of gold are fine enough to
enter these pores of glass, and that without any supernatural
influences.

While, as before stated, there is no necessity for resorting
to such a hypothesis, we may say that the essential, spiritual
life germs, if such can be assumed to exist, may be, for all
that we know, as many times smaller than the atoms of gold
as atoms of gold are times smaller than bullets. No one
can show that this may not be so.

Then again, suppose that these ultimate atoms, which no
man ever saw, were of irregular shape, interstices may exist
even larger than if all were globular, and thus the porosity
of the substance be even greater than in the former supposed case. That interstices must exist is an inevitable
consequence of the atomic theory as generally received.
Thus these experiments of learned men in Europe and
America,— with these infusions of hay, and of turnip, and a
dozen other infusions, both animal and vegetable, in sealed

bottles, — even if life was apparently generated there, would by no means prove that an immaterial principle of the germs of life did not go through the pores of the glass into these infusions. I do not claim that this is so ; but it shows that what some learned men have received as a demonstration falls very far short of it.

Since writing the above I have seen Rudolf Schmid on " The Theories of Darwin," and on pp. 138, 139 find the following : " This inexplicability would still exist, if what is quite improbable should happen, namely, that the experimental attempts at *artificially producing organic life* should be successful, and if thus the question as to the *generatio æquivoca*, which during the past decades so much alarmed the minds of scientists and theologians, should be experimentally solved and answered in the affirmative. For in view of the hopes of a possible explanation of life, which is expected to be the reward for the success of these attempts, Zöllner is fully right in saying : 'That the scientists to-day set such an extremely high value on the inductive proof of the *generatio æquivoca*, is the most significant symptom of how little they have made themselves acquainted with the first principles of the theory of knowledge. For, suppose they should really succeed in observing the origin of organic germs under conditions entirely free from objection to any imaginable communication with the atmosphere, what could they answer to the assertion that the organic germs, in reference to their extension, are of the order of ether-atoms, and, with these, press through the intervals of the material molecules which form the sides of our apparatus ?' "

Doubtless the reader already knows that the atomic theory is merely an hypothesis, and that we do not know whether the atoms (if they exist) are all alike and material, or whether a part are material atoms and others ether-atoms. Again, among the sixty-five supposed original chemical elements, what, for instance, is the difference between an atom of hydrogen and one of nitrogen?

So of the various kinds of life-germs which we are able to screen out of fluids, in what do their differences consist?

Where these life-germs originate, or how they happen to be everywhere present, I do not attempt to explain. But it has been proved by Pasteur's and Tyndall's experiments that these life-germs, so far as we are now acquainted with them, can easily be prevented from getting into solutions by wads of cotton-wool.

Sometimes, however, it has been exceedingly difficult to so perfectly filter infusions that all the visible suspended particles of matter will be removed. After going through a score or more sheets of filtering-paper, visible particles will still remain. Yet porous earthen-ware will screen out such life-germs; and thus we have no need of laying much stress upon any supposed spiritual essence which may go through what are called solids. Dr. Tyndall says (pp. 80, 81, " Floating Matter ") : "Infinitesimal as these particles are, however, they may be separated by mechanical means from the liquid in which they are held in suspension. Filters of porous earthen-ware, such as the porous cells of Bunsen's battery, have been turned to important account in the researches of Dr. Zahn, Prof. Klebs, and Dr. Burdon Sanderson.

" In various instances it has been proved that, as regards the infection of living animals, the porous earthen-ware intercepts contagia. For the living animal, organic infusions or Pasteur's solution may be substituted. Not only are ice-water, distilled water, and tap-water thus deprived of their powers of infection, but, by plunging the porous cell into an infusion swarming with Bacterial life, exhausting the cell, and permitting the liquid to be slowly driven through it by atmospheric pressure, the filtrate is not only deprived of its *Bacteria*, but also of those ultra-microscopic germs which appear to be as potent for infection as the *Bacteria* them- selves The precipitated mastic particles before described, which pass unimpeded through an indefinite number of paper filters, are wholly intercepted by the porous cell.

"These germinal particles abound in every pool, stream, and river. All parts of the moist earth are crowded with them. Every wetted surface which has been dried by the sun or air contains upon it particles which the unevaporated liquid held in suspension. From such surfaces they are detached and wafted away, their universal prevalence in the atmosphere being thus accounted for. Doubtless they some- times attach themselves to coarser particles, organic and in- organic, which are left behind along with them ; but they need no such rafts to carry them through the air, being themselves endowed with a power of flotation commensurate with their extreme smallness and the specific lightness of the matter of which they are composed."

Prof. Owen, as quoted by Hitchcock (p. 304), more than thirty years since wrote : "Thus each leaves, by the last act of its life, the means of perpetuating and diffus- ing its species by thousands of fertile germs. When once the thickly tenanted pool is dried up, and its bottom con- verted into a layer of dust, these inconceivably minute and light ova will be raised with the dust by the first puff of wind, diffused through the atmosphere, and may there re- main long suspended, forming, perhaps, their share of the particles which we see flickering in the sunbeam, ready to fall into any collection of water, beaten down by every

summer shower into the streams or pools which receive or
may be formed by such showers, and, by virtue of their
tenacity of life, ready to develop themselves whenever they
may find the requisite conditions of their existence. The
possibility, or, rather, the high probability, that such is the
design of the oviparous generation of the infusoria, and such
the common mode of the diffusion of their ova, renders the
hypothesis of equivocal generation, which has been so frequently invoked to explain their origin in new-formed natural or artificial infusions, quite gratuitous." (Owen's "Lect.
Comp. Anat.," vol. 2, p. 31.) It is doubtless from these
very minute floating germs that life in the infusions which
have been deprived of all living existences must come. But
this still leaves the question how these "germinal particles"
first came to be in every pool, stream, and river unanswered.
Science has not demonstrated how these myriad forms of
germinal life which constitute so large a proportion of the
"floating matter of the air" are themselves generated, or
decided whether they are first generated in the water. It is
generally thought that the first appearance of terrestrial life
was in the water, that in the water living organisms were
first created or developed. It is, however, useless to make
positive assertions on this point, in our present state of knowledge. Certainly the advocates of "spontaneous generation" have no warrant for assuming that these animalcules
which are so numerous in water are "spontaneously generated" in the water. We do not know for a certainty
whether these germinal particles are first in the air and fall
into these pools, and in this way fill the pools with living
particles, or whether they are first generated in the water,
and from these wafted into the atmosphere. Nor is it necessary that we should know whether they first originate in the

air or in the water, so long as we know the fact that in both air and water these germs exist in almost infinite numbers.

The advocates of "spontaneous generation" have made hundreds, and, perhaps, thousands, of experiments, and sometimes have thought they proved it beyond a doubt. One exhausted the air from a glass vessel, and let no air into the vessel except what passed through quicksilver, supposing that no life-germs could go through so dense a medium as quicksilver; but living things appeared in his solution, and he thought he had a case of genuine spontaneous generation. But M. Pasteur, upon investigation, found that quicksilver itself might become permeated with these living germs.

I have referred to faultiness of experiments as a frequent cause of misleading the believers in "spontaneous generation," and I can favor my readers no better than by quoting freely from Prof. Tyndall to show how these mistakes are likely to occur. He says (pp. 124, 125, "Floating Matter") : "During the course of this inquiry some eminent biologists have been good enough, from time to time, to look in upon my work, and to give me their views regarding the evidential force of the experiments. To Prof. Huxley, moreover, I am indebted for undertaking the examination of a number of the hermetically sealed tubes. Thirty of them were placed in his hands, none of them being regarded as defective. A close examination, however, disclosed in one of them a mycelium. No faultiness could for a time be discovered in the tube; the sealing appeared to be quite as perfect as that of its sterile fellows.

"Once, however, on shaking it, a minute drop of liquid struck my friend's face, and he soon discovered that an orifice of almost microscopic minuteness had been left open in the nozzle of the tube. Through this the common air had been sucked in as the liquid cooled, and hence the contamination. It was the only defective tube of the group of thirty, and it alone showed signs of life.

" The statement of this fact before the Royal Society, by Prof. Huxley, brought to my mind a somewhat similar experience of my own. One morning in November I lifted one of the hermetically sealed tubes from the wire on which it was suspended, and, holding it up against the light, discovered, to my astonishment, a beautiful mycelium at the bottom. Before restoring the tube to its place I touched its fused end, and found it cutting sharp. Close inspection showed that the nozzle had been broken off; the common air had entered and the seed of the mycelium had been sown. Two other instances, one like that observed by Prof. Huxley, have since come to light. In one of them a minute orifice remained after the supposed sealing of the tube. The other case was noticed when the tubes were returned from the Turkish bath. One of them contained a luxuriant mycelium. It was noticed that the liquid in this tube had singularly diminished in quantity, and on turning the tube up it was found cracked at the bottom.

" No case of pseudo-spontaneous generation ever occurred under my hands that was not to be accounted for in an equally satisfactory manner."

Much more might be written on this point, but the examples here given are samples of hundreds of like experiments with like results. But I will add one more quotation from Tyndall (p. 224, "Floating Matter"). He says, "The source of the contagium was also indicated by the following experiments.

" A large number of retort-flasks, embracing infusions of snipe, wild duck, partridge, hare, rabbit, mutton, turbot, salmon, whiting, mullet, turnip, and hay, had remained over from my stock of 1875. After a year's exposure to the temperature of our warm room not one of these flasks showed the slightest trace of turbidity or life. On the 7th of December the sealed ends of forty of them were snipped off in the laboratory. Five days afterwards twenty-seven of them were found swarming with organisms, — a considerably higher percentage than that obtained by the same process in the same laboratory a year previously.

"It is needless to dwell with any emphasis on the obvious inference from all this, namely, that the contagium is external to the infusions, that it is something in the air, and that at different times we have different amounts of aerial interspace free from the floating contagium."

It would seem that these experiments ought to settle the question.

When a writer has won a high reputation for careful scientific investigations his statements will justly have great weight; and when his experiments seem to demonstrate the truth of a theory, then the majority of men will believe that he has made no mistake in his conclusions; yet when no one can know with certainty what the actual truth is in a disputed case like the origin of life, great men may support a wrong theory as well as men of less eminent attainments. Careful students who have clear heads are quite as likely to hold actual truth as men of genius who deal largely in theories which are the creations of their own imaginations.

The writings of great men prove this, for they are largely composed of articles correcting the mistakes of still greater men.

Huxley says ("Critiques and Addresses," p. 281) : Dr. Hæckel "conceives that all forms of life originally commenced as *Monera*, or simple particles of protoplasm, and that these *Monera* originated from not-living matter.   Some of the *Monera* acquired tendencies towards the Protistic, others towards the Vegetal, and others towards the Animal, modes of life.   The last became animal *Monera*."

Then these animal monera went through twenty-two distinct stages, till the perfect man was produced.   But no proof, beyond certain statements and suppositions which appear reasonable to Hæckel, is given.   As it seems so to him, — and no man has proved that he is not right in many of his suppositions, — he has a right to his own opinions ; and so have other men, who cannot accept his conclusions, a right to their opinions.

Dr. Wainwright, in opposing the views of Hæckel (pp. 77, 78, " Scientific Sophisms "), states that " Du Bois Reymond has incurred the . . . wrath of Hæckel by declaring this genealogical tree (Stammbaum) to be as authentic in the eyes of a naturalist, as are the pedigrees of the Homeric heroes in those of an historian."

Hæckel is more positive in his statements than most men of such high intellectual attainments usually are.   Generally when really great men propound such or similar theories they do not pretend that they can demonstrate them to be true.   They propose them as conclusions which should be drawn from other facts which they know to be true.   If these hypotheses seem reasonable to a majority of scientific men they are generally accepted without actual demonstrations.   But trouble comes when second or third rate men (claiming to be scientific) read these hypotheses and then restate them as facts which have been proved, and thus mislead those who listen to them.   So long as we carefully distinguish between facts and mere suppositions we are not in danger ; but when we mistake suppositions for facts then danger comes.

Let us then consider facts, and see where the boundaries of our knowledge are fixed. First, in regard to the boundaries which limit microscopic observation : —

Much of the matter which floats in our atmosphere is too fine to be seen with the most powerful microscopes, and yet a concentrated beam of light will reveal the presence of these motes. But if these motes are too small for microscopic observation, any accurate description of their shapes or composition is impossible. Yet many of these very minute motes are believed to be living germs, which breed disease, or parasitic life if they get access to proper material, such as wounds in animals or men.

Here are limits to be constantly kept in mind when studying matters pertaining to the origin of life. The original germs of life may be much smaller than anything which can be discerned with the microscope.

It should also be borne in mind, that, with the microscope, one investigator may see what another can never see. And another man may think he sees what no man ever did see or ever will see. The imagination often supplies investigators with mistaken material. Now about the examination of the smallest and simplest particles of organic matter, viz., protoplasm.

According to Stricker (Wainwright, " Scientific Sophisms," p. 132), protoplasm is many-shaped. " We have club-shaped protoplasm, globe-shaped protoplasm, bottle-shaped protoplasm, cup-shaped protoplasm, spindle-shaped protoplasm ; " and he describes twelve other shaped protoplasms. Sometimes it is fluid, sometimes semifluid and gelatinous ; sometimes of considerable resistance.

" Then there is nerve protoplasm, brain protoplasm, bone protoplasm, muscle protoplasm, and the protoplasm of all the other tissues, no one of which but produces its own kind, and is uninterchangeable with the rest." Lastly, " We have to point to the overwhelming fact that there is the infinitely different protoplasm of the various infinitely different plants and animals, in each of which its own protoplasm, as in case of the various tissues, but produces its own kind, and is uninterchangeable with that of the rest."

Query : Are these protoplasms really different in kind, or is the difference in the moulding forces? The protoplasm from which the sugar-maple is developed and that from which the deadly nightshade grows may be entirely different protoplasms ; and this may be the reason why each never gets the protoplasm which belongs to the other. Why do weeds in the garden always draw from the soil only their own kind of protoplasm? Why does wheat always draw only its own kind, while the grass draws another kind? Why do different kinds of grasses never interchange their own kinds? Does it not seem probable that there may be a different kind of vital principle for each and every species of plant and animal, which transmutes the same or similar kinds of protoplasm, so as to make them contribute to the support and growth of each different species of plants and animals?

This action of growth seems to be mechanical ; but under what law of mechanics do they make this choice of substance, and never make a mistake in their choice? So of animals. There is a certain something which places a clear distinction between the building up of men and animals, and also between the different races of animals. There is no danger that horses will ever assimilate the protoplasm belonging exclusively to sheep, nor that sheep will ever produce dogs, nor dogs produce birds. Nature has fixed these bounds, and never mistakes them.

From the fact that the first outlines of human beings and all other animals in the ovum appear precisely alike, and cannot be distinguished from each other, and that each is a single cell, certain evolutionists carrying out analogy assert that the original ancestral form of man and all other animals was a one-celled organism. But it is legitimate to ask such to show proof of the correctness of this assertion.

The word cell is here used not to represent the ultimate particles of protoplasm but the elementary forms of organic matter somewhat in mass. A cell generally consists of concentric layers of cell-wall, protoplasm, etc., in one distinct organism.

The ovum is a single cell before fertilization, but fertilization entirely changes the character of the ovum, as it afterwards becomes a many-celled organism, and the number of cells continues to increase with its development.

Dr. Hæckel says (pp. 136, 137, vol. 1, " Evolution of Man ") : " Even under the highest magnifying power of the best microscope, there appears to be no essential difference between the eggs of Man, of the Ape, of the Dog, etc. This does not mean that they are not really different in these different Mammals. On the contrary, we must assume that such differences, at least in point of chemical composition, exist universally. Even of human eggs, each differs from the other. In accordance with the law of individual variation, we must assume that 'all individual organisms are, from the very beginning of their individual existence, different, though often very similar.'"

I am somewhat surprised at this confession of Dr. Hæckel, for I should suppose that, to be consistent with his general

theory, he would have contended that these ova, which
originally looked alike, were, indeed, alike at first, but that
all the differences manifested afterwards by different races of
animals were simply modifications received from the particular
animals through which they received their development. It
is probable, however, that the Doctor looked farther, and
saw what effect this theory of original individual differences
would have in another direction.

Sure enough, why should there not be individual differences
from the very beginning of life ? But where is this beginning?
Certainly it is before the ovum gets to be a one-hundred-
and-fiftieth of an inch in diameter, as it is generally, when
examined with the microscope.   Probably at this time it
has thousands, and, perhaps, millions, of molecules in its
organism ; and the innate composition of the ova of the
man, dog, horse, etc., may be as different as the hundreds
of chemical combinations, which can be made from a few
simple chemical constituents, some of which combinations,
as water, may be perfectly harmless ; while others, like
sulphuric acid, gunpowder, or corrosive sublimate, may be
peculiarly destructive.   So the differences of the very natures
which are contained in these eggs which look alike may be
originally as great as we find them in adult men, dogs, and
horses.

The original natures inhere in the ova, and we have no
reason to suppose that the differences in their original natures
are not as real in these ova as they are in the mature animals.

CHAPTER IX.

THIS CHAPTER CONTAINS A SHORT HISTORY OF DISCUSSIONS
CONCERNING THE SUBJECTS CONSIDERED IN THE LAST
CHAPTER, AND EXTRACTS FROM THE RECORDS OF EX-
PERIMENTS MADE BY PROF. TYNDALL UPON GERMI-
NATING FLUIDS.

THE writings of Aristotle generally controlled the science
of natural history for two thousand years, and in fact
Aristotle may be called "the Father of Natural History."
Aristotle denied "the eternity of the individual," and contended that the individual came into existence "in the act of
generation, and perished at death."

But if Aristotle was right in this supposition, of which he
gave no proof, that does not answer the question, "Whence
is life?" For two thousand years succeeding Aristotle the
doctrine of "spontaneous generation" was generally accepted
by scientific men. Caterpillars and insects which infest
trees and vegetables were supposed to be spontaneously generated. Because putrefying flesh was infested with worms,
or other living creatures, the supposition was that these came
spontaneously. No one was able to show that this was otherwise until A.D. 1668, when Dr. Francisco Redi, of Tuscany,
while watching meat ready to decay noticed flies alight upon
it, and suspected that the maggots which followed were in
some way connected with these flies. He then placed meat
in jars so covered that the flies could not get access to it,
and found that, although it putrefied, no maggots came. He

then put gauze over the mouth of the jars, and he found that the flies hovered over the meat, and laid their eggs on the gauze, and they hatched out there, but no maggots came in the meat. Other physicians and philosophers continued these observations and experiments; and though improvements in the microscope helped to dispel the illusions of centuries respecting the generation of the larger insects, etc., yet the animalcules found in stagnant water were still believed to be spontaneously generated. For about two hundred years succeeding, many distinguished men were ranged on each side of the controversy, and not until within the past twenty years have anything like positive results been reached on this question.

As late as 1872 Dr. H. C. Bastian published his views on abiogenesis, and strongly advocated the doctrine of "spontaneous generation." Speculations concerning the origin of bacterial life become intimately connected with the germ theory of diseases.

Do diseases originate themselves? or are they propagated as vegetable and animal life are propagated? Do putrefactive germs breed from previous germs? Or do they originate spontaneously? Closely connected with the germ theory comes the "antiseptic system of surgery" of Prof. Lister, which has rendered surgical operations comparatively safe which, a few years ago, were exposed to extreme peril. Prof. Lister, like Pasteur, Dr. Budd, Prof. Tyndall, and others believes that all putrefactive diseases originate from disease-germs which float in the air and readily attach themselves to any person or substance which is susceptible to their action. Dr. W. B. Carpenter writes, in the "Nineteenth Century," of Prof. Lister's theory (as quoted in "Popular Science Monthly," Dec., 1881, p. 248): "Among the most

immediately productive of its results may be accounted the
'antiseptic surgery' of Prof. Lister, of which the principle
is the careful exclusion of living bacteria and other germs
alike from the natural internal cavities of the body and from
such as are formed by disease, whenever these may be laid
open by accident or may have to be opened surgically.
This exclusion is effected by the judicious use of carbolic
acid, which kills the germs without doing any mischief to
the patient; and the saving of lives, of limbs, and of severe
suffering, already brought about by this method, constitutes
in itself a glorious triumph alike to the scientific elaborator
of the germ-doctrine and to the scientific surgeon by whom
it has been thus applied."

M. Pasteur has cultivated various disease-germs as one
would cultivate grain, and has discovered processes by which
these germs may be rendered malignant, and in almost every
case produce certain death to such as become inoculated with
the deadly virus; and he has also discovered ways of render-
ing the same comparatively harmless.   His experiments have
been of immense advantage in stamping out deadly diseases
among the flocks of France.   He has also discovered the
destroyers of the grape-vine of France.   He proved them to
be propagated by living germs, and provided a remedy
against them.

The remarks of Dr. Carpenter are so directly in point
and of such practical importance that I shall quote freely
from his article.   He says of the transmission of disease-
germs among flocks of sheep: "One of the first questions
examined by Pasteur was the cause of outbreaks of 'charbon' in its most deadly form among flocks of sheep feeding
in what appeared to be the healthiest pastures, far removed
from any obvious source of infection.   Learning by the in-

quiries he instituted that special localities seemed haunted, at distant intervals, by this plague, he inquired what had been done with the bodies of the animals that had died of it, and learned that it had been customary to bury them deep in the soil, and that such interments had been made, it might have been ten years before, beneath the surface of some of the very pastures in which the fresh outbreaks took place. Notwithstanding that the depth (ten or twelve feet) at which the carcasses had been buried seemed to preclude the idea of the upward travelling of the poison-germs, the divining mind of Pasteur found in *earthworms* a probable means of their conveyance, and he soon obtained an experimental verification of his idea which satisfied even those who were at first disposed to ridicule it. Collecting a number of worms from these pastures, he made an extract of the contents of their alimentary canals, and found that the inoculation of rabbits and Guinea-pigs with this extract gave them the severest form of ' charbon,' due to the multiplication in their circulating current of the deadly *anthrax-bacillus*, with which their blood was found after death to be loaded.

" Another mode in which the disease-germs of anthrax may be conveyed to herds of cattle widely separated from each other and from any ostensible source of infection was discovered by the inquiries prosecuted, a few years ago, by Prof. Burdon-Sanderson at the Brown Institution, in consequence of a number of simultaneous outbreaks which occurred in different parts of the country. It was found that all the herds affected had been fed with brewers' grains, supplied from a common source; and, on examining microscopically a sample of these grains, they were seen to be swarming with the deadly *bacillus*, which, when it has once found its way among them, grows and multiplies with extraordinary rapidity."

Pasteur and others struck upon the idea that the violence of such diseases might be mitigated by inoculation, in the same way that inoculation against small-pox has been practised. Having cultivated the charbon-virus until it was of proper strength, he tried it upon various animals with success, until the Provincial Agricultural Society of France thought best to make a test of the value of his theory upon a scale of considerable extent. The result is described as follows in the language of Dr. Carpenter :—

"Accordingly, a farm and a flock of fifty sheep having been placed at M. Pasteur's disposal, he 'vaccinated' twenty-five of the flock (distinguished by a perforation of their ears) with the *mild* virus on the 3d of May last, and repeated the operation on the 17th of the same month. The animals all passed through a slight indisposition, but at the end of the month none of them were found to have lost either fat, appetite, or liveliness. On the 31st of that month all the fifty sheep, without distinction, were inoculated with the *strongest* charbon-virus, and M. Pasteur predicted that on the following day the twenty-five sheep inoculated for the first time would all be dead, while those protected by previous 'vaccination' with the mild virus would be perfectly free from even slight indisposition. A large assemblage of agricultural authorities, cavalry officers, and veterinary surgeons having met at the field the next afternoon (June 1), *the result was found to be exactly in accordance with M. Pasteur's predictions.* At two o'clock *twenty-three* of the 'unprotected' sheep were dead; the *twenty-fourth* died within another hour, and the *twenty-fifth*, an hour afterward. But the twenty-five 'vaccinated' sheep were all *in perfectly good condition;* one of them, which had been designedly inoculated with an extra dose of the poison, having been slightly indisposed for a few hours, but having then recovered. The twenty-five carcasses were then buried in a selected spot, with a view to the further experimental testing of the poisonous effect produced upon the grass which will grow over their graves. But the result, says the reporter of the 'Times' (June 2) 'is already certain; and the agricultural public now know that an infallible preventive exists against the charbon-poison, which is neither costly nor difficult, as a single man can inoculate a thousand sheep in a day.'"

To show the extreme importance of this theory in regard to other diseases, I quote further from Dr. Carpenter: "These wonderful results obviously hold out an almost sure hope of preventing the ravages, not merely of the destructive animal plagues that show themselves from time to time among us, but of doing that for some of the most fatal forms of human infectious disease which Jennerian vaccination has already done — as shown by Sir Thomas Watson in these pages — for what was once the most dreaded of them, small-pox."

It scarcely seems too much to expect that before long, as Prof. Lister last year suggested, "An appropriate 'vaccine' may be discovered for measles, scarlet fever, and other acute specific diseases in the human subject;" for already, as I have been informed by one of the most distinguished of the United States members of our Congress, researches have been there made, with very promising results, on the "cultivation of the *diphtheritic* virus, — the mortality from which, in England and Wales, during the last decade, has averaged nearly three thousand annually, being, for seven years, 1873–1879, *half as great again* as the mortality from small-pox during the same period." I may here add that M. Pasteur has now secured a world-wide reputation for his successful treatment of the dreadful disease of hydrophobia by means of vaccination.

Much more might be said on this point, and its importance will appear more clearly when we consider that the "black death" which carried off one-third of the population of Europe some five hundred years ago, was, doubtless, propagated by disease germs which floated through the atmosphere. Dried disease germs will live through all extremes of heat or cold ever experienced in our climate, and probably will retain their destructive vitality, if kept dry, for centuries. I see no reason why they may not (like the grain taken out with the Egyptian mummies and planted) grow into a regular crop after lying dormant for thousands of years, during all which time their vitality may remain unimpaired.

The plague which has so often afflicted parts of Europe was a sort of contagious fever, accompanied by carbuncles and buboes. The last visitation to Southern Europe was in 1815 and 1816, and we may hope it may never again visit the earth; yet I see no reason why its germs may not still exist, and only favorable circumstances may be wanting to induce its return. Each kind of disease-germs breeds only its own kind, and for each kind of contagious disease a separate class of germs exists; and if these germs are not self-originating, or, in other words, cannot be spontaneously generated, then the question how they do originate assumes great importance.

Shultze and Schwann, in Germany, tried many experiments to show the effect of the exclusion of the air in preventing the appearance of living organisms in decomposable fluids. Dr. Carpenter continues : "But the discovery of the real nature of yeast and the recognition of the part it plays in alcoholic fermentation gave an entirely new value to Shultze's and Schwann's results, suggesting that putrefactive and other kinds of decomposition may be really due, not (as formerly supposed) to the action of atmospheric oxygen upon unstable organic compounds, but to a new arrangement of elements brought about by the development of germinal particles deposited from the atmosphere.

"It was at this point that Pasteur took up the inquiry, and, for its subsequent complete working out, science is mainly indebted to him ; for, although other investigators — notably Prof. Tyndall — have confirmed and extended his conclusions by ingenious variations on his mode of research, they would be the first to acknowledge that all those main positions which have now gained universal acceptance, save on the part of a few obstinate 'irreconcilables,' have been established by Pasteur's own labors. These positions may be briefly summarized as follows : —

1. "That no organic fluid undergoes *spontaneous* fermentation or decomposition, even in the presence of atmospheric air, any such action being originated and maintained only by the developmental action of definite organic germs.

2. "That different kinds of fermentation (using that term in its large sense) are produced by organic germs of different species. Thus, while *torula* sets going the alcoholic fermentation in a saccharine wort, other fungoid germs will set up the acetous, and others, again, the putrefactive, fermentation, when introduced into fluids of the same kind.

3. "That many different kinds of germs — notably those

of the *bacteria*, which induce putrefactive fermentation — are constantly floating in the ordinary atmosphere, so as to be almost certainly self-sown in any organic fluid freely exposed to it.

4. "That, if these germs be removed by mechanical filtration, or be got rid of by subsidence, or be deprived of their potency by chemical agents which destroy their vitality, the most readily decomposable organic fluid may be subjected to the freest contact with the air from which the germs have been thus eliminated without undergoing any change.

5. "That as there is no such thing as fermentation without the presence of germ-particles, so there is no such thing as the spontaneous origination of such germs, each kind, when sown in the liquid, reproducing itself with the same regularity as in higher plants, and thus continuously maintaining its own type.

6. "That such germ-particles, when dried up, can not only maintain their germinal power for unlimited periods, starting into renewed activity so soon as the requisite conditions are supplied, but that, in this state of dormant vitality, they can be subjected to influences which would destroy the life of the growing plants, — such as very high or very low temperatures, the action of strong acid or alkaline solutions, and the like."

It will be seen that these statements cover a very wide field. The air we breathe is permeated with fine floating matter, and about one-half of this floating dust is composed of organic matter, the very smallest particle of which may carry the seeds of life or death to organic matter subject to its influences. This has been proved by taking solutions which have been put up in hermetically-sealed vessels, and which have remained perfectly clear, and devoid of the least appearance of life for months; but by placing the smallest particle of this dust in these infusions, they will teem with living organisms within forty-eight hours.

These floating particles, which can be seen by a concentrated beam of light, are so exceedingly minute that they cannot be seen by the best microscope. In proof of this I quote from Prof. Tyndall's "Floating Matter of the Air" (p. 78) : —

"'Potential germs' and 'hypothetical germs' have been spoken of with scorn, because the evidence of the microscope as to their existence was not forthcoming. Sagacious writers had drawn from their experiments the perfectly legitimate inference that in many cases the germs exist, though the microscope fails to reveal them. Such inferences, however, have been treated as the pure work of the imagination, resting, it was alleged, on no real basis of fact. But in the concentrated beam we possess what is virtually a new instrument, exceeding the microscope indefinitely in power. Directing it upon media which refuse to give the coarser instrument any information as to what they hold in suspension, these media declare themselves to be crowded with particles — not hypothetical, not potential, but actual and myriad-fold in number — showing the microscopist that there is a world far beyond his range."

Thus we have in the concentrated beam of light a revealer of what would otherwise forever remain concealed. But we must bear in mind that these minute atmospheric germs probably are not the bacteria of disease but simply the germs from which the bacteria are bred. And yet not all these germs are necessarily deleterious in their influences.

All water which is exposed to the common air is pervaded with these germinal particles, which fall into it from the air, if such germs are not indigenous to the water. From the immense number of germs in a closed room, we might infer that every part of the surface of the water must constantly be becoming filled with them. Tyndall has estimated that in a room fifteen by twenty feet, divided into horizontal spaces six inches apart, the number of germs that fall daily are over 30,000,000. He says : "At all events, 30,000,000 of germs daily would be an exceedingly moderate estimate of the number falling into thirty layers of tubes."

It is true that some are sceptical in regard to this great number of germs, but surely there are enough to infect any and every particle of fermentable or putrescible matter which is left exposed to the air. These germs may be much more plenty in one place than in another, as was proved by the experiments of Tyndall in 1876, when he found it very difficult to perfectly sterilize infusions in a certain room ; but in a shed built only eight yards from this room he found no difficulty in sterilizing them. In the laboratory where he had used some old hay the germs remained very abundant for a long time afterwards ; but the shed built only eight yards distant had not been infected by the hay-germs, and germs were comparatively few there. Perhaps no one article has more vigorous life-germs in it than old hay, and the infusions are often hard to sterilize. Well may Tyndall say, as he does on p. 179 : —

"Let us compare results and draw conclusions. At a distance of eight yards from the shed, viz., in the laboratory, infusions both of beef and cucumber refused to be sterilized by three hours' boiling. Indeed, I have samples of both infusions which have borne five hours' boiling and developed multitudinous life afterwards. But the upshot of this experiment in the disinfected shed is, that every tube of the two chambers, though boiled for only five minutes, contains an infusion which, at the present hour, is as limpid as the purest distilled water.

"What shall we say, then? Is the infusion in the laboratory endowed with a generative force denied to the same infusion in the shed? Irrespective of the condition of the air can a linear space of eight yards produce so remarkable a difference? It is only the confusion of mind still prevalent in relation to this subject that renders such a question necessary. Let me add that it suffices simply to wave a bunch of hay in the air of the shed to make it as infective as the laboratory air. Even the unprotected head of my assistant when his body was carefully covered sufficed in some cases to carry the infection."

In some localities high above the sea level meat never putrifies, though exposed to the air and even the sunlight In some places in the north-western territories of the United States when the settlers kill an ox or a deer they are accustomed to hang the meat on a tree some twenty feet above the ground, fully exposed to the winds, and it does no putrefy, and why? Doubtless there is nothing to cause putrefactive germs to float so high above the ground. Bu place meat in a cellar there at the same time and it wil putrefy. These germs seem to float near the ground, bu not high above it.

Edward King states that at the monastery at St. Bernard in Switzerland, the dead never putrefy. After describing the manner of gaining entrance to the morgue there, and looking at the dead in the dim light, he writes concerning the first one which attracted his attention as follows (" Boston Journal," Oct. 9, 1882) : " Pretty soon you discern that the face belongs to the body of a woman, and the woman is clasping to her breast the form of a tiny babe. The mother is seated on the ground, and appears to be dazed by the light pouring down into her darksome habitation. But oh, the horror of her face ! Here is death without decay ; here, eight thousand feet above the sea-level, putrefaction is unknown."

Not only in the Alps and among the Rocky Mountains, but wherever the air or insects do not bear putrefactive germs, putrefaction is unknown. Floating disease germs are abundant during the existence of widespread epidemics. A fact which seems to indicate some connection between disease-germs and bacterial germs may be mentioned in regard to experiments made by Tyndall during the years 1875 and 1876. During the latter part of 1876 epidemics were quite general in London. Tyndall then found it much more difficult to sterilize infusions and keep them sterile than in 1875, when there was a time of general health. This of itself is not proof that these general epidemics, or the germs of these epidemics, were the direct cause of this difficulty of sterilizing the infusions, but the two certainly went together.

The germs of contagious diseases are generally minute vegetable organisms ; but similar kinds of organisms produce somewhat different results, or are sometimes modified by their surroundings.

If such germs get access to dead animal matter they produce putrefaction ; but, if to living animals, they may produce fever or inflammation.

Prof. Tyndall says : " A contagious disease may be defined

as a conflict between the person smitten by it and a specific organism, which multiplies at his expense, appropriating his air and moisture, disintegrating the tissues, and poisoning him by the decompositions incident to its growth."

But as late as 1875, at a meeting of the Pathological Society, Dr. H. C. Bastian admitted the coexistence of *bacteria* and contagious disease; but, "instead of considering these organisms as ' probably the essence or an inseparable part of the essence ' of the contagium, Dr. Bastian contended that they were 'pathological products' spontaneously generated in the body after it had been rendered diseased by the real contagium." (Tyndall, "Floating Matter," p. 93.)

That is, although these germs are always present in zymotic diseases, Dr. Bastian contended that they were the result of the disease, instead of being the cause.

In treating diseases it is important to understand whether these bacteria are the *cause* or the *result* of the disease; for if they are simply the *result* of the disease, it is of little avail if we destroy them; but if they are the cause, it is of immense importance that they, if possible, be destroyed, that through their destruction diseases may be stayed.

There can be no putrefaction nor fermentation without these germs, and hence, without them, there can be no diseases which are in their nature fermentable or putrefactive.

Prof. Tyndall says ("Floating Matter of the Air," p. 263) : "The most striking analogy between a *contagium* and a ferment is to be found in the power of indefinite self-multiplication possessed and exercised by both. You know the exquisitely truthful figures regarding leaven employed in the New Testament. • A particle hid in three measures of meal leavens it all. A little leaven leaveneth the whole lump.

"In a similar manner, a particle of *contagium* spreads through the human body and may be so multiplied as to strike down whole populations. Consider the effect produced upon the system by a microscopic quantity of the virus of small-pox. That virus is, to all intents and purposes, a seed. It is sown as yeast is sown; it grows and multiplies as yeast grows and multiplies, and it always reproduces itself."

Such germs may be scattered by the breath, or through perspiration, or be carried in the garments. It matters little, however, how they are carried (as to their practical effects), for they are no respecters of persons, provided they find parties or substances which are susceptible to their influences. These germs being seeds, the person attacked by them receives them as a field does the seeds of grain or vegetables. It matters not whether these seeds are large enough to be seen by the eye, or so fine that they cannot be seen even with a microscope; they are still seeds, and their progeny often increase and multiply as rapidly as do thistles when sown in a rich soil. I cannot better close the consideration on this point than by quoting from Prof. Tyndall's "Floating Matter of the Air," pp. 254, 255 : —

"Thus far, I think, we have made our footing sure. Let us proceed. Chop up a beefsteak and allow it to remain for two or three hours just covered with warm water; you thus extract the juice of the beef in a concentrated form. By properly boiling the liquid and filtering it you can obtain from it a perfectly transparent beef-tea. Expose a number of vessels containing this tea to the moteless air of your chamber; and expose a number of vessels containing precisely the same liquid to the dust-laden air. In three days every one of the latter stinks, and, examined with the micro-

scope every one of them is found swarming with the bacteria of putrefaction.   After three months, or three years,
the beef-tea within the chamber, if properly sterilized in the
first instance, will be found as sweet and clear, and as free
from bacteria, as it was at the moment when it was first put
in.   There is absolutely no difference between the air within
and that without, save that the one is dustless and the other
dust-laden.   Clinch the experiment thus.   Open the door of
your chamber and allow the dust to enter it.   In three days
afterwards you have every vessel within the chamber swarm-
.ing with bacteria, and in a state of active putrefaction.   Here,
also, the inference is quite as certain as in the case of the
powder sown in your garden.   Multiply your proofs by
building fifty chambers instead of one, and by employing
every imaginable infusion of wild animals and tame ; of flesh,
fish, fowl, and viscera ; of vegetables of the most various
kinds.   If in all these cases you find the dust infallibly
producing its crop of bacteria, while neither the dustless air
nor the nutritive infusion, nor both together, are ever able to
produce this crop, your conclusion is simply irresistible that
the dust of the air contains the germs of the crop which has
appeared in your infusions.   I repeat there is no inference
of experimental science more certain than this one.   In the
presence of such facts, to use the words of a paper lately
published in the ' Philosophical Transactions,' ' it would be
simply monstrous to affirm that these swarming crops of
bacteria are spontaneously generated.' "

In a former chapter I stated that there is no reliable evidence that "spontaneous generation" now exists, and that
there is no credible evidence that any life now is produced
except from antecedent life.   That completes one step.   From
analogy we may infer that if the doctrine of " spontaneous

generation" is false now probably it was always so; and that the laws of nature as regards the production of life have never changed since they were first instituted.

Life only from antecedent life is the present law. But this does not inform us whence life originally came. There must have been a beginning of terrestrial life. But the great fountain of life may have had no beginning. There must have been during past eternity a time or point when life could not be derived from antecedent life. It seems that there must have been a first life, — and nothing can be before the first.

Nothing now occurs without an antecedent cause. But there must have been a point or time when there could not be an antecedent cause; and thus we seem to be again forced back upon a self-existing cause, or "cause of causes." It seems to me that all life had its origin in the great first life. Here we have to deal with original causes, concerning which it is said that we can know nothing.

It is true that the human mind cannot comprehend original causes, but it can, in a measure, understand the force of the declaration made to Moses: "I am that I am." And until some man can show a cause for the origin of life which is more likely to be true, we must look to the great "I Am" as the fountain from which all terrestrial life came.

The Duke of Argyll, quoted before (p. 272, "Reign of Law"), says: "It is the great mystery of our being that we have powers impelling us to ask such questions on the history of Creation, when we have no powers enabling us to solve them. Ideas and faint suggestions of reply are ever passing across the outer limits of the Mind, as meteors pass across the margin of the atmosphere; but we endeavor in vain to grasp or understand them. The faculties both of reason and of imagination fall back with a sense of impotence upon some favorite phrase — some form of words built up out of the materials of analogy, and out of the experience of a Mind, which, being finite, is not creative. We beat against the bars in vain. The only real rest is in the confession of ignorance, and the confession, too, that all ultimate physical Truth is beyond the reach of Science."

And emphatically there is no place where we intellectually " beat against the bars in vain " with greater certainty than with the question, " Whence is life?" unless we are willing to refer its origin to the Great First, or Self-existent Life.

CHAPTER X.

DEVELOPMENT OF LIFE.

THE questions already discussed lead to further inquiries concerning inherited traits of character and the increased development of the brain during past ages.

Where shall we find a limit to the increasing size of the brain and the consequent enlargement of intellectual capacities?

The brains of vertebrate animals have been increasing in size and activity for many thousand years. The average European human brain of the males is now larger than it was one hundred years ago.

Prof. Marsh, in his lecture on "Vertebrate Life in America," shows that there was a general increase of the size of brains as long ago as the Tertiary period. On p. 48, he writes : "The real progress of mammalian life in America, from the beginning of the Tertiary to the present, is well illustrated by the Brain-growth, in which we have the key to many other changes.

"The earliest known Tertiary mammals all had very small brains, and in some forms this organ was proportionally less than in certain Reptiles. There was a gradual increase in the size of the brain during this period, and it is interesting to find that this growth was mainly confined to the cerebral hemispheres, or higher portion of the brain. In most groups of mammals, the brain has gradually become more convoluted, and thus increased in quality, as well as quantity. In some, also, the cerebellum and olfactory lobes, the lower parts of the brain, have even diminished in size. In the long struggle for existence during Tertiary time the big brains won, then as now; and the increasing power thus gained rendered useless many structures inherited from primitive ancestors, but no longer adapted to new conditions."

If we believe that men have been developed from a lower race of animals during the long past ages, may it not be reasonable to presume that in future ages men may become developed into a still higher race of beings? Why may they not become as much superior to any of the present races of men as these are superior to any of the present species of apes? This would be carrying development analogies as at present expounded to their legitimate conclusions.

However, it would seem evident that a limit to this increasing brain development and expanding intellectual power must be reached some time, and certain facts, taken by themselves, would seem to indicate that this limit is already nearly reached in man. I will briefly state some of these facts: —

First. The tendency of the highest civilization is to decrease rather than increase the size of the female brain. The size of the female brain in London, Paris and Berlin is now less than it is among women in localities where society is less highly organized. The brains of males and females among savage or semi-savage races are nearly equal in size; but in London and Paris the average female brain weighs about five ounces less, or about ten per cent. less, than the average male brain. Of course, the female brain becomes more convoluted and of finer quality in highly civilized communities than among the uneducated tribes or races.

Second. It is seldom that women of very high intellectual abilities now marry men of very strong mental cast; and, on the other hand, it is quite uncommon for a man of a very intellectual cast to select a wife with marked intellectual power; hence men of extraordinary mental gifts are not to be expected from such unions. A large proportion of the women of the strongest intellectual abilities never choose to marry, and of those who do choose to marry, few have children, or, if they have children, it is seldom more than one or two.

The author of " Conflict in Nature and Life " says, on p. 424 : " This is to be observed in the many unfortunate marriages of literary and other intellectual people. If they secure in connubial relations intellectual equality and companionship, there is apt to be no issue, in which case marriage fails of its end. It is a matter of common remark, that the distinctively intellectual marry the unintellectual, and fail completely of companionship, and hence the unhappiness of so many of this class in their marriage relations."

Now, if high intellectual and moral qualities are inherited, and women of genius have no children, or if the men of genius do not marry women of strong intellectual power, how are very high intellectual and moral qualities to be transmitted from parents to children? The intellectual and moral qualities of the mother show quite as plainly as those of the father in the children.

Some careful students assert that there are no very marked examples of men of genius who did not have intellectual mothers. By intellectual as applied to mothers who produce men of great intellectual strength, I do not mean

necessarily what are commonly styled educated women, but
mothers who have well-developed brains, with strong and
vigorous mental make-up, so that if their lives were given to
literature or science they would rank among the intellectual
women of the age.   It is not education that is inherited,
but the ability to become educated, or the mental constitution on which to engraft an education.   .

The desire for offspring is a natural one; but, if the intellectual organs largely predominate, it is quite natural that
the desire for children should be weak, in fact so weak that
highly intellectual women naturally strive to avoid the cares,
risks and responsibilities of maternity.   Besides, the pains
and risks of maternity are much less with those who have
a good amount of physical exercise in the open air than
with those who live in luxury, or have more mental and less
physical exercise.   Nature here points the way, and those
who attempt to go counter to the way she has marked out
will not succeed in riding over her decrees.   In fact, her
decrees in this respect are unalterable, and the anathema of
sterility is written against such as flagrantly disobey her
mandates.

Again, intelligence and the size of the brain bear a
striking relation to each other.   If the brain in both parents
is developed to a great extent, and the offspring inherit this
extreme development, births will be correspondingly more
difficult.   This will prevent the production of children with
heads above a certain size; and here again nature has set
up a bound that cannot be leaped over.

Dr. Dunglison (in "Human Physiology," vol. 2, p. 447)
says : "The records of the Dublin hospital showed that there
died during the process of parturition, . . . and probably
as a consequence of the injuries to which they were sub-

jected, 151 male children for every 100 female. There was thus an excess of 50 male deaths amongst every 250 children, or 20 in every 100, referable, according to Dr. Simpson, to the greater size of the head of the male infant." Further, he adds, " we may take it for granted that, on a low computation, one in every 50 children dies during labor." According to further computations, of the 500,000 children born in Great Britain, about " 6,500 of the offspring die during labor, and one-fifth of that number are lost in consequence of the sex and size of the male child." "In Great Britain, therefore, the lives of 1,300 infants are lost annually in childbirth from the operation of this agency."

Not only the risk of the child's dying during labor will be increased as the size of its head becomes greater, but the risk to the mother in labor will be augmented by the increase of the size of the head.

After stating that the number of male births in Europe is about 106 to 100 female births, Darwin says (p. 243, "Descent of Man"): "Prof. Faye remarks that 'a still greater preponderance of males would be met with if death struck both sexes in equal proportion in the womb, and during birth. But the fact is, that for every 100 still-born females, we have, in several countries, from 134.6 to 144.9 still-born males. During the first four or five years of life, also, more male children die than females; for example, in England, during the first year, 126 boys die for every 100 girls, a proportion which in France is still more unfavorable.' . . . We have before seen that the male sex is more variable in structure than the female; and variations in important organs would generally be injurious. But the size of the body, and especially of the head, being greater in male than female infants is another cause; for the males are thus more liable to be injured during parturition. Consequently the still-born males are more numerous."

But there is still another serious bar to the upward intellectual progress of men. Statistics show that with largely increased size and activity of the brain come certain mental diseases. Melancholia, insanity and a disposition to suicide are alarmingly on the increase among the highest-cultivated races. These almost universal accompaniments of the highest civilization tend to thin out those who might otherwise become the most intellectual.

But, in regard to the necessity for large brains through which to manifest great mental power, the objection is made that some men with small heads accomplish more than others with large heads; so what is the necessity of laying so much stress upon the size of the brains? Some men with small bodies have more muscular strength than other men with large and apparently well-developed bodies. But does this indicate any general advantage of small bodies when muscular power is needed? As a general rule (as all know) a well-built man weighing two hundred pounds has more muscular power than another of similar proportions who weighs one hundred and fifty pounds. The same general rule applies to mental power, in connection with the size of a man's brain. Some brains are of finer texture, better distributed, more convoluted, and consequently more active; but general rules concerning size and quality apply to both brain and muscle.

We find the assertion that certain great men have had small heads, and from this fact an attempt has been made to discredit the theory that size represents the measure of power in the intellectual faculties; but I have yet to learn (as a general rule) anything which shows that size is not very important in the brain, if we wish for intellectual power.   If the size of the brain is of little importance, why is it that those whose brains weigh less than thirty-five ounces are almost invariably idiots?

The most conspicuous exception to the general rule concerning large brains is exemplified in J. F. L. Haussman, a German mineralogist, whose brain was under the average weight, it being only forty-three and one-quarter ounces, or over five ounces less than average weight of the brains of his countrymen.   But Haussman died at the age of seventy-seven, or at an age when the brain weighs nearly ten per cent. less than in early life.   At the age of thirty-five probably his brain was nearly the average weight.

I have not seen a likeness of Haussman, but I believe such would show that his head was long and narrow, and with a large part of it in front.   The nearest case to this that I have known is that of J. G. J. Hermann, the German philologist, whose brain weighed forty-six and one-half ounces, or two and one-half ounces less than the average weight ; and yet he became quite learned, and very popular with German students.

Soon after Gambetta's death many newspapers published the statement that his brain weighed only forty-six ounces, or three ounces less than the average weight of the brain among educated Frenchmen.   *Per contra*, the statement was published later that Dr. Laborde, who examined Gambetta's brain, reported to the " Faculty of Medicine " that " the brain was of exceptional size," and highly convoluted in " the regions assigned as the centre of the power of language."   This latter statement seems much more likely to be true than the former.   However, a brain of average size, having a large proportion of it in the frontal region, will give much more intellectual acumen and force than a brain considerably larger if a large proportion of it is in the regions representing the animal passions.

We do not look for any strong intellectual force if the brain is not well developed in the frontal regions. Not only the quality of the brain but its proper shape has much to do with the manifestations of mental power. These, properly correlated with size, will give a general measure of brain power.

Bain supposes that all our intelligence, including memory, is located in the gray substance which envelops and enters in among the convolutions of the brain. This gray matter averages about one-tenth of an inch in thickness in the average healthy human brain. But supposing that in exceptional cases this gray matter should be double the average thickness, and be of good quality, should we not naturally expect extraordinary manifestations of mental power, according to the size of the brain?

The writer has frequently heard it stated that the heads of Lord Byron and Napoleon were small; but Huxley states that the brain of Byron weighed 1807 grammes, or over sixty-three and a half ounces, or over fourteen ounces more than the average brain of Englishmen.

Napoleon's biographer states that the head of Napoleon was one of the largest and best formed he ever saw. The brain of Napoleon weighed slightly less than Byron's, or a little over sixty-two ounces.

According to Prof. Calderwood's published tables, the brains of Daniel Webster and Louis Agassiz each weighed only about fifty-three and a half ounces, or four and a half ounces above the average brains among the most cultivated races. But Dr. W. A. Hammond says that "Webster's brain (allowance being made for disease which existed) weighed sixty-three and three-fourths ounces;" and further, that his "cranium was the largest on record, being one hundred and twenty-two inches." And the writer has seen it stated elsewhere that the brain of Webster weighed over sixty-two ounces; and he believes the larger figures are correct. Prof. O. S. Fowler, who measured Webster's head, writes, "The author found Webster's massive head to measure over twenty-four and a half inches." Fowler also states that his forehead was uncommonly high.

Quatrefages states that it has been reported that the brain of Oliver Cromwell weighed over seventy-eight ounces; but, he adds, "There is not the certainty we should wish for about these figures."

But it should be borne in mind that the weight of the brain does not always bear the same ratio to the skull capacity; that is, the specific gravity of the brain in certain persons is greater than in others.

Fowler states that the head of Napoleon Bonaparte measured over twenty-four inches in circumference. Dr. Gall states that "Moderns have (in their pictures) left Napoleon's head in its natural size, but placed it on a body of colossal proportions, to make it conform to their ideas of proportion."

Ben. Franklin's head measured considerably over twenty-four inches in circumference. Cuvier's brain weighed over sixty-four and a half ounces, and, going through the whole line of illustrious men, we find, as a general rule (with very few exceptions) that large brains, if well proportioned, indicate great mental force; but a man with a brain of only average size, if it is uncommonly active, may exhibit considerable acumen. But I doubt if a profound and comprehensive thought ever originated in a brain of much less than average size. No doubt that thorough investigation would put to rest all assertions that great power can be found in small brains, unless in very exceptional cases, and these will be as exceptional as instances of small men or small animals possessing surprising strength and activity.

To illustrate, we may find a pugilist weighing one hundred and twenty pounds who may beat an ordinary man weighing two hundred pounds, and this on account of his superior training and activity. The same rules may be applied to mental manifestations, or brain power.

Here, then, is an important point regarding the brain structure. But if the brain and nervous system are developed out of due proportion to the muscular system, so that the rest of the body is incapable of furnishing proper sustenance to the brain, then disastrous results are sure to follow ; and here is another limit which cannot be passed.

But, says one, the law of Evolution, through which the less useful disappears, and the most useful is preserved, will so adjust the mutually dependent conditions of mind and body that a general improvement in both physical and mental capacity may be confidently looked for.

But nature has apparently set certain bounds to this development, through the well-known fact that generally the less developed races increase faster than the highly developed races. In many civilized communities the higher classes are running out, and they would, before long, become extinct if it was not for the admixture of their blood with that of descendants of lower classes. Says a very vigorous writer : "In France there is greater prolificacy among the inhabitants of the poorer than among those of the richer departments. The aristocracies are everywhere running out, as in the Roman empire, and they would become extinct but for constant accessions from the ranks below ; and some come up from almost the very bottom. Reigning dynasties are not apt to last long, and once a family has reached the pinnacle of human greatness its doom is written."

As an example of this, take the Bourbon family, which one hundred years ago controlled about half the thrones in Europe. Where now are its prominent descendants?

Look at the increase of the former slave population in the United States. Where and when has a highly educated and highly developed race increased and multiplied as rapidly as they did? Who now rear the largest families? — the laboring men, farmers, and mechanics, or those who live in habits of laborious study?

In order to facilitate the production of a superior class of children and the rearing of prosperous families there must be a somewhat befitting sympathy between the parents. This sympathy is much oftener wanting among the highly educated classes. Delauney says ("Popular Science Monthly," December, 1881) : "The biological considerations we have adduced explain to us why the two sexes tend to diverge from each other as we proceed from the lower to the higher classes. Both sexes among peasants and working-people having nearly the same moral and intellectual faculties, they can sympathize with each other, and have no reason for becoming estranged. It is different among the intelligent classes, where the two sexes, in consequence of the increasing preeminence of man, not having the same ideas, the same sentiments, nor the same tastes, cannot understand each other, and form separate coteries. Moralists have long taken notice of the separation, which is of force in the family and in the meetings of men and of women, which seem to be increasing from year to year."

It will be said that this divergence should not be allowed to exist. Very true; but human beings will consult their own tastes. If we assert that such divergences are evidence of depravity, that does not change natural laws.

Nature will not lessen her demands at the requests of philosophers or military chieftains. Her demands must be paid to the uttermost farthing. Without care the whole tendency of animal and vegetable nature is to revert to the original type. It is only through struggles that beneficent development takes place. Without this continual struggle the descendants of present highly developed races of men would go back towards the original type much faster than they came up from that condition. By original condition I do not mean that they came from a radically different race, but that without this struggle the tendency is to revert to the primeval condition of man.

We are told that the general course of Evolution is forward, and that every succeeding generation is becoming, on the whole, better and more wisely developed. But it is a question whether we have at present any living men who are superior in mind or in real philosophic strength to Thales, who flourished six hundred years before Christ, or Socrates, four hundred years before Christ, or Plato his disciple, or Democritus, or Zeno the Stoic, or Aristotle. I fail to perceive one whit of gain in two thousand years in the vigor of thought, clearness of expression, or acuteness in metaphysical reasoning. And if the present generation had been placed here with no printed books, and no greater facilities for education than were common two thousand years ago, I do not believe the living world would show itself superior to, if it would equal in intellectual strength, that of two thousand years ago. Let this expectation of any surprising intellectual development from the present tendency of thought be given up. A vigorous and apparently well-informed writer contends that the ancient Greeks as a race were superior in intellectual ability to the present race of Englishmen; and much may be said which seems to accord with his statement. Another fact is well worth considering. We have no reliable secular. histories which date back over four thousand years. The oldest written language, notwithstanding extravagant claims to a very high antiquity of some Oriental languages, probably does not date back five thousand years. How did it happen that the ancient Greeks, within about two thousand years after the invention of the first written language, became developed to such a height of intellectual vigor that there should be no perceptible gain in intellectual acumen or strength during the next two thousand years, if men had been æons in becoming developed from animals to real men? Is it not strange that there should be such a sudden stop in the growth of intellectual acumen so soon after the race of men got so fairly away from brute life as to become capable of leaving historical records?

It may be asserted that, with proper educational privileges, two thousand years is long enough to develop a race from a very low to a very high state of intelligence. Granted; but then let us go back more than a thousand years prior to the Grecian development, or to within a thousand years of any generally acknowledged date of the first written language, or to the time when it is generally believed that Moses, the Hebrew law-giver lived. Can any one justly assert that any man has lived during this century who has shown a greater intellect than the laws and precepts attributed to Moses would indicate that he possessed? His civil code is the basis of much of our present law, and in many respects it has not been improved upon.

If it is asserted that this was in consequence of Divine inspiration, I shall not deny that; but, inspiration or no inspiration, God has never used weak intellects to lay foundations of laws and customs destined to last thousands of years among the most learned and enlightened nations. Even if the Pentateuch was written from traditions by some one who lived in later ages, — as some suppose, — that does not lessen the great prominence of Moses as an actual law-giver.

Moses exhibited intense intellectual vigor, and no higher has been seen during the past thirty-four hundred years.

We are not warranted in expecting that men will soon make a decided gain in their general intellectual strength.

But, to make a wider application of this principle, we see that the course of development or degradation of races of men is quite similar to that of the rise and fall of families. But the time required for the rise and fall of a race is much longer than that for the rise and fall of a single family. The family may be taken as a type of a race. All must see that a certain amount of development or degradation exists in many directions. This accords with the general principles of Evolution, and apparently applies not only to men but to the whole animal creation.

But whatever one's opinion concerning the past development of the human race may be, and if we believe that the race has nearly reached its limit of physical and intellectual development, may we not at least fondly hope that in moral ideas and moral character men will yet reach a much higher plane than has ever been reached by any class of men? If the course of nature generally tends towards higher ends, why, at least, should not the moral sense and moral faculties be allowed to reach a much higher standard than has heretofore been reached by any people?

Who knows but the hopes of a blissful immortal life, which were long ago cherished by heathen philosophers like Socrates and Cicero, and in later ages by millions of Christians, may be the silent outspeakings of this possibly universal law of nature?

Hope has always claimed that "there's a good time coming."

Who can properly estimate the moral possibilities which lie as yet undeveloped in the womb of the future? There is certainly abundant need of and opportunity for a great improvement in this direction.

PART II.

ETHICAL SPECULATIONS AND INQUIRIES.

ETHICAL SPECULATIONS AND INQUIRIES.

CHAPTER XI.

TO WHAT EXTENT WILL ONE'S BELIEF MODIFY HIS MORAL CHARACTER?

SOME assert that the influence of belief, especially religious belief, is merely nominal.

A distinction should be drawn between what a man *believes* and what he professes to believe. It is not profession, or what a man professes, that has lasting power, but the belief which is ingrained in the character will have a powerful effect upon his whole life.

If a man believes that by investing in certain property he will become rich, does any one suppose that such belief will not influence his acts? In religious matters, if a man hardly knows whether he believes or not, but simply falls in with the current, as many do, and professes to believe with the majority, because it is easier to go with than against the current, such belief is of little value, and will be likely to change as soon as his surroundings change. But if a man has a firm conviction that a certain course is right, and also determines to be himself right, then his belief avails much towards giving character to his whole life.

It has been said that Washington believed that "honesty is the best policy ; " and doubtless he was correct.   But if a man's honesty does not spring from a higher motive than common policy, it will not be of a very high type.   The same rules apply to a man's belief in a future life and its rewards or retributions.   If he really believes that he will consciously exist in a future world, and that what he does here will have an important effect on his future happiness, most certainly this belief will exert a powerful influence in shaping his acts.   But if he has simply a half-conscious idea that he may possibly exist, or perhaps not exist, then such a belief cannot have any marked influence on his character.

Hugh Miller says : " That belief in the existence after death, which forms the distinguishing instinct of humanity, is too essential a part of man's moral constitution not to be missed when away ; and so, when once fairly eradicated, the life and conduct rarely fail to betray its absence."

The belief of a nation will influence the character of its laws and habits, for nations are made up of individuals. If the individuals of a free nation believe in honesty and integrity the rulers will feel this influence, and we may expect an equitable enforcement of just laws.

The decline of religious belief is now making itself very apparent in European countries, controlling, in some respects, their politics.   Formerly, in Italy, the words of the pope and the priesthood, in many respects, had the force of law. But times have wonderfully changed.   Many who once bowed submissively now care little what the pope and priests may say.   Those who have relapsed from belief into non-belief are very different from what they formerly were, and new motives must be supplied in order to influence their acts. Some, who formerly believed in the immortality of the soul, now believe that the death of the body is the last of them. If you wish to keep such in a right course it will not do to appeal to the motives which formerly influenced them. It ever has been very dangerous to the welfare of the state for lawless classes not to feel some sense of moral responsibility ; for you can never tell to what excesses such may go while unrestrained by religious or moral belief. This is more especially true when the immoral become atheistic. But I would not advise preaching untruth to control even the immoral, for untruth is not to be defended. "Truth is mighty and must prevail," and no lasting good can come from teaching error. But it is not teaching error to proclaim to its fullest extent the doctrine of moral responsibility.

I am well aware that many have tried to show that there is no unvarying moral standard, and have further attempted to show that all our ideas of right and wrong are connected with remembrances of pleasures or pains ; or are the inherited echoes of pleasures or pains experienced by our ancestors in connection with various courses of conduct. Referring to this idea, Mansel says (p. 143, "Metaphysics") : " Pleasure and pain, so far as they are objects of desire and aversion, do not probably lie in the things by which they are caused, but in the actions by which those things are brought into contact with the person affected. But the actions, and, in some degree also, the feelings which prompt them, may be exhibited in another point of view not merely as pleasant or painful, but as right or wrong. The existence of these terms, or their equivalents, in every language, indicates a corresponding phenomenon in the universal consciousness of mankind which no effort of ingenuity can explain away. Indeed, the very ingenuity of the various attempts that have been made to identify the conception of right with that of expedient, or agreeable, or any other quality, is itself a witness against them ; for no such elaborate reasoning would be required were it not necessary to silence or pervert the instinctive testimony of a too stubborn consciousness."

Even if the present popular assumption that our moral intuitions and tendencies are inherited, or have descended to us as the unconscious effects of pains or pleasures experienced by our ancestors, is correct ; or if they are inherited as directly as the peculiar qualities of a pointer dog are, that fact in no wise changes another fact, viz., that a certain course of conduct will (all things considered) be the very best course a man can take. That best course is the only perfect one, and is imperatively demanded by a perfect moral standard.

Even if our moral sentiments and feelings have been changed or modified in the progress of Evolution through many generations, that fact does not obliterate or change the other probable fact, that the Deity, or some being or power which established the very laws of nature, has predestined this very course from the very beginning, and thus this very course of development may be in accordance with an original design.

The course of development which has resulted in our present moral intuitions or sentiments may have come through natural laws ; but full compliance with these laws may constitute conformity with a perfect moral standard.

Perhaps a better appreciation or more correct apprehension of moral laws may yet become developed as education and general intelligence increase.

Loss of belief in moral responsibility, with the unprincipled, leaves the impression that they may do as they please, no matter how inhuman or wrong the objects they wish to accomplish, provided they have physical force sufficient to accomplish their purposes. We see this principle of action cropping out in Ireland, Germany, France, Italy, and, in fact, to some extent in almost every civilized country.

It was reported ("Contemporary Review," 1882) that in a debate in the Italian Parliament on matters pertaining to the welfare of the poorer classes in Italy, Signor Giovagnoli said: "In times past religious belief helped to mitigate the sufferings of the poorer classes. But now that science has done away with religious delusions even the poor aspire in this world to their share of happiness, of bread, of meat, and of wine; and unless science can also do away with the delusion of these necessities, social violence will make short work of legislation and legislators."

The atheistic scout the idea that their teachings tend to encourage social violence. But what does the history of the past show? The prophecy of Signor Giovagnoli, "that social violence will make short work of legislation and legislators," will probably come true, provided unprincipled masses ever become strong enough to overpower proper authority, if science dispels all of what he calls "religious delusions;" for, under such circumstances, the partially dependent classes will not submit, as they formerly submitted, and will, as far as possible, take matters into their own hands, regardless of right or wrong. Ignorant men cannot be governed by philosophical appeals, for they do not comprehend such appeals; but history abundantly proves that they can comprehend the commands of unprincipled adventurers who promise bread or blood, and greater influence, both social and political.

This view concerning the actions of masses maddened by wrongs, either real or supposed, and their well-known brutality under such circumstances, well accounts for the blasphemous and atheistical utterances of the most fanatical of the Communistic leaders. They well know that the first step towards getting the ignorant and vicious populace into condition to be impelled to deeds of violence and outrage is to destroy in their minds all idea of moral responsibility. No prominent people or nation having clear ideas of moral responsibilities ever existed which did not also have some sense of religious responsibility.

Thus the statement of the signor, above quoted, properly translated, means this : that, all hopes of immortality being given up, the unprincipled and vicious classes will have nothing but present fear to restrain them ; and if they should lose their lives while in open violation of law or right, it would be of no great consequence, for that would be the end of them, and hence they could be as outrageous as they desire, without any lasting harm to themselves. Let the idea get firmly implanted in the minds of the majority of a people that there is no conscious hereafter, and before long the probable result will be violence and brutality such as the world has never witnessed except in the worst states of barbarism.

I am aware that the assertion has been made that there are some four hundred millions of Buddhists who are practically atheists, and do not believe in immortality, and that they live peaceably and cultivate the moral virtues. But such an assertion concerning their atheism and disbelief in immortality needs to be received with many reservations.

First, — the Buddhists might be properly called agnostics, rather than atheists; for they do not deny that there was a first cause, but simply leave inquiries into this out of view. They inculcate practical duties rather than inquiries into what is beyond the comprehension of mortals.

It is true that, in a certain sense, they do not believe in immortality, but they do believe in a future life, and their belief in ten billions of years of happiness in one of their heavens, or ten millions of years of misery in one of their hells, ought to be a pretty good substitute for a belief in immortality, or at least a sufficient inducement to avoid their hells by a virtuous life, and to gain their heaven by proper devotion to the tenets of Buddhism.

Their *Nirvana*, instead of meaning annihilation, as that word is commonly understood, is very different from that, and is rather an absorption into the infinite than absolute non-existence. But they expect to be dead to all earthly pleasures and pains; and this, in principle, is not very different from that perfectly inactive state of rest which some Christian teachers in former times talked about, viz., a Sabbath of inactivity rather than one of activity.

For practical purposes, Buddhism enjoins the performance of moral duties and living a virtuous life, and also urges their necessity in a manner quite similar to that employed by the apostle Paul; and thus the assertion that the belief of Buddhists is nearly equivalent to modern atheism is very far from being true.

We can imagine in a faint way what the result of genuine national atheism would probably be, from what was done during the French revolution, though only a fraction of the violent agitators there were entirely free from traces of this so-called "religious delusion." Had it not been for the little of this restraining influence left, probably three murders would have been committed where there was one, and the horrors of such a situation can be better imagined than described.   Though I use the term "religious delusion," let it not be understood that I believe pure religion has not a real existence.

Religious sentiments are, in some sense, a part of man's very nature.   I am aware that revolting crimes have been committed under the plea of defence of pure religion.   It is too true that fanaticism and bigotry, both religious and political, have been the parents of grievous evils.   One might well exclaim, "O Religion!" as well as "O Liberty! what crimes have been committed in thy name!"

When scientific men deal with mathematical or other problems which can be demonstrated, we may generally put confidence in their conclusions; for, if they make mistakes in their reasoning, such mistakes may be pointed out.   But the moment scientists enter the regions of speculation their conclusions are no more reliable than the conclusions of speculative theologians.   Both are right so long as they confine their statements to known facts; but both may be entirely in error in their speculative conclusions.

We are answered that the honest scientist is seeking for truth alone and he has no reason to deceive the people.

What reason has the honest theologian to deceive people?   There are scientific delusions as really as there are religious delusions; and when they enter the regions of speculation both parties are equally likely to arrive at false conclusions. Let us disabuse ourselves of the idea that delusive ideas pertain exclusively to religious beliefs.   The history of so-called scientific speculations shows that the fallacies of scientific hypotheses have been very extensive.

But to return to the consideration of the political effects of a disbelief in religious and moral obligations. We are aware of the ready answer, that eminent atheists do not show a blood-thirsty disposition. Granted; but men of their social and intellectual position are above the pinchings of want, and they are educated to a degree which enables them to see the untold evils that must result from a communistic outbreak, accompanied, as it would be, by outrages upon those called the upper classes; for they themselves belong to the upper classes, and their own personal interests are involved as directly as those of any other class, and hence we see them on the side of law and order.

But, in case of a communistic rising, they could not control the result of their own teachings; and if in such a case they attempted to control the violent, they would fall before blind fury as soon as other persons.

We are told that under a free government there is no danger of such outbreaks. Let us not deceive ourselves. We are also reminded of the benefits of intelligent instruction and the great blessings that flow from general education; and to that I say amen, provided the education is of the proper kind; but I have no sympathy with those who wish to let the moral education of children take care of itself.

Much has been written about letting the generous natures of children be developed; but if they are brought up without moral restraint, how will their natures be developed?

If all the wishes of children are gratified, what kind of men shall we have? In the majority of cases we shall have poor specimens of humanity. The passions of all need moral restraint, and unless children receive some kind of moral as well as intellectual teaching they seldom become valuable citizens.

One very singular fact connected with all philosophical inquiry into mental and moral acts is the mutual dependence of several apparently diverse beliefs. For instance, nearly all philosophers who believe in the existence of an Omnipotent Creator also believe in a future conscious existence.

Nearly all who believe in a Creator believe also in the existence of an absolutely unvarying moral standard, and that moral laws are as permanent and certain in their operations as the general laws of nature. Doubtless, if we could perfectly comprehend all truth, we could understand what this standard requires, and all would be obliged to agree not only to the existence of this standard, but also to what men should do to conform to its requirements.

It must not be understood, however, that a perfect moral standard would require that all persons should act alike in all cases ; for of necessity there must be different positions and circumstances in life. For instance, it might be in conformity with a perfect moral standard for one who is famishing with hunger to take and eat food, which under ordinary circumstances, would belong to another.

Again, those who believe in an absolute moral standard generally believe in the immortality of the human soul. At first sight there would not seem to be any necessary or logical connection between morality, God and immortality. But why should those who generally reject belief in the existence of an eternal moral standard and an eternal Law-giver at the same time disbelieve in the soul's immortality ?

Many atheists believe in morality and in the performance of moral duties ; but as their standard of morality can admit of no obligations to any higher power than humanity itself, it cannot be an unvarying standard, for humanity is constantly changing.

But what is morality? What constitutes an act a moral one? The lexicons tell us that " morality is the relation of conformity to the true moral standard, or rule." But what is this standard which is called the true? On what basis does it rest, and in what does it consist? What is the real foundation on which the moral quality of an act must stand, and what is the abstract quality which expresses the difference between a moral act and an immoral one? There must be something in the very nature of things which underlies the principles upon which morality apparently rests. What is that foundation?

I am aware that many think it is not scientific to suppose the will of the Deity can have anything to do with the absolute moral quality of an act, and that the real quality is the same whether the act is in accordance with the will of the Deity or not. Such a position is satisfactory to such as do not believe the Deity ever made a revelation of His will to man. These assert that inasmuch as what seems moral to one may seem immoral to another, therefore there cannot be an absolute code of morals which is applicable to all men. Some trace all evil to selfishness, and others all good to unselfishness. Still others assert that the moral quality of an act is entirely dependent upon its utility.

Now I suppose that any act, which, taken in all its bearings, tends to the best good of mankind and their ultimate happiness, cannot be otherwise than moral ; and it is also, in one sense, an act of highest utility. And, further, I cannot believe that the performance of any act which is strictly moral can be of ultimate injury to the doer, when we take into consideration all its bearing. An objection may be noted in the case of a person who sacrifices his present interests, or his life, for the good of others. In case of one whose life is voluntarily sacrificed to save others the question may be raised how that can result in good to the one sacrificed? That raises another question which leads into realms that lie beyond the reach of human experiences, and hence, from want of any certain knowledge on this point, we must leave the question unanswered, or else refer its answer to a power or being wiser than we are. I cannot believe, however, that the principle of self-sacrifice has been placed in mankind except for wise reasons. But it seems natural to suppose that a perfect moral standard must be in harmony with the physical laws of the universe, or with what are called the laws of nature, for both are believed to be established by the same power.

Following out this idea, we may suppose that, as a general rule, men who live up to the highest moral standard which commends itself to the judgment and reason of intelligent and enlightened men enjoy better health and live longer than those who are careless in regard to these things. Also, that the man who attempts to live up to the standard of morals set up by Jesus Christ will enjoy better health, and that (other things being equal) in consequence of this better health he may expect a longer life and much greater happiness than one who disregards this high standard of morals.

The very fact that such physical and mental results follow high moral action seems to indicate, even if we assume that utility, or conformity with the laws of nature, forms the true basis of morals, that the maxims of Jesus, judged by either standard, are of the highest order of utility. And this fact, again, would seem to indicate that the origin of these maxims may be found in the very highest wisdom. Can we then wonder that so many believe that these maxims and precepts were dictated by wisdom from above?

Of course, believers in the teachings of Christ and his apostles will readily acknowledge that some necessary logical connection must exist between belief and non-belief in God and belief or disbelief in the existence of the human soul.

In regard to the question whether there is an unalterable moral standard, it seems evident that there can be no definite answer unless we first decide in our minds whether there is an Infallible Law-giver; or, in other words, we should first decide whether there is preponderING evidence of the existence of an Infinitely Wise Being or Power which established the laws that govern the universe. If such a Being exists, He may prescribe a standard which will be in complete harmony with universal laws. But if there is not clear evidence of the existence of such an Infinitely Wise Being or Power, then an unalterable moral standard may not be supposed to exist; for with changing circumstances or surroundings the quality of moral actions will be likely to change.

Kant held that neither the existence of God, nor the immortality of the human soul, nor the freedom of the will could be demonstrated through any scientific arguments or speculations; and yet he believed in God, and in moral and religious obligations, though rejecting much which is taught as theology. He also believed in an unvarying moral standard, and in the freedom of the will, without which freedom these moral laws could not be obeyed; and, further, that without the existence of "God and the soul's immortality there would be no final cause or motive for human conduct." "He further believed that men may be placed in a state of felicity agreeable to morality, provided by and to be obtained through God, in another and a better life."—("Penny Cyclopædia.")

Kant's opinion, though not capable of demonstration, cannot be refuted, and if the teachings of science are set up against a moral standard, one assertion will balance the other. Science is not genuine if it has no demonstrable basis; and thus I believe that what is falsely called science may be at fault rather than belief in an infallible moral standard. Science should be definite, clear, and not delusive, and that which claims to be scientific, if it leads away from a proper moral standard, — if an unchangeable moral standard is not a myth, — must be falsely called science. Much, however, is taught for science which cannot be disproved, but which, whether so intended or not, does tend to undermine ideas of any direct responsibility to a Supreme Intelligence. Doubtless some, who dislike to lessen conscientious regard for moral obligations, do teach what in most minds must raise questions which will of necessity cause them to doubt the existence of real moral obligations.

Take for instance the question of the descent of man from the lower animals (provided it is shown that he has so descended), and this, with many, will have (though not justly) a direct bearing upon the question whether there can be any absolute standard of moral responsibility; for they will ask, if there is such a responsibility, where is the line between the brute and the human which marks the bounds of moral responsibility? This would seem like trying to draw a line between daylight and darkness. Where in the twilight does this line come? If the stronger and fiercer animal commits no wrong when it mutilates or drives away its weaker or less courageous relative, how can it be said that man does wrong when he commits a similar act, if he has descended from a like animal?

Does not this look like the doctrine that " Might makes right? " If the higher animals which appear to have in kind the general mental qualities that men possess commit acts of violence without incurring moral guilt, why should men, who are simply higher developed animals, be held morally responsible for like acts? Human governments hold madmen and fools irresponsible, where men of intelligent and sane minds are held guilty, if they commit acts of violence. But on what law can this distinction be founded, if there is no absolute standard?

Every intelligent man at some time during his early childhood has been considered irresponsible, but with the increase of intelligence there came a time when he became responsible. Doubtless some reach a state of partial moral responsibility long before it is reached in all respects ; and perhaps some never reach that state in all respects. Probably in no two children will this moral responsibility be reached exactly alike, or at exactly the same age. A similar state may possibly have been reached between the brute and the human at some time during past ages, provided men have been developed from the brutes.

But we ask at what stage of the evolution of man from the brute does moral responsibility commence? To whom does this responsibility or moral obligation run? Does it run to men, or to a higher power? How can it run to a higher power when we deny that there is a Supreme Lawgiver? This is a practical question, for we want to know where moral responsibility commences and where the consciousness of right or wrong commences. Is conscience an

inborn faculty, or is it entirely the result of education? Is
it in the very composition of our natures?

Again, if conscience is inborn, is it a safe guide? Surely,
if it is badly educated, all must know that it is not a safe
guide. Then what is its value? Its natural voice would
seem to be, "Be right, do rightly, act rightly;" and even
though it is not an infallible guide, men ought to be thank-
ful for its warnings, for on just such warnings the safety
and welfare of society largely depend.

It seems to me that in man the sense of right and wrong is
inborn; but the standard according to which this inborn faculty
acts is greatly modified or changed by circumstances of birth,
education, and other surroundings. But these surroundings,
while they modify the standard which men in different
localities accept, in no wise change the actual and absolute
moral standard, any more than men of different ideas of
geology can change the geological strata. The strata are
there, and no man or set of men can place the granite above
the limestone formations. The same Almighty Power
which placed the granite on its everlasting foundations and
in its present position has also (I believe) set up an equally
solid and stable moral standard. But a difficulty occurs
when men who are warped by their own desires and interests
attempt to interpret or explain that standard; for the
standard they accept and act upon is apt to be somewhere
nearly on a plane with their desires. Hence the word imperfect, both in their standards and their acts, may be
justly written against the lives of all men who make or set
up their own notions for a moral standard. And hence the
necessity of some standard to which all can appeal as the
one unerring moral standard.

I think no one will dispute the desirability of such a

standard, provided we could tell its exact limits and bounds. We have the " data of ethics " from able writers ; but the very ablest of moral philosophers who argue from the light of science or of reason differ greatly among themselves in regard to the real force and position of these data. It seems evident that no perfect moral standard can be of human origin, for the moment we leave the demonstrable for the unknown, theories which look perfect to one seem very imperfect to another, and thus endless discussions result. We need to deny the assumptions of a considerable part of what is supposed to be scientific concerning fundamental moral principles, because many of these rest upon questionable hypotheses rather than demonstrations.

If, as claimed by Herbert Spencer and others, our moral ideas are based simply upon inherited instinct or impressions handed down through the experience of many generations, it does not seem probable that there can be any demonstrable moral standard ; for the strength of these inherited impressions will increase or decrease with the state of civilization and other surroundings. But, if moral impressions and ideas come entirely through inherited instinct, how does it happen that some men of very limited opportunities for education, and whose parents have not shown any extraordinary strength of moral development, have been so greatly ahead of all their contemporaries in the strength, depth, and clearness of their moral apprehensions?

Take the case of Jesus Christ, for instance, and look at it from the Spencerian stand-point. Here we see a man having only limited opportunities for education, surrounded by and brought up among a people held under bondage by the Romans, burst forth as a moral light high above all other men who preceded or succeeded him. Leaving out of view everything concerning his supposed miraculous birth and his Divine nature, and not affirming or denying anything concerning the nature of the miracles which the evangelists state that he performed, or whether he rose from the dead, as believed by Christians, we will now look at him merely as a man, as this evolutionary theory necessitates. I ask, how did it happen that Jesus Christ inherited such a wonderful depth and clearness of moral sense that he stands in this respect high above every other moral teacher who has ever lived?

Some have attempted to show that his moral precepts were not of much higher order than those of other teachers; but until the works of such teachers are produced such assertions lack a proper foundation. Passages have been quoted from Confucius, Buddha, Zoroaster, Plato, and Socrates containing excellent moral precepts. Perhaps those quoting these precepts think they have made out a probable case; but, in so far as the writer is informed, all such quoted passages have failed to reach anywhere near the sublime moral heights of the teachings of Jesus.

Such authors and quotations have to meet statements of candid infidels, who, having no belief in Christianity, yet have freely confessed that the moral teachings of Jesus are high above all the teachings of other men. Besides, some four hundred millions of the human race are nominal Christians, and the nations called Christian comprise the most highly educated and cultivated races on the globe. This fact indicates that great numbers of intelligent men believe that the utterances of Jesus are in a moral sense the highest ever proclaimed by man. This is a kind of testimony that no denials can shake.

I am aware that the three hundred and seventy millions of

Buddhists may (as far as numbers go) be set over against the number of Christians, and that both Jesus and Buddha taught that total unselfishness is a high moral quality ; yet when we compare the results and the reasonableness of their lives and their teachings, we see that they are not at all comparable. Buddhists teach that Buddha, during one of his many lives, at one time saw a tigress and her cubs famishing with hunger, and he carried his benevolence so far as to give his body to satisfy their hunger ; which certainly was benevolence run mad. We find no such unmeaning benevolence in the teachings of Jesus.

Again, in and beyond his moral teachings, Jesus asserted the existence of a kind, compassionate, and forgiving Heavenly Father. But such a Deity has no existence in any other religion. Forgiveness is the peculiar attribute of the Deity whom Jesus claimed to be his Father.

Is it not exceedingly strange that this child of poor parents, who, it is supposed, worked at the trade of a carpenter until within three years of death, should, during those last three years of his life, flash out meteor-like, and shed a moral light which threw all moral lights which preceded into comparative darkness? Can we believe that such a clear and strong moral light was inherited from his peasant parents? If so, from which of his parents did he inherit such extraordinary moral strength? There is nothing in the record to show this, except that his reputed father, Joseph, was a just man, and that he and his wife, Mary, were careful to conform to the Jewish forms of worship. The record does not indicate that either his parents or grandparents had any very strong development of the moral faculties.

It is true that in the genealogy from David through Solomon several prominent names appear ; but in none do I recognize any moral exhibitions at all comparable to those of their immortal descendant.

Every observing student of human intelligence knows that mental tendencies are to some extent inherited, and several men of extraordinary intellectual and moral strength have appeared during the ages who probably inherited a tendency towards those lines of thought in which they have become eminent.   But most of these have given a lifetime to study in the departments of science, literature or moral teachings, through which they became distinguished.   But in Jesus we meet a man concerning whom there is no record of any considerable previous intellectual or moral training, who, near the commencement of his public life, delivered a speech on the side of a mountain, which, for high moral principles and deep insight into the inner nature of man, is without a parallel in any other human effort.   Surely the production of such a man must indeed be wonderful, and one is inclined in all soberness to ask, Is it not as easy to believe the story of the unusual manner of his procreation as to believe that such extraordinary moral powers were simply inherited in such an age of moral darkness?   However, the record asserts that Jesus claimed to be the Son of God, and that he taught as he was directed by his Father.

Perhaps one here may be inclined to ask whether, from a philosophical point of view, that last statement may not furnish a clue to the probable reason why the moral and religious light of Jesus shone with such exceeding brightness.

The writer expects that exceptions will be taken to the question put in this way, and that some will see in it lingering traces of old religious beliefs and old-fashioned teach-

ings.   But it is pertinent to ask, If these former beliefs and
teachings accord with actual truth, shall they be disregarded
because they are now thought to be rather old-fashioned?
Did not the very best men who lived in those former times
assent to these teachings?

CHAPTER XII.

ETHICAL SPECULATIONS AND INQUIRIES.

ONE reason why so many are pleased when anything is discovered which seems to contradict formerly accepted opinions concerning religious theories and beliefs is because 'of the spirit of the times, which cannot brook spiritual dictation, and because so many seem to connect in their minds the very idea of religion with dictation in spiritual matters.   But such greatly err when they confound religion with certain doctrines which dogmatic expositors of religious doctrines formerly taught, and which many modern expositors would have men believe it is a sin to doubt.

If such apparently irreverent ones would remember that the essence of religion consists in the worship of God and love for our fellow-men, they would see that religious feelings should be cultivated rather than opposed.   But I am not surprised at wrong conclusions on this subject when I recollect that religious teachers are men, — and some of them selfish too,— and that some, perhaps unconsciously, use religion or religious feelings for their own advantage rather than for the good of their fellow-men.   Such desire to impress upon the minds of less independent thinkers the belief that they (being the expositors of the will of God) should be obeyed, and that to act contrary to their instructions is to rebel against God. Thus who can wonder that when anything occurs which gives these dogmatic teachers a set-back it naturally pleases those who have observed their ill-advised assumptions? Some, by thinking they are in the service of God, and thus are speaking for or in the place of God, may perhaps honestly come to the conclusion that, of right, they should be listened to and obeyed. But if those who object (and justly too) to such a state of things will consider that religion is one thing and the teachings of any man or class of men may be quite another thing, they will not be willing to encourage a spirit which naturally leads the minds of men away from that reverent belief and trust in the Deity which certainly is a source of much enjoyment to the faithful believers in God.

But however consoling a belief in the existence of an All-Merciful and Overruling Providence may be, I think there is no doubt that there is need of being decidedly sceptical in regard to much which is now taught for scientific truth; yet some are disposed to be extremely uncharitable towards those who do not accept their speculative dogmas, however much they may praise the independent and philosophic spirit of religious sceptics. The fact that religious sceptics have fared badly at the hands of professed religious men is no excuse for scientific uncharitableness. Religious sceptics do not need any defence at my hands; but in justice to them it may be truthfully said that they have not done so badly for pure religious belief as many think. On the contrary, on account of sceptical objections, religious men have been obliged to look carefully to the foundations of their belief, and thus they know much better what can be really defended as truth than they would if these objections had never been raised.

All have a right to ask the why concerning what they are requested to believe. Again, if there were no objectors, much of religious belief would degenerate into mere superstition. If there were no sceptics, religious pretenders would have a very wide field to work upon, and superstition, instead of truth, would largely prevail. When a man becomes afraid to doubt what a religious or scientific pretender claims to be the truth he becomes the slave of the pretender's whim. When one feels that if he doubts the words or teachings of a religious teacher he is to be condemned, he ceases to be a reasonable being, and might just as well be a Mohammedan or a Buddhist, as far as his personal responsibility for his belief is concerned; for in respect to belief, he is not really himself, but is an offshoot, or echo, of the priest or the pretender. Why may he not as well believe in and worship Buddha as any other deity, so long as his personal responsibility for belief is lodged in some other person, while he neither understands nor comprehends the reasons why he should believe the doctrine taught? If this position is denied what barriers have we against the most absurd superstitions?

The apostolic injunction is that every one should " be able to give a reason for the hope that is in him." But suppose that one gives as a reason for his faith something which does not correspond to any rational conception, what shall we say? Such answers are not unfrequently given, and we should pronounce the party who gives such reasons insane, provided he talked as strangely and illogically concerning matters of every-day life. This fact proves a stumbling-block to many, and they seem inclined to think that one belief may be as good as any other, in regard to the foundation principles of ethical doctrines.

The question has been asked, Why, if there is a God, He has not revealed Himself in such a manner that no one can have a doubt concerning His existence, or the character and requirements of His laws? Has the thought ever occurred to such inquirers, that possibly if the Deity and all His laws were so plainly revealed that no one could be able to doubt, perhaps there would be no such thing as moral responsibility? If evidence of such a demonstrative nature is presented that whether one is willing or not he is compelled to know, — where is the chance for the exercise of either faith or choice? Can there be moral responsibility where there is no opportunity for the exercise of choice?

If one is *compelled* to believe and acknowledge just laws, should he have moral credit for such acknowledgment or obedience? All observing persons know how readily men receive what they wish to believe, and how naturally they reject what they do not wish to believe.

If the Deity should reveal Himself to every one, whoever he may be, and whatever his moral disposition is, so that he would be compelled to fully comprehend the origin and operations of all laws, and also fully understand the results of obedience or disobedience, would not men, under such circumstances, be morally mere machines?

It may be said in reply that men now know that physically they are under the complete dominion of law, and yet they often disregard the laws of health, and hence it is evident that *knowledge* does not always cause men to act wisely, or lessen their responsibility. That is true; but in regard to physical laws, men would act wisely if something in their physical organizations or in their mental operations did not incline them to act unwisely. So as to moral laws, doubtless all would yield cheerful obedience to them if there was not something in the moral proclivities of men which inclines them to disobedience. Mere physical laws are not generally supposed to have any moral quality, hence their applications are different from those of the moral laws, and cannot be directly applicable to the question under discussion. Persons may be reckless even when they know they are dealing with inexorable and irrevocable laws ; but their recklessness in regard to the consequences of the violation of physical laws cannot relieve them from the obligations of moral laws.

I repeat, what in substance I have before said, that we should bear in mind the fact that if it was the purpose of the Deity that men should enjoy moral freedom, He could not, in wisdom, so order His providence as to render the existence of moral freedom impossible.

It is well known that M. Pasteur has done more than any other living man to show that all terrestrial life has been developed from life-germs previously existing. I have before remarked that the belief in the doctrine of " spontaneous generation," or that life inheres in the very composition of matter itself, tends to create many strange views on the real position of man's place in nature. The belief that life comes only from antecedent life tends to modify the views which scientists hold concerning the relations which men sustain towards an Intelligent Ruler of all terrestrial affairs.

The speeches of M. Pasteur, the eminent physiologist, chemist, and scientist, and of M. Dumas, the distinguished chemist, were very gratifying incidents connected with a meeting (held in April, 1882) by the French Academy, of which the foremost literary and scientific men of France are members. Among others who took part in the discussion were Ernest Renan, the eminent sceptical writer, and H. A. Taine, the materialistic philosopher. The discussion, instead of being purely scientific, included the consideration of the question of the immortality of the soul and of the existence of an Intelligent and Omnipotent Creator. This brought a conflict between faith and positivism, spiritualism and materialism, and raised the question whether mind or matter takes precedence ; and the whole involved ideas concerning the finite and infinite.

According to the usual course of exercises at the meetings of the Academy, it became the duty of Pasteur, Dumas, and Renan to make speeches, the speech of Pasteur, according to custom, being a eulogy upon the life and character of M. Littré, to whose seat, made vacant by his death, Pasteur had succeeded. M. Littré was a strong materialist and positivist, a devoted follower of Compte, yet his belief consisted largely of negation ; that is, not so much of what he did know as what he believed he did not know. M. Pasteur's arguments are worthy of the widest circulation, and I will now quote certain extracts from his speech as published in the " Edinburgh Review " of July, 1882.

He says of M. Littré, who was an admirer of Compte : " The fundamental principle of Auguste Compte is to set aside all metaphysical inquiry into first and final causes, to reduce all ideas and all theories to fact, and to restrict the character of certainty to experimental demonstrations. His system includes a classification of the sciences, and a pretended law of history expressed by the assertion that the conceptions of the human mind pass successively through three states, — the theological, the metaphysical, and the scientific or positive."

The reporter further continues : —

" M. Littré found a certain repose of mind in the absolute denial by the positivists of all metaphysical truth. He was, in fact, what is now called an agnostic. Without denying the existence of God and the immortality of the soul, he dismissed them from his thoughts as subjects incapable of scientific demonstration."

. To this M. Pasteur replies : —

"As for myself, holding that the words ' progress ' and ' invention' are synonymous, I ask by what new philosophical or scientific discovery the soul of man can be torn from these lofty themes? They seem to me to be eternal, because the mystery that infolds the universe, from which they emanate, is itself eternal. . . .

"Beyond this starry firmament, what is there? More skies and stars. And beyond these? The human mind, impelled by an irresistible power, will never cease to ask itself, what lies beyond? Time and space arrest it not. At the farthest point attained is a finite boundary, enlarged from what preceded it ; no sooner is it reached than the implacable question returns, returns forever in the curiosity of man. It is vain to speak of space, of time, of size unlimited. Those words pass the human understanding. But he who proclaims the existence of the infinite — and no man can escape from it — comprehends in that assertion more of the supernatural than there is in all the miracles of all religions ; for the conception of the infinite has the twofold characters that it is irresistible and incomprehensible. We prostrate ourselves before the thought, which masters all the faculties of the understanding, and threatens the springs of intellectual life, like the sublime madness of Pascal. Yet this positive and primordial conception is gratuitously set aside by positivism, with all its consequences on the life of human society.

"The conception of the infinite in creation is everywhere irresistibly manifest. It places the supernatural in every human heart. The idea of God is a form of the idea of the infinite. As long as the mystery of the infinite weighs upon the mind of man, temples will be raised to it, be the object of adoration Brahma, Allah, Jehovah, or Jesus. Metaphysics are but the study of this commanding notion of the infinite."

Pasteur took strong ground in favor of a belief in the Deity as an Omnipotent Creator, and also in the immortality of the soul. He was answered by Ernest Renan in an eloquent speech, which, however, was considered a failure in so far as it was an attempt to answer the statements of Pasteur.

Dumas stated most pointedly and positively that there was something connected with a man's existence which could not be accounted for by chemistry.

M. Dumas' reported statements are as follows : —

"The physician and naturalist may teach what is physical in man ; that his nerves are sometimes instruments of pain, and that his body is but dust. That is their business. But philosophy and eloquence should cast their mantle of purple and gold over the baser aspects of life. It is their business to strengthen the heart of man and raise his soul to immortality."

"But the discoveries of science in our own age prove that none but the ignorant can suppose that the whole book of wisdom has been revealed to us. The source of life and its essence are unknown to us. We have not seized that mysterious link which connects the body with the mind, and constitutes the unity of individual man. We have no right to treat man as an abstract being, to disdain his history, or to attribute to science an influence over the direction of the moral axis of the world which its progress does not justify. We have, it is true, conquered the earth, measured the track of the planets, calculated the mechanism of the heavens, analyzed the stars, resolved the nebulæ, and followed the eccentric course of comets ; but beyond those stars, whose light is centuries in reaching us, there are other orbs whose rays are lost in space ; and farther, farther still beyond all limits and all computation, are suns which we shall not behold, and innumerable worlds hidden from our eyes.   After two thousand years of effort, if we reach the utmost extremity of the universe, which is but a point in the immensity of space, we are arrested on the threshold of the infinite, of which we know nothing.   'The nature of man, his present and future existence, are mysteries impenetrable to the greatest genius, as well as to the rest of mankind,' said D'Alembert, at the height of his fame. ' What we know is but little,' said Laplace on his death-bed. Those were the last words of the illustrious rival of Newton. Let them also be mine."

The "Edinburg Review" remarks upon the above as follows : —

"These are, in other words, the sentiments expressed by M. Dumas and M. Pasteur.   And who are they who hold this language ?   The one is a chemist, conversant with all the known properties of natural bodies and the marvellous combinations of the atomic theory which reduces them all to a few primitive elements.   The other is a physiologist who has refuted the theory of " spontaneous generation," and established on a solid basis that life alone can impart life.   They have both travelled as far on the road of natural science as it will take them ; they have even enlarged the bounds of physical knowledge.   But, arrived at that term of man's labor, they acknowledge that an infinite horizon of thought, of action, of forces, and of power lies beyond the scope of sensuous observation. He studies nature with a careless eye and a benighted mind who does not perceive that the supernatural lies in it and above it. For when all is said that science can teach, and all is done that skill can achieve to cultivate the earth and bring forth its fruits, one gift remains without which everything else were vain — that gift which the Supreme Creator has reserved absolutely to Himself — that gift which man and every living creature can take away, but can never restore — that gift without which this earth would be no more than the cinder of a planet — the mystery and the miracle of LIFE. Life is everywhere ; without life nothing would exist at all ; matter would be the *caput mortuum* of the universe. With the diffusion of life creation begins ; and of that act all but a supernatural power is incapable."

Speeches like those of Pasteur and Dumas seem like a new departure, in an institution like the French Academy, but straws show which way the current is setting, and to my mind the reception these speeches had indicates that the materialistic current, which refers the origin of all things to unconscious, unthinking, and purposeless destiny, has reached its limit, and that there are indications of a change towards more reverent and reasonable views.

Although Pasteur eulogized Littré's character, and his faithfulness to what he believed to be true, he was obliged to disagree decidedly in the matter of belief with the man he eulogized. Pasteur is a firm believer in the existence of the Deity, and also of the immortal existence of the human soul. M. Littré did not absolutely deny that an Omnipotent Creator exists, but he denied that we can have any definite knowledge or evidence that such a Being exists ; and hence followed a disbelief in the immortality of the human soul. Hence he denied that we can have any direct evidence of the existence of a soul or mind separate from man's physical organization.

This striking peculiarity of belief appears in the writings of almost every one who rejects the idea of the existence of a soul separate from the body. Most of these do not attempt to show that such a thing cannot exist, but simply to say that we cannot, from scientific demonstrations, prove that a soul does exist. This position is entirely negative, and does not in the least help to explain how the invisible power that exists in every living man comes to be in him. It is true that we have never seen any manifestation of life or intelligence unless it was connected with a material substance; but the fact that spiritual existence (or souls, if such exist) cannot make its influence felt by men except through physical or material organisms by no means shows that it cannot exist in a separate state. This last statement materialists must admit to be true. It is also true that the power of manifesting intelligence increases and decreases with the growth and decay of the physical organs. In the infant, intelligence seems feeble, and also in extreme old age, when we speak of the aged as losing their faculties. It appears to me that, in the case of the aged, this is simply a loss of power in the brain and nervous system, the physical organs through which intelligence is manifested to other parties. Pressure on the brain may destroy all consciousness, and with that all power of manifesting intelligence; but a removal of that pressure may at once bring back to the brain and nervous system the power of intelligent manifestations, and with it memory of occurrences long past. The power of intelligence must have existed either in or out of the man during the time when no manifestations of intelligence could be manifested, as is proved by the immediate return to memory of occurrences which took place long ago, on the removal of the pressure.

The point I now make is this : The fact that the mind can make no manifestations of its existence while a certain pressure is on the brain does not show that the mind is not still in existence ; for, as soon as the pressure is relieved, memory returns. Then, if mind exists somewhere during the life of the individual while it cannot be manifested, what right have we to deny that it can exist in other states where it can make no manifestations which we can see?

What right have we to say that the functions of the mind can be suspended for a time, and again resumed, and acknowledge that this invisible power still existed during its suspension, and yet deny that it may exist under other circumstances when we cannot see its manifestations?

If we deny that intelligence can exist when we cannot see it, or if we assume that the soul cannot exist because we cannot see it, carry this denial to its legitimate conclusion, and deny the existence of intelligence in the living man when we cannot discover indications of either life or intelligence. If the intelligent principle while temporarily inactive does not exist in the man while he is in a state of unconsciousness, where does it exist during this time? — It certainly cannot have been dead and brought to life again.

Take for instance the case of a person apparently drowned, who remains unconscious for an hour or more. After being restored to consciousness he has a perfect recollection of every circumstance up to the time of his loss of consciousness, and then for an hour or more there is a perfect blank, and he can remember nothing which occurred during that interval of time ; but, on regaining his faculties and returning to his normal condition, memory and every other quality of intelligence return, and become as clear and strong as ever. Where was the mind during his state of unconsciousness? Did it still exist in the body, or was it out of the body? Its principles must have existed somewhere, or else a new creation is necessitated to bring back a return of memory and the other intellectual attributes.

Again, take a person in a profound sleep. He may be perfectly unconscious of everything around him, but is the action of the mind suspended or dormant while he is in this condition? Dreams show that the mind itself may be still active, while to all outward appearance the man has no consciousness. Through the condition of sleep his mental connection with the outer world seems completely severed; but the mind itself may not be even sleeping, as its activity in dreams abundantly indicates. This shows that there is a perfectly active mental condition when no man can see any manifestations of mind.

Who can look at the mass of humanity, and see its individuality of character, and behold one man, from youth to old age, in mental and moral respects different from every other man, and not see that there is a kind of personal identity in his actuality, which we call character, that cannot be accounted for by any mere physical causes? Physiologists may dissect as carefully as possible, and find no material difference in the quality of the brain, heart, and muscles; but distinct and definite characteristics cleave to the man from youth to old age which neither chemistry nor any other physical cause can account for. When one dies a distinct individuality is stamped out. Of what does this individuality consist? Explain it, if you can, by merely physical science. What trace of character can you find by disscetion, except in the shape or quality of the brain, which an invisible entity has taken as its organ of communication with the outer world? What is this something which we call mind, or intelligence? What makes the different moral characters and dispositions which are distinguishing characteristics of various individuals of society?

Who can tell what makes one man's disposition, thoughts, and desires so different from those of every other man? Explain this if you can without acknowledging in him the existence of an invisible and intelligent force entirely distinct from the like force which exists in any other individual of the human race.

Many believe this force to be a soul, or something inseparably connected with a soul. Those who deny the existence of a soul leave us in the dark concerning these distinguishing qualities in human character.

CHAPTER XIII.

SOUL AND MIND.

THE principle of Atavism must be admitted to exercise a very strong influence upon particular men, and even races of men. How often we see a very marked trait developed in a man when you can scarcely find a semblance of that trait in father, mother, grandfather, or grandmother, but by looking back several generations you will find the trait strongly developed in some ancestor, and it has jumped over several generations, and now all at once it crops out in a very marked manner.

We all know the tendency of various diseases to descend from father or mother to son or daughter, as, for instance, scrofula or consumption, or in mental tendency to insanity, and in fact to many other peculiarities. The sins of the parents are "visited upon the children to the third and fourth generation," and we might even say to the tenth generation.

All know that there is an invisible and distinguishing something pertaining to every individual man, and the question is, how this came to be in him. To say that it is inherited does not in the least inform us how these invisible and peculiar kinds of forces came to be originally implanted in man.

We may deny the existence of that which we cannot see; but it may be as reasonable for a blind man to deny that light exists because he never beheld it, as it is for man to

deny the existence of an intelligent cause of human intelligence and human individuality.   Intelligence is not a myth,
neither can the cause of intelligence be other than a reality.
Our denials of this will not in the least change actual facts
which pertain to human existence, or alter the mysterious
connection which exists between the invisible entity which we
call mind or intelligence, and our physical organization.   To
me it seems to be folly to assert the positive non-existence of
an entity like the soul because its existence cannot be demonstrated by physical science, when in actual fact the matter
under consideration is beyond and entirely outside the domains of the physical sciences.   To claim as some do that
all of the acts of the mind or the soul are properly under
physical laws is begging the whole question ; for the physi-
cist must first show that the soul (if it exists) is composed
of a material substance in order to bring it under physical
laws.

We are told that the idea of an immaterial essence is unthinkable; and some go even farther, and assert that what
is unthinkable is also impossible.   This is a mere assertion,
and I deny its truth, and on this point my assertion is a
positive one ; while the evidence upon which the other assertion rests is entirely of a negative character.

What is unthinkable to one may not be so to another of
a different grade or order of intelligence.   It would be the
highest folly and self-conceit for a near or short sighted
man to assume that a certain object could not exist because
it is not manifest to his vision, when a far-seeing man could
readily see the object.   I think there is as real a difference
in the range of the intellectual vision in different men as
there is in the power of their physical vision ; and the reason
why some are so confident that certain invisible essences or

entities or powers cannot exist is probably because of some peculiarity of their mental or moral vision.

Of unthinkable things, take, for instance, certain matters pertaining to space. We cannot comprehend the idea of space being limited; for, if we attempt to do this, we must think of what is beyond this limit. Neither can we comprehend the idea of unlimited space. But space exists, and it must be either with or without limit, notwithstanding, in either case, the idea of placing any definite limit is unthinkable. Time, also, must either have had a beginning, or it did not have one. But how there could be such a thing as a beginning of time is incomprehensible; and yet we cannot comprehend its opposite, viz., that time can be without a beginning. Is there, therefore, no such thing as time?

If it is answered that time is necessarily limited, it being only a part of eternal duration, and hence must have a beginning and end, this answer gives merely a verbal turn; for it gives no idea of the length of time's duration or of how it merges into eternity. But if one will still insist upon this difference between the words time and eternity, then let us shift the word, and use eternity instead of the word time, and ask whether we can conceive of a beginning or end of eternity. Is there then no eternity?

We cannot prove our personal identities; yet what sane man doubts his personal identity? Notwithstanding all the sophistries used in attempting to show that we do not know that we are the same individuals we were ten years since, our consciousness, with memory added, tells us that we are the same; and these testimonials concerning our personal identities are stronger than a thousand scientific sophisms. Upon this point Dr. Reid (as quoted by Jackson, p. 184) writes as follows : —

" All men agree that personality is indivisible ; a part of a person is an absurdity. A man who loses his estate, his health, an arm, or a leg, continues still to be the same person. My personal identity, therefore, is the continued existence of that indivisible thing which I call myself. I am not thought, I am not action, I am not feeling ; but I think and act and feel. Thoughts, actions, feelings change every moment ; but *self*, to which they belong, is permanent. If it be asked how I know that it is permanent, the answer is, that I know it from memory. Everything I remember to have seen, or heard, or done, or suffered, convinces me that I existed at the time remembered.

" But though it is from memory that I have the knowledge of my personal identity, yet personal identity must exist in nature, independent of memory, otherwise I should only be the same person as far as my memory serves me ; and what would become of my existence during the intervals wherein my memory has failed me ? My remembrance of any of my actions does not make me to be the person who did the action, but only makes me know that I was the person who did it."

It is well to have enough of scepticism in our mental constitutions to prevent being imposed upon by superstitious fears ; but universal doubt must result in gigantic evil.

David Hume writes concerning Pyrrhonism, or universal doubt, as follows (" Essays," p. 381) : "A PYRRHONIAN cannot expect that his philosophy will have any constant influence on the mind ; or, if it had, that its influence would be beneficial to society. On the contrary, he must acknowledge, if he will acknowledge anything, that all human life must perish, were his principles universally and steadily to prevail. All discourse, all action, would immediately cease ;

and men remain in total lethargy, till the necessities of nature unsatisfied put an end to their miserable existence."

Yet the same Hume, when under another state of feelings, writes as follows (I quote at second hand) : "The *intense* view of these manifold contradictions and imperfections in human reason has so wrought upon me, and heated my brain, that I am ready to reject all belief and reasoning, and can look upon no opinion even as more probable or likely than another. Where am I, or what? From what causes do I derive my existence, and to what condition shall I return? Whose favor shall I court, and whose anger must I dread? What beings surround me? And on whom have I any influence, or who have any influence on me? I am confounded with all these questions, and begin to fancy myself in the most deplorable condition imaginable, environed with the deepest darkness, and utterly deprived of the use of every member and faculty.

"Most fortunately it happens, that since reason is incapable of dispelling these clouds, Nature herself suffices to that purpose, and cures me of this philosophical melancholy and delirium, either by relaxing this bent of mind, or by some avocation, and lively impression of my senses, which obliterate all these chimeras. I dine, I play a game of back-gammon, I converse, and am merry with my friends ; and when, after three or four hours' amusement, I would return to these speculations, they appear so cold, and strained, and ridiculous, that I cannot find in my heart to enter into them any farther."

It seems to me that men may as well attempt to prove that they are their own grandfathers as attempt to show that many of the current negations concerning our personal identities are true, or that the assumption that our physical systems constitute the most important element of ourselves is founded in reason.

If it is conceded that the soul consists of a material substance, then it may be entirely subject to physical laws. But that is just what is not conceded; and until this part of the question is agreed upon there cannot be commonly conceded foundation truths from which to proceed in our discussions.

The question has been asked, if the mind "is composed of highly refined or etherized matter, at what stage of this refinement does it become so refined as to be able to think?" To say that there may be realities which are immaterial is by no means a contradiction; for instance, a shadow. We may be answered that a shadow is not an entity, but is the mere absence of light. However this may be, the shade of a tree is an agreeable and pleasant reality in a hot day, as many a weary traveller on a hot and dusty road can testify. There is certainly a sweet and refreshing potentiality in this absence of light, and hence, negatively, a sort of recuperative force. It may be answered that the shadow is in itself absolutely nothing, and hence cannot be a force; that this refreshing potency is simply the result of arresting the enervating action of too much sunlight; but the fact still remains that without the absence of these rays of the sun through their interception (from which the shade is inseparable) this refreshing power could not exist. Or, in other words, this refreshing force or power being inseparable from the shade (dispute about it as we may), the shade still remains a reality appreciable by our senses. It has shape and outlines, which are distinguishing characteristics of reality. We hope, however, that the reader will not understand this to be a practical confession of our belief that the soul may be a mere shadow or shade.

There may be other immaterial realities, for all we know, which are not appreciable by or through our senses, and it is neither wise nor philosophical to assert that this cannot be so. Thus arises the question, what things may be immaterial, and yet realities — as a thought or sensation, for instance.

Scientific men generally believe that thought is accompanied by molecular action of the brain ; in fact, some assert that thought is caused by the action of matter under unalterable laws. Please observe, however, that there is a vast difference between saying that thought is accompanied by the action of matter and saying that thought consists of the action of matter. We may concede that molecular action of the brain may accompany thought, but not that thought consists of such action.

If thought is produced by the action of matter alone, guided by natural laws, then the same mental result should always be produced by the same material causes when all the conditions are the same. But does the same force or agency applied to our minds always produce the same result, even when the conditions, so far as we can see, are the same?

One man hears a statement of a fact, and receives it as such, and another, sitting by his side, rejects it, not believing it to be a fact. Both have the same evidence, given in the same way ; but the results produced are exactly opposite. Why should the same fact cause one to love and rejoice, and another sorrow or hate? Are there opposite material forces of nature struggling in the brains of different persons? Or have they immaterial principles, viz., souls that are possessed of different moral states, with affections running in opposite directions, which cause these directly opposite results? Which looks most reasonable?

Dr. Maudsley says (p. 152), speaking of different beliefs : " Our beliefs, sane or insane, are not the results of reason, but have their roots in that unconscious part of our nature of the state of which the feelings are the indices."

It is exactly this unconscious part of our nature that we need information about. The conscious parts of our natures may be observed and reasoned about. But what is this " unconscious part of our nature"? May it not be the soul itself which originates or modifies our mental and moral tastes, habits of thought, likes and dislikes? And, *per contra*, may not voluntary acts tend to modify the moral state of the soul?

The question whether men are responsible for the moral state of the " unconscious part of their natures " forces itself upon us. Why do certain men naturally tend towards one kind of moral or immoral actions, and others naturally tend towards other and opposite kinds of actions? Can a man mould or modify this " unconscious part " of his nature? If not, why the feeling of guilt when we are inclined to do what we know to be wrong? I think that our voluntary acts do modify the condition of this unconscious part, as surely as indulgence in the use of intoxicating liquors will modify the digestive organs, which also do their work unconsciously.

There seems to be a reflex action in both cases. The disordered stomach often craves intoxicants, and in turn these intoxicants tend to increase abnormal cravings. Indulgence in certain lines of thought tends to create a mental passion running in the same direction.

Here comes before us the actual fact of voluntary thought.

Why can a man generally think of any subject if he chooses to do so?   Why the consciousness of a free will, if all the acts of the will are necessitated by a power outside of the mind, and by the laws that govern matter?   Is not the very consciousness of freedom of choice to be taken into account when we make up our verdict?   Does not reason itself depend largely on our consciousness for its basis?   What man can say that he is sane, or that he can reason correctly, except that his reason and consciousness act harmoniously together?   It is the merest delusion to say that reasoning can be sound which ignores facts of consciousness.

But, again, why has a man a conscience?   And why a feeling of moral obligation?   Can we throw these out of account when we make up our verdict in regard to our thoughts, consciousness, and physical organization and their dependence on or independence of each other?   What kind of mere matter can cause a sense of right and wrong?   It is useless to assume that *all* moral feeling comes from education, for if it does all who are educated precisely alike will have the same moral feelings.   In our practical dealings, we know better than to be deceived by any such fallacy.

While we admit that mind cannot make manifestations of its existence that men can perceive, except through the action of the brain and nervous system, we do not believe that any material substance can be equivalent to a thought, or to the mind.   Mind and the soul seem to be spiritual; and the life and the soul in man may be inseparable; and if we consider life to be more than a mere process, or condition of matter, both may be as actually immaterial as a thought or a desire. Why should any one suppose that the mind, which is the parent of the thought, consists of a material substance any more than its children, the thoughts?

As an actual fact we neither know what the real nature or essence of either mind or matter is ; and, in one sense, it does not matter whether the mind or the soul is highly etherized matter or is actually immaterial; and I do not believe it can be demonstrated whether it is the one or the other, or whether it is either. Some hold to the opinion that it is highly important to show that the soul is immaterial, because they fear that unless this can be shown one great foundation principle on which the doctrine of the soul's immortality rests is in danger of being undermined. But I do not share in this fear.

We can conceive abstract realities which are not material, as justice, equity, and truth. These may be called qualities rather than entities, though we speak of justice, etc., with a fair appreciation of what truth, justice, etc., are. There is no lack of power to conceive of immateriality, as space, for instance, which, for all that we know, may exist as an absolute void, notwithstanding the statement that such an idea is unthinkable. As before mentioned the ground taken by some that what is unthinkable or inconceivable cannot be true is simply an assumption ; for, as we have before stated, it is incomprehensible how space can exist without limits, and it is also unthinkable that space can have any limits. But space does exist, either with or without limits, and I suppose it must be without limits.

Some have asserted that the very existence of space must have succeeded motion, which is simply another assumption. By space I mean simply "room," or "extension, considered independently of anything which it may contain ; " and this extension may be an absolute void. Space, in this sense, eternally existed, and never was created, nor can it ever be annihilated. Thus, from its very nature, space must be eternal in the future as well as in the past. Empty space certainly cannot be material.

Justice, equity, space, etc., are not entities in a sense equivalent to or like what are called imponderable agents in nature, as electricity, for instance ; for we do not deny that electricity may be a material substance. But who can tell the composition of electricity, or weigh it? Yet it is a mighty power, and it can be tasted, which fact would seem to indicate that it may be material.

But who can weigh or feel a thought through any of the senses? Does any one claim that thought is a material substance?

Who can weigh that invisible power which underlies sound? That invisible energy which causes vibrations in the atmosphere which we call sound will shake mighty structures when the right tone is struck, and that out of all proportion to the apparent power which causes that tone.

As an illustration of this invisible power, take the atmospheric vibrations caused by the small animal called the howling monkey. He often makes a noise which can be heard two or three miles, causing cubic miles of the atmosphere (which weigh millions of tons) to sensibly vibrate. He forces the air through a small aperture in the roots of his tongue, and the cavity — not larger than an English walnut — between his lower jaw and under his tongue is the place where all these intense vibrations originate.

So the vibrations of a string which weighs less than a quarter of an ounce (if what is called the tone of the arch is struck) will cause an arch which weighs many tons to shake so that the vibrations can be detected by the sense of touch. A very small mechanical power originates these vibrations. But how does such an immense apparent increase of power arise from such apparently insignificant original mechanical powers?

Certain musical sounds cause particles of dust or sand to range themselves in regular mathematical figures on a plate of glass. The same sounds or vibrations move inanimate matter, and also ravish the ear and the very soul with their melodies.

It is true that the air which vibrates is a material substance; but the air is not that original invisible power which causes these powerful vibrations which make sound perceptible through our sense of hearing.

Some have quibbled over the meaning of the word sound, and used it in a sense so restricted that there can be no sound unless there be ears to perceive the vibrations which cause sound. But I have used the word sound according to the second definition of Webster, viz., "The impulse or vibration which would occasion sound to a percipient if present with unimpaired organs;" and, when used in this sense, with the same propriety it might be asserted that there can be no light unless there are eyes to see it, as to say that there can be no sound unless there are ears to hear. What school-boy does not know that the fact that a blind man cannot see nor a deaf man hear in nowise alters the fact of the existence of light or the existence of a power which underlies conditions which produce what we call sound? An invisible and indescribable power seems to underlie the cause of sound-waves. What is this energy or power? This power seems to correspond to the "noumenon" of Kant, while sound appears to be the "phenomenon;" but is this "noumenon," or underlying force a material substance?

Memory, what is it? How wonderful! How are the records of passing events stamped into the mind? What an intertwined and intertwisted network of impressions must be on the brain, if all our hopes, fears, loves, hatreds, joys, and sorrows are material substances! When a scene not thought of for twenty years before "rushes on the recollection," what a clearing off of the tracks of other materials must there be, if thoughts and memories are material substances! Yet there are those who contend that for every fact stored in the mind an infinitesimally small cell exists, representing that fact, in the gray matter of the brain, and that only a limited number of these cells can be accommodated in the brain of any man. Thus when some new fact is acquired and treasured some old fact must be crowded out to make place for the new fact, provided the spaces in the brain allotted to storing facts are previously full. This is quite similar to the position assumed by Bain.

To further explain I will quote from Bain, "Mind and Body," extracts from pp. 91, 93, 94.

"For every act of memory, every exercise of bodily aptitude, every habit, recollection, train of ideas, there is a specific grouping, or coördination, of sensations and movements, by virtue of specific growths in the cell junctions."

"In the next place, Acquisition has a limit, determined by the amount of the nervous substance, that is, the size of the brain.

"We are apt to be carried away with a vague notion that there is no limit to acquirement, except our defect of application or some other curable weakness of our own. There are, however, very manifest limits. We are all blockheads in something; some of us fail in mechanical aptitude, some in music, some in languages, some in science. Memory, in one of these lines of incapacity, is a rope of sand; there must be in each case a deficiency of cerebral substance for that class of connections. Then again there is a tendency in acquisitions to decay unless renewed. Hence a time must come in the progress of acquisition when the whole available force of growth is needed in order to conserve what we have already got; when, in fact, we are losing at one end as much as we gain at the other.

"It is further to be remarked that much of our mental improvement in later life is the *substitution* of a better class of judgments for our first immature notions, these last being gradually dropped. There is not necessarily more room occupied in the brain by a good opinion than by a bad, when once the good opinion is arrived at."

In regard to recollection, or the recalling of events long past, he says, p. 89: "It must be considered as almost beyond a doubt that '*the renewed feeling occupies the very same parts, and in the same manner as the original feeling*,' and no other parts, nor in any other manner that can be assigned."

Hence, under this theory of new cell-growths for every new fact acquired, a very rapid growth or increase of these material cells, when one is rapidly learning new facts, is necessitated. But it needs further evidence than I have yet seen to convince me that this is the way in which our memories are stored. The fact that the gray matter of the brain is largely composed of very minute cells cannot be denied; but whether these cells represent acquired facts is a question.

But to make a fair and reasonable presentation of Bain's theories of memory I shall quote further from his "Mind and Body" certain ingenious calculations in regard to nervous elements, etc. This is worthy of attention, because it is, perhaps, as concise and clear a statement of the materialistic view of memory as has been made : —

" Let us make a rough estimate of the nervous elements, — fibres and corpuscles, — with a view to compare the number of these with the number of our acquisitions.

" The thin cake of gray substance surrounding the hemispheres of the brain, and extended into many doublings by the furrowed or convoluted structure, is somewhat difficult to measure. It has been estimated at upwards of three hundred square inches, or as nearly equal to a square surface of eighteen inches in the side. Its thickness is variable, but, on an average, it may be stated at one-tenth of an inch. It is the largest accumulation of gray matter in the body. It is made up of several layers of gray substance divided by layers of white substance. The gray substance is a nearly compact mass of corpuscles, of variable size. The large caudate nerve-cells are mingled with very small corpuscles, less than the thousandth of an inch in diameter. Allowing for intervals, we may suppose that a linear row of five hundred cells occupies an inch; thus giving a quarter of a million to the square inch, for three hundred inches. If one-half of the thickness of the layer is made up of fibres, the corpuscles or cells, taken by themselves, would be a mass one-twentieth of an inch thick, say sixteen cells in the depth. Multiplying these numbers together, we should reach a total of twelve hundred millions of cells in the gray covering of the hemispheres. As every cell is united with at least two fibres, often many more, we may multiply this number by four, for the number of connecting fibres attached to the mass; which gives four thousand eight hundred millions of fibres. Assume the respective numbers to be (corpuscles) one thousand, and (fibres) five thousand, millions, and make the comparison with our acquisitions as follows : —

" With a total of fifty thousand Acquisitions, evenly spread over the whole of the hemispheres, there would be for each nervous grouping at the rate of twenty thousand cells and one hundred thousand fibres.

" With a total of two hundred thousand Acquisitions of the assumed types, which would certainly include the most retentive and most richly endowed minds, there would be for each nervous grouping five thousand cells and twenty-five thousand fibres."

But suppose there are material cell-growths in the brain corresponding to all acts to be remembered (as Bain supposes), it by no means follows that the mind, or the memories stored in these cells, is also material. The mind itself is connected in some way with the brain ; but the mind is one thing, and the brain, the organ of the mind, is quite another thing.

We say of one man that he thinks quickly, and of another that he thinks slowly. Now if thought consists of action which is similar to the action of electricity, then as different substances transmit electricity with greatly different velocities, so the sensations of different men may travel with different velocities, according to the fineness of their nervous structures.

This principle probably goes through the mental constitutions. For instance, if two men at the same instant should see the flash of a gun which was aimed at them, one might think quick enough to drop out of danger before the shot arrived, while another, whose nervous conductors were of coarser make, might not think quick enough to get out of danger.

It is well known that electricity moves with vastly different velocities according to the media through or by which it is transmitted. It is also stated that electricity moves upon the nerves of men with just the same velocities as nervous sensations do. This may be from sixty to one hundred feet per second. Thus the velocity with which sensations travel must be somewhat dependent upon the quality, structure, or texture of the nerves, and thus it would travel with much greater velocity in one man than in another who possesses a different quality of nerves.

If you strike the feet of two men at the same instant, one might be conscious of the blow, and move within two-thirds the amount of time it would take the other to be conscious of it.

Also, people remark upon the different sizes, qualities, and characters of brains and bodies which different men inherit. But why wonder at this? In the brains and bodies of children from the same parents there may be, both in size and quality, a difference similar to that found in different apples from the same tree. Both the bodies and the brains of children descend from the parents in a manner quite similar to that of apples from the parent tree, and they are produced under the action of natural laws quite similar in their operations. Some apples are sound and others not sound; some are small and others large; some are healthy and others unhealthy. So the brains and bodies of some children are large, others small; some healthy, others diseased; some strong, others weak; some active, others inactive; and this constitutes no anomaly in nature.

But in youth, as well as in men, the will, the intentions, and voluntary habits so operate as to vary to some extent these analogies.

Thus, in regard to the performance of moral duties, we say generally that men are morally responsible for making or not making the best possible use of both their inherited and acquired abilities, and also for capacities which they have had opportunities of acquiring. But no two living beings are in all respects just alike either mentally or physically. No two men look just alike, and the qualities of their physical systems are never just alike, to say nothing of the difference in their mental constitutions. Even the waste matter that each person loses through the pores of the physical system in the process of living is different in each and every individual. This is so different in each person that a dog can tell the difference between the waste matter which is thrown off by his master and that thrown off by any other person; otherwise the dog could not, by the scent, distinguish his master's track from that of any other individual. The same rule applies to the waste thrown off by birds and different animals. A dog trained to hunt partridges or quail does not mistake the scent of a rabbit or other animal for that of the quail. All odors which strike the olfactory nerves are believed to be composed of particles of matter; and every flower which scatters its aroma is constantly wasting particles which compose its substance.

Thus many things which generally pass for immaterial substances, as odors, for instance, are supposed to be material. But this by no means shows or even indicates that the soul, or that indescribable something which makes every man different from every other man, is not ethereal, or spiritual.

In view of the preceding thoughts we now come to the consideration of our concluding speculations concerning moral responsibilities, which are believed to be incumbent upon every rational man.

All must see that the moral responsibilities of men must to some degree be dependent upon the position they hold in respect to moral freedom, or the freedom to choose or refuse to perform acts which have either a moral or immoral quality. If both mind and matter are subject to the natural laws in the same way, and to such an extent that they must be as they are, and cannot be in any other way, then this subjection will go far towards breaking down or destroying our general ideas concerning the different qualities of acts which are termed moral and immoral.

But before inquiring into this idea of the actual necessity of moral evil, or its opposite, let us consider some facts which may be familiar to us from our daily observation, and ask, what renders a man's act one of moral responsibility? For there may be a vast difference in the extent of moral dignity or turpitude of similar acts according to the circumstances influencing one in the commission of various acts. The same temptation to do wrong may be great to one and very slight to another. It will be the stronger just in proportion to one's liking for the forbidden act or his indifference in regard to its moral character. One may try to resist temptation, and another may have no desire to resist; one may possess a strong desire always to do right, and the other not care whether he does right or wrong. A case of actual fact will illustrate : —

Some twenty-five years ago two men worked together in a manufacturing establishment in Boston. Both were married men. One was particularly careful of his reputation, scrupulously honest, and was in every respect considered strictly moral. The other was a libertine, and boasted (as is altogether too common in certain places) of his lack of care concerning the moral quality of his acts, or whether he had the good opinion of his fellow-men or not. One day a travelling phrenologist called where they were engaged, and wished to examine their heads and give phrenological charts.

The two men agreed between themselves to submit to an examination ; but it was also privately understood between them that both were, if possible, to mislead the phrenologist and give him an incorrect idea as to their personal characters. The libertine was to act the role of a very moral and pious character, in order to test the skilfulness of the phrenologist.

The first to be examined was the moral man. The phrenologist gave him an excellent character, commending his faithfulness to his family, and said he was careful of his language, avoiding all profane and irreverent talk. It was strongly intimated to the examiner that he had made a radical mistake in the character he had given ; but he insisted that he knew he was correct in his estimation of character, for no man could be produced with such a phrenological organization who was unchaste or immoral, and from that statement he would not vary. When told that he ought to hear the profanity indulged in when matters went wrong in that man's department, he replied, " That man cannot swear ; no man with his phrenological organization was ever in the habit of doing so."

The libertine then sat for examination. The first remark of the phrenologist was, in substance, Here is a man who will not be faithful to one wife ; and in other respects he gave a correct portrayal of his character. The writer was present, but was suspicious that some one had before informed the phrenologist concerning the characters he would find. However, the libertine did not mistrust that such was the case ; and after the phrenologist had left, he said : " Now you see that men are not responsible for being as they are. You are acting out your nature according to the organization of your brain, and you cannot be otherwise than as you are

now.   I also am acting out my nature just as it was originally intended that I should."

To this the reply was substantially as follows : " Now,
B——, you know better than that.   You know that you and
I have like passions ; but when tempted to do wrong I determine to do no wrong.   You can do the same if you desire
to do so ; but, according to your own daily confession, you
do not care whether you do right or wrong in the matter of
the gratification of your passions.   This has been your habit
until it has become a sort of second nature.   If you wished
to restrain yourself, and could not do so, then there might
be truth in your assertion that you are acting out you: nature
as the Creator intended you should.   Or, if you were so
created that it was impossible for you to desire to do differently, then again you might be excused for violating most
of the commands in the Decalogue."

The excuse of this libertine is substantially the same that
has been made in all past ages by those who have been
accustomed to violate all moral laws and the proprieties of
every-day life since Cain asked, " Am I my brother's
keeper ? "   They have always claimed that they were simply
following out propensities in their very natures, and hence
are accustomed to assert that the fact that such propensities
are implanted relieves their acts from the strength of moral
turpitude.

If one inherits such an organization that it is impossible for
him to wish to do right, or to care if he does wrong, so that
under no circumstances could he desire to do better, then
there would be an apparent excuse, and that excuse would
be *moral imbecility*.   But that could not be so in this libertine's case, for no one was quicker than he in detecting
wrong in others, and quicker in pointing it out.   Hence the

pretence, that when he was acting immorally he was carrying out just what the Creator intended he should, was without truth behind it, and was simply pretence.

Although this libertine had a brilliant intellect he went from bad to worse, until about twenty years later he became a wreck morally and physically, and filled a drunkard's grave. Can any one believe that the Creator deliberately endowed this man with brilliant parts and then intentionally beclouded his moral nature for the purpose of sending the helpless victim to a drunkard's grave? To me such an idea seems preposterous; and yet that would be the logical result of the position he took in regard to his moral responsibilities.

I am aware that many good men have contended that the foreknowledge of the Deity is equivalent to a decree, or predestination, and that the Deity would never create a man unless he intended at the time of his creation that all of his misfortunes, sorrows, and crimes should take place in regular appointed time and order. But such an assumption is beyond my power of comprehension.

The doctrines of Reprobation and the damnation of unbaptized infants were also formerly taught by excellent men; but it has always seemed to me that while with one breath such teachers described the Deity as "merciful and gracious," with the next breath they clothed him with the attributes of a fiend.

W. E. H. Lecky, on pp. 96, 97, "History of European Morals," writes: "That a little child who lives but a few moments after birth, and dies before it has been sprinkled with the sacred water, is in such a sense responsible for its ancestors having six thousand years before eaten some forbidden fruit that it may with perfect justice be resuscitated and cast into an abyss of eternal fire in expiation of this ancestral crime, that an All-Righteous and All-Merciful Creator, in the full exercise of those attributes deliberately calls into existence sentient beings whom He has from eternity irrevocably destined to endless, unspeakable, unmitigated torture, are propositions which are at once so extravagantly absurd and so ineffably atrocious that their adoption might well lead men to doubt the universality of moral perceptions. Such teaching is in fact simply demonism, and demonism in its most extreme form. It attributes to the Creator acts of injustice and of barbarity, which it would be absolutely impossible for the imagination to surpass, acts before which the most monstrous excesses of human cruelty dwindle into insignificance, acts which are in fact considerably worse than any that theologians have attributed to the devil."

How good men with good general judgments and benevolent dispositions ever could have brought themselves to believe such contradictory doctrines concerning the " Just and Merciful " is more than my philosophy can comprehend. If such beliefs now obtained credence with any considerable number of intelligent and reflective men it would seem to indicate that human nature is sadly in need of a rapid upward moral development, or else the advocates of the doctrine of "total depravity" will have the best of the argument. It does not seem possible that one of a reflective and philosophical mind, unless his moral sense was in a certain sense perverted, could believe in the Doctrine of Reprobation as it was once taught.

The reason why such doctrines formerly obtained so general belief is because a class of theologians assumed that certain attributes must of necessity belong to the Deity, and then, by carrying these assumptions out to their apparently logical conclusions, they arrived at absurd results.

The fallacy in such reasoning lies in its starting-point, viz., the assumption that certain attributes must of necessity belong to the Great Overruling Power, when in fact neither theologians nor any other persons can know positively what the complete attributes of the Unknowable and Unsearchable are ; and thus we are ignorant just where we seem the most to need information.

But, strangely enough, certain theologians, even in this nineteenth century, continue to assert that a disbelief in certain assumed tenets which they teach constitutes a heinous sin. What monstrous credulity must human nature be endowed with to allow such absurd assumptions to frighten men out of their undoubted right to honestly and conscientiously think for themselves in religious matters ! It is, however, true that when a man rejects an important and evident moral truth because his moral state is such that that truth is repulsive to him he does violence to his moral nature, and hence will be likely to fall in with grievous error.

CHAPTER XIV.

CONCLUDING SPECULATIONS.

THE real issues or points now to be decided are, first, whether men are possessed of a spiritual nature, or, on the other hand, whether men are simply intelligent animals and nothing more.

If man has nothing but animal nature, and death is the last of him, and he becomes convinced that such is the fact, then it is evident that pleasure, present or prospective, will naturally be his highest aim ; and, in fact, this is all that can reasonably be expected of him. The idea of duty as such implying any moral quality under such circumstances cannot have deep-seated influence with thinking men.

Yet, even if men are mere animals, it is better that animals should so conduct themselves as to gain general confidence in, rather than distrust of, each other ; and they should be friendly, rather than hate each other. If life on this earth is all the life allotted to men it certainly is best that men should make the most of their friendships and social amenities. Thus the having of rules for the regulation of conduct towards each other is by no means useless.

But that the belief that certain acts are right and opposite acts wrong is universal among intelligent men I think will not be denied. Even savages have their moral and property laws, however they may vary between themselves in regard to what these laws should be. One may think a certain course right, and another think a like course wrong; yet, from his point of view, every one who is not an idiot has certain ideas of wrong and right. Can we then doubt that a sense of right and wrong inheres in our very natures?

Doubtless man is so made that he naturally connects moral conduct with the enjoyment of happiness, — for I believe that this is founded upon a law of nature; but some carry their ideas of right and wrong beyond the point where they expect to experience happiness; and such are willing to suffer intensely rather than yield up their convictions of right. Something like wilfulness often shows itself in this connection. To illustrate this point I will quote from J. S. Mill's " Examination of Sir Wm. Hamilton's Philosophy," p. 131, in which he says: "If I am informed that the world is ruled by a being whose attributes are infinite, but what they are we cannot learn, nor what the principles of his government, except that the highest human morality which we are capable of conceiving does not sanction them, convince me of it, and I will bear my fate as I may. But when I am told that I must believe this, and at the same time call this being by the names which express and affirm the highest human morality, I say in plain terms that I will not. Whatever power such a being may have over me, there is one thing which he shall not do : he shall not compel me to worship him. I will call no being good who is not what I mean when I apply that epithet to my fellow-creatures; and if such a being can sentence me to hell for not so calling him, to hell I will go."

Here, certainly, Mill carries his ideas of right and wrong far beyond the place where he can expect to experience happiness, and proves that he would be willing to be tortured rather than fall down and worship a false god, or one whose character he could not reverence. What pleasure could he expect to experience from thus being tortured; and all this on account of his deep sense of right and wrong? Surely his sense of right and wrong must be very clearly cut, or he would not be willing to endure so much simply for an idea which may be a delusion, if it can be traced simply to inherited notions.

Mr. Jackson, in his "Prize Essay," remarks upon this peculiarity of Mr. Mill's reasoning, and says (p. 224) : " We are equally sure that 'Godliness is profitable for all things,' and that 'Honesty is the best policy.' But then we are quite sure also that the final cause of godliness is not profit, nor its essential nature a love of gain; and that policy is not a true description of honesty, nor the being politic the true and proper aim of the honest man. And Mr. Mill, when his moral sentiments asserted themselves, felt these certainties as elements of his inner life. Rather than worship a Being whose unknown moral attributes fell beneath, not the dictates of Utility, but the purest instincts of his own inmost morality, Mr. Mill goes on to declare that he is willing to suffer the horrors of Eternal death. Hell is better than a violation of his own moral nature. Can this be a declaration deduced from the supreme law of Interest? Is it not rather a foundation maxim of independent morality? Violate such foundation maxims, says the independent moralist, and you need not even speak of 'Going to hell,' hell will come to you! Sooner or later you will find its undying torments within you."

Probably this sense of right and wrong is a part of the very nature given us from the Eternal Fountain of all morality and intelligence. The fact of inheritance of certain peculiarities is not doubted; but I must doubt the truth of the assertion that our moral sense is entirely dependent upon ideas of utility, or upon inherited ideas of pain or pleasure experienced by our ancestors. The very fact of the universal prevalence of the moral sense in intelligent men seems to point to the origin from whence all that is valuable in humanity must have been derived, or to the Power which has constituted Man a Morally Responsible being.

This opens the question as to who is responsible for the acts of men. Those who contend that an All-Wise Intelligence has absolutely and arbitrarily decreed everything which comes to pass, in such a way that nothing can or ever could happen otherwise than it does happen, virtually make this Intelligence the cause of all the deeds committed. Such deny moral freedom to man except in the sense that he has the power to choose one way and only one way, and thus, of necessity, he must choose as he does. This appears to destroy his moral responsibilities. But, says one, why did a wise God create man, when he must foreknow at the time of his creation all the trouble man would experience, as well as all the suffering he would have to endure? You ask me too hard a question; but I will suggest some thoughts connected therewith. In the first place we must understand what the design was in creating man, before we shall be able to pass upon the benevolence or otherwise of man's creation. What purpose did the Deity have in his creation? If He intended to create man a morally responsible being, He must of necessity give him a certain kind of freedom, or he could not be morally responsible. In this supposed case, it is also true, that, after purposing to make man a moral being, and creating him such, the Deity could not prevent him from making use of such moral freedom as He had bestowed upon him. It also appears to be true, that the Deity could not make man morally free, and yet at the same time place him under complete and absolute necessity; because, according to the proper signification of the words freedom and necessity, these very terms themselves imply a contradiction.

Now, upon this hypothesis (if it is a correct one), the Deity was in such a position that he must endow man with the power of doing wrong (if man chose to do so), or man could not be held morally responsible; for otherwise he would be morally a machine. If God chose to make man morally responsible, he could not absolutely and arbitrarily prevent him from doing wrong provided he desired to do so. This seems too plain to need argument. Now whether it was a benevolent act to create man as he is cannot be decided until we can first decide what the final history and destiny of the human race is to be. If there is to be an eternal state of conscious existence (as the Christian and also many heathen and infidel philosophers have believed), where all the wrongs endured in this world shall be righted, that is a very important consideration to be taken into the account.[1]

But if all the existence man has is confined to his present life upon the earth, that is quite another thing, and brings in other considerations. But until we can decide these preliminary questions we shall not be in a position to sit in judgment (as some irreverently seem ready to do) upon the

---

[1] In all ages since men have had any clear conceptions concerning man's responsibilities there have been philosophers who have thought there must be a conscious state of existence after death, in order to make equitable adjustments for the sufferings and miseries which good men have suffered while on the earth; and also that there must be a state of retributive justice, where those who have caused untold miseries on the earth will at least have to reflect on the consequences of their previous wickedness; because otherwise they could not see how equal justice could be meted out or distributed. Thus the doctrine of future rewards and punishments has been held by many among barbarous tribes, and by many learned heathens, and also by some infidel philosophers, as well as by believers in a Divine revelation.

acts of the Almighty Creator. But suppose the present life is all that man has, and our hopes of immortality are mere pleasant dreams, shall we then conclude that man experiences more sorrow than joy, more injustice than justice? Rather, do not a majority of men experience happiness nearly in proportion to the number and quality of their virtuous acts?

Who does not cherish life such as it is and for what it is? How few, in a sane state of mind, are ready to lay life down rather than stay even in this state of sorrow! The majority of our sufferings are more mental than physical, and many of our sorrows arise from disappointed hopes or ambitions; and often they arise from desires which we have no right to cherish. If we go back and lay all this trouble at the door of the Deity, our reason will not bear us out in our accusations. Reason proclaims that if the Deity is a perfect being He cannot be the author of moral wrong; and if we are under complete necessity, and mere moral machines, it would appear to be the Creator who acts when man commits acts which would be criminal if man was free, but which seem to be no more criminal than the falling of a brick upon one's head would be if man is under complete necessity.

But we are conscious that we have a certain amount of freedom, and this very consciousness is the very highest authority in a matter like this; and no amount of metaphysical reasoning can beat this consciousness of freedom out of us when we act in practical every-day life; and it seems to me that this very fact should convince every man that, in his immoral acts, he is not irresistibly driven to their commission; and that it is absurd to assume that lying back of man's will there is a series of causes forcordained which have unconsciously or consciously forced man to choose to do immoral acts. Even if one's moral sense may become so blunted that he does not think he does wrong when he grossly abuses his neighbor, no intelligent man's moral senses ever become so blunted that he cannot feel that he is wronged when his neighbor wrongs him.

Thus the assumption that men are under complete moral necessity in regard to deeds performed, however supported by apparent reason, leading as it does to absurd conclusions, cannot be a correct one. That men, in consequence of an unholy or vitiated bent of mind arising from an unhealthy moral condition of the " unconscious part of their natures," may sometimes seem to be impelled to perform acts of wickedness is true ; but who can show that men are not generally morally responsible for the disposition or bent of this "unconscious part of their natures "?   Have not voluntary acts of wickedness often modified this " unconscious part of their natures " greatly for the worse ?

Much connected with the origin and abstract nature of our mental and moral conceptions as well as concerning the origin and nature of life and the soul is shrouded in mystery, and it has been impossible for the intelligence of man to logically and harmoniously account for many seeming contradictions.   Yet I have no doubt that if our minds ever become sufficiently capacious and sufficiently enlightened, all these seeming contradictions may appear no contradictions, but in perfect harmony with each other.

There can be really no contradictions in the laws established by Infinite Intelligence in accordance with Infinite Wisdom, whether these laws relate to our mental, moral, or physical natures.

Upon the supposition that man is under complete moral necessity, David Hume writes, what would be likely to suggest itself to a thinking mind, as follows ("Essays," pp. 368,

369) : " The ultimate author of all our volitions is the Creator of the world, who first bestowed motion on this immense machine, and placed all beings in that particular position, whence every subsequent event, by an inevitable necessity, must result.

" Human actions, therefore, either can have no moral turpitude at all, as proceeding from so good a cause, or, if they have any turpitude, they must involve our Creator in the same guilt, while he is acknowledged to be their ultimate cause and author. For, as a man who fired a mine is answerable for all the consequences, whether the train he employed be long or short; so, wherever a continued chain of necessary causes is fixed, that being, either finite or infinite, who produces the first, is likewise the author of all the rest, and must both bear the blame and acquire the praise which belong to them. Our clear and unalterable ideas of morality establish this rule, upon unquestionable reasons, when we examine the consequences of any human action; and these reasons must still have greater force when applied to the volitions and intentions of a Being infinitely wise and powerful.

Ignorance or impotence may be pleaded for so limited a creature as man ; but those imperfections have no place in our Creator. He foresaw, he ordained, he intended all those actions of men which we so rashly pronounce criminal. And we must therefore conclude, either that they are not criminal, or that the Deity, not man, is accountable for them. But, as either of these positions is absurd and impious, it follows that the doctrine from which they are deduced cannot possibly be true, as being liable to all the same objections. An absurd consequence, if necessary, proves the original doctrine to be absurd ; in the same manner as criminal actions render criminal the original cause, if the connection between them be necessary and inevitable."

And Hume's thoughts, as expressed on p. 371, are worthy the consideration of such as rashly presume to hold the Deity morally responsible for faults which their own inmost moral natures tell them they are themselves morally responsible for. Hume adds: "These are mysteries which mere natural and unassisted Reason is very unfit to handle; and whatever system she embraces she must find herself involved in inextricable difficulties, and even contradictions, at every step which she takes with regard to such objects. To reconcile the indifference and contingency of human actions with prescience, or to defend absolute decrees, and yet free the Deity from being the author of sin, has been found hitherto to exceed all the power of philosophy. Happy, if she be thence sensible of her temerity, when she pries into these sublime mysteries, and, leaving a scene so full of obscurities and perplexities, return, with suitable modesty, to her true and proper province, the examination of common life, where she will find difficulties enough to employ her inquiries, without launching into so boundless an ocean of doubt, uncertainty, and contradiction."

We cannot deny that a consciousness of guilt and feelings of sorrow are natural to all men with whom we would be willing to trust our interests, whether these interests be our property, reputation, or even our lives. Every man who can be safely trusted is sensible to such emotions. Whence do these originate, if behind them there are no realities which they represent? Philosophize and dispute and doubt as we may, we cannot flee from our own natures. These very natures themselves indicate our moral responsibility; and if by sophistries and special pleadings, aided by our own unhallowed desires, we convince ourselves that we are not morally responsible, our very inmost natures themselves rise up in eternal protest against such a conclusion. The whole organization of society, all law, all duties between man and man, presuppose moral responsibility. Why so natural the detestation of men guilty of unnecessary cruelty, ingratitude, treachery, theft, and murder, except upon the principle that these men are responsible for their acts? We do not deceive ourselves upon this point in our every-day acts. When we can show that black is white, and make the worse appear the better reason, then with a like consistency may we try to lessen or moderate our detestation of meanness, moral turpitude, treachery, falsehood, and crimes against nature. But the reflective mind cannot help asking a still farther question, viz., If man is morally responsible for his acts, and he has violated moral laws, what shall he do to make amends for such violation? Is it in his power to make any such amends?

Then another question arises: If we are under moral laws are the operations of those laws ever suspended? Are moral laws, like the physical laws, unbending, and inevitable, in their consequences? Some contend that in the moral world, as in the physical world, man must take the full consequences of his acts, without any abatement of their severity. If these consequences are punitive, and must be expiated to their full extent whether the offender tries to make reparation for his misdeeds or not, then such a rule would shut off all chance of forgiveness by the Supreme Law-giver. But, if a man trespasses against his fellow, the aggrieved one may, and not unfrequently does, forgive the offender, when he has made the best reparation it is in his power to make. Shall the Deity, in this respect, have less liberty than man, when the offender against moral law atones as far as he is able for his guilt?

Superstitious savages as well as enlightened Christians have some idea of propitiating an unseen power. Every prostration before a heathen idol is an indication of a belief in some kind of propitiation. Where does such a belief come from? Is it all delusion? If one believes that there is no just basis from which such or similar impressions may arise, however misguided heathen devotees may be, let him show, if he can, that such, or similar impressions do not comport with the very nature of the human mind.

Similar impressions are found among intelligent and learned men. Is the human mind so constituted that it must necessarily be the sport of delusion? If so, are those who talk confidently concerning moral and religious delusions of others sure that they are not themselves the subjects of delusion? Let them prove that they are not themselves deluded before they assume that they are right and that millions of other intelligent men must be wrong. Let them show (if they can) that the Deity cannot forgive, and that penalties for sins may not be remitted to the truly penitent, before they presume to *assert positively* that the consequences of every wrong act must of *necessity* be fully expiated through the personal sufferings of the offender.

But I can see no philosophical reason why infractions of moral laws should not be followed by inevitable penalties as certainly as violations of physical laws. When we violate both a moral and a physical law in the same act, the physical part of the penalty must certainly be paid.

But David said (addressing the Deity), "But there is forgiveness with Thee, that thou mayest be feared." Does any one know that David was mistaken when he wrote this?

Unaided reason is entirely incompetent to deal success-fully with this problem; and if the reason of David was assisted, or if he was under inspiration, might not he have understood more concerning this question than a modern speculative moralist can?

Still another question arises : If the penalties for broken moral laws must be fully expiated and endured without mitigation, is it possible that one who was not the real offender can, through his own consent, be treated as the offender, and thereby the real offender escape the penalty which, as a result of his acts, became justly due?

We are accustomed to hear about settling moral and religious questions upon a scientific basis ; but the answer to this last question lies outside the domains of physical science. Yet questions concerning penalties for broken laws are often discussed, and are worthy of serious consideration. It is, however, of the highest importance that we learn how to avoid violating the laws of our being, both physical and moral.

To many these questions seem puerile, but, in view of the consequences which may follow, reasons for their careful consideration should not be lightly treated, — especially when millions of intelligent men who are as likely to be right in their opinions as we are believe these questions to be of supreme importance.

After all that has been written concerning speculative be-lief, and the desires warping the opinions of men, the reader may possibly desire to know what belief the writer has.

By speculative belief I mean that which is theoretical and has its roots in something which transcends the bounds of experience. Speculative reasoning soars into the region of the unknown. This may be distinguished from belief which rests on the teachings of purely physical sciences, though ninety-nine out of every hundred of those who profess to base their opinions upon the teachings of physical science are more or less influenced in these very opinions by their own speculations.

The substance of the writer's speculative belief, so far as it relates to the origin of life and all finite existences through a great originating Power, is substantially as follows: He believes in an Overruling Power endowed with Infinite Intelligence and Infinite Benevolence. That this Power, or Being, caused the heavens and the earth to exist, either by an Almighty fiat, or through the action of natural laws which He constituted and ordained; and, further, that He caused to exist all the planets, suns, and stars, and that the whole universe, both animate and inanimate (as well as the interests of all on this tiny ball which we call the earth), is under His constant and direct supervision; that we see manifestations of His power equally in the budding of the trees, the beautiful flowers, the mighty ocean, the gentle zephyr, and the hurricane's blast; that all the powers of nature are subject to Him, and nothing can exist contrary to what He has ordered. Though the nature of this Power is incomprehensible, yet it is personal, or akin to what we term personal, and not a mere blind force. (I use the word "personal" because it expresses the idea, so far as we can comprehend it, nearer than any other word in our language; and yet I do not suppose that the *personality* of Deity is of such a nature that man can comprehend it.)

Many events in life (so-called providences) which seem mysterious, and in certain respects harsh or cruel, are by this Power ordered in mercy to the world at large.

There is reason to believe that the Creator has arranged

this world in the best manner possible for the ultimate happiness and welfare of His creatures, when we consider how these creatures are constituted.

Yet it must not, however, be forgotten that actions of so-called natural laws often modify greatly the characters and constitutions of men as well as animals.

Terrific storms which carry death and destruction into certain localities are also, when considered in their whole effects, instruments of purification, and thus probably of mercy to the world. Even in sudden taking off of men who are beloved, useful, and honored, this Omnipotent Power is, in general, carrying out His programme of mercy. Some providences may, and actually do appear to bear hard on individuals. Some wicked men appear to prosper, and others seem never to get proper retribution for their crimes, or for the sorrow they may have caused. Good men suffer in a mysterious way, and appear to be cruelly afflicted; and, looking at this life only, there seems to be a lack of equity. But this apparent lack of equity is not real, but only apparent; for, in order to draw just and full conclusions of the equity, we must take into consideration the whole duration of man's existence.

The doctrines of Evolution, which imply the existence of an active developing force behind all the phenomena of life, and which in general tend to raise the lower to a higher and better state of existence, themselves teach that this Power, in thus raising the lower to a higher state, is now exerting a benevolent influence. Even the taking away of the poorer to make way for the better is in itself an act of benevolence; and thus the operations of what are called the stern and unfeeling laws of nature result in actual good.

So many things indicate the mercy of God that we cannot reasonably doubt in cases which seem to be exceptions to the exercise of this merciful care that these apparent exceptions are seeming exceptions. But, to square all the sufferings and wrongs of men, and make all things equitable, there should be another state of existence, where wrongs suffered in this world will be righted, and justice tempered with mercy will forever exist. In a perfect being justice must be an essential attribute; and thus no man has suffered or ever will suffer injustice at the hands of a being in whom perfection is centred.

Man is the highest intelligence on the earth, but there may be on the planets intelligent beings of a much higher order than any on the earth; and on the planets which are believed to accompany the great fixed stars there may be still higher orders of intelligence. From our limited capacities we do not know a thousandth part of what might be known, and the most learned man on the earth does not know a thousandth part of what would be known in regard to matters of daily occurrence if his mind were sufficiently capacious to comprehend these matters. Other and higher intelligences may understand the mysterious connection between souls and bodies as well as the engineer or the builder of a locomotive understands its construction and powers. No man understands the hidden causes of life except as he refers them to the Creator of all things. A horse sees a railroad train, but does not comprehend its moving power; so we see life developed, but do not understand its secret moving power.

The writer here makes a digression, because some writers assert that we have no reason to believe that other planets are inhabited by higher orders of intelligences than are on the earth, or by any order of intelligent beings; and they seem to consider it a kind of treason to revelation not to believe that all the wondrous machinery of the universe was made for man's especial benefit. While admitting that terrestrial nature is in a certain sense arranged for man's benefit, it may also, in a similar way, be arranged for the benefit of the brute creation, and in fact for all animate existences. The arrangements of the solar sytem are so adjusted as to develop life in all its multifarious forms; but when one asserts that this little planet called earth, which is like a mustard-seed when compared with the universe which can be seen by the aid of the telescope (to say nothing of what is beyond the reach of telescopic vision), is of more importance than the rest of the universe, he virtually asserts that a pin's head may be of greater importance than the most magnificent edifice on the face of the earth; but when a man asserts that he belongs to the highest order of intelligences which live anywhere in the solar system he exhibits egotism and vanity, not to say exceeding folly. It is true that we know nothing absolutely concerning life on other planets, but analogy would teach us that the larger planets would not be made entirely subservient to the smaller ones; and when we see the laws of gravitation called into action we see at least the importance of the greater weight of matter; and, for all that we know to the contrary, this may also teach us that the animated existences there may also be as superior in intelligence as their habitation is greater. Certainly no man knows that this may not be so.[1] But, leaving this digression, I will proceed.

---

[1] The writer is aware that some have undertaken to show that the planets Jupiter and Saturn are too far removed from the sun, and in too cold a region, to support life. Others have asserted that for various reasons Jupiter and Saturn are not now in a condition to support life of intelligent beings, and that ages must elapse and vast changes come before animal life can be developed there; that these planets are now in a condition similar to what the earth was during the period of coal

With all man's boasted intelligence he has so limited a mental scope that he cannot comprehend the springs of life, and thus it is the highest folly to be dogmatic in those matters of life concerning which no demonstrations exist. It is also unphilosophical for any man to shut his eyes to the facts connected with his mysterious being, and with positiveness deny the existence of an intelligent Creative Power which has constructed all these mysterious things, including the mental, moral, and physical constitutions of men. Man's personal existence and moral obligations are matters of consciousness, and hence (concerning these facts) contain the most positive evidence he is capable of receiving.

Jesus Christ taught that there is not only an Eternal God, but that man is a being destined to an Immortal Existence. Many millions of intelligent and honest men have fully credited these teachings, and enjoyed in anticipation, through faith and hope, the joys of a heavenly home. Science cannot throw any light here ; and if the longings for eternal life have no real basis to rest upon, but are mere delusions, where do these delusions originate ? Are they not implanted in the very constitution of our natures ? How can we justly account for such a general impression and expectation in the minds of a large majority of intelligent men if these impressions and hopes are delusions ? This problem is of the highest importance.

In 1821 Lord Byron wrote, in answer to a letter informing him of prayers in his behalf, as follows : "Indisputably the firm believers in the gospel have a great advantage over

---

formation, viz.: That they are thickly enveloped by clouds and vapors, generated by their internal heat; that these clouds prevent radiation of heat into space, and also prevent the rays of the sun from penetrating directly to their bodies, and hence with an atmosphere so loaded with vapor, at the present time, that they must be unfit for the abodes of living ·animals, — all of which may or may not be so.

all others, for this simple reason : that, if true, they will
have their reward hereafter ; and, if there be no hereafter,
they can but be with the infidel in his eternal sleep, having
had the assurance of an exalted hope through life, without
subsequent disappointment, since (at the worst of them)
' out of nothing, nothing can arise,' not even sorrow."

Dr. Raymond, the founder and president of Vassar Col-
lege, in his youth, gave little thought to the subject of his
being, but when twenty years old he began to think it was
high time that he should have some definite idea, if possible, of the questions, Whence? Whither? And we find
entered in his " Book of Comments " the following passage : —

"Is the religion of Christ a delusion, or is it not? I fear
to think it is, and I fear to think it is not; for if it is a
reality, it is an awful one to me ; and if it is nothing but a
mockery, what is the truth? What am I? Whither am I
tending? For what purpose is existence? To what shall
I direct it? By what principles of action shall it be
governed?"

Different men come to different conclusions, and give
different answers to such questions. Science can give no
answer. Faith or non-faith must enter largely into
reasonings when the attempt to answer is made. With
Dr. Raymond, faith and reason conspired to make him
believe that the religion of Christ was not a delusion,
and hence he became a consistent Christian worker.
Another man with the same evidence before him might
turn out a confirmed sceptic. Why such a difference in
conclusions from the same evidence? Let no sceptic
assume, in a matter of scientific uncertainty like this,
that the sceptic is the greater philosopher. But it is almost

universally the fact that religious sceptics do claim that they are sounder philosophers than the believers in the Christian religion. But is such a claim philosophical?

In order to become a real believer in an immortal existence faith, and not science, must be the prevailing power. Hence if one cannot believe what cannot be demonstrated he must be a sceptic. But what then would become of a large portion of *scientific* theories which have gained general assent? They must certainly be doubted, for they are based on *unknown* premises, premises *assumed*, just as really as those in the belief in immortality.

Many physical facts which are known by experience cannot be accounted for upon any known laws of nature, unless we accept supposed bases for facts, or treat them as facts, although no one knows whether these supposed bases be existent facts or not. If the statement that a great multitude of testimonies to belief in anything which cannot be demonstrated to be fact does not show this belief to be founded in truth is correct, then many scientific theories which are generally received as true must be regarded as unproved, and those who put confidence enough in such theories to make them the basis of action in practical life must be regarded as no philosophers, unless believers in immortality may be considered to have equally strong philosophical grounds for their belief. This idea has been before stated, but it will bear repeating again and again, in these days of professed disbelief in what cannot be *demonstrated* to be true. We cannot however find an intelligent and sane man who does not believe in much which cannot be demonstrated to be true.

Without faith in things which are uncertain, the chief moving springs of our active lives would become paralyzed.

All persons are, to some extent, sceptics, and all, to some extent, exercise faith.

All need humility when inquiring into the mysteries of our existence. With reverent awe we may justly inquire, Whence? Whither? and Where do our moral, religious, and educational responsibilities begin and end?

The force, strength, and extent of moral responsibilities appear greater to some than to others who are equally intelligent. To some the moral bearings of human conduct seem of the greatest importance, while to others they appear of very little consequence. Some walk carefully and reverently in the presence of the unknown ; while others go heedlessly on, all the more carelessly the more solemn and mysterious the truths or facts are which ought if possible to be clearly apprehended. Men are rushing forward in the world like an army into battle, and the different feelings with which each meets the responsibilities, cares, and obligations of life are as manifest as the different emotions of soldiers going into battle. An old soldier said he had seen men of great physical power, and possessing undoubted courage of a certain kind, show unmistakable signs of fear before going into battle.

Men who, in a pugilistic contest, would gladly fight any man in the regiment, shed tears like children, and had to be forced into line before the fight commenced. They were not afraid of what they could see, but the destructive power of an unseen bullet terrified them. On the contrary, men with less physical vigor, and who appeared to be quite timid, went into the battle without any visible signs of fear, and apparently as unmoved as if going to parade.

Courage is thus shown to be of two essentially different kinds, the one meeting unseen dangers calmly, the other

meeting them with trembling.   Now what makes this difference?   Is there a different kind of intelligence, which mani-
fests itself in such strangely different ways? or has conscience
something to do with this difference?

No man can foretell how he will act in trying circumstances.   But there may be a vast difference between seen
and unseen dangers, and the cautious and prudent man will
hesitate before unnecessarily meeting the unseen.   The
organ of hope in some men is so large as to lead them to
expect *they* will escape injury while others may be less
fortunate.

A statement may appear to be true, and yet not be true.
Also, a thing may apparently exist, and not really exist.   So
an act may seem to be performed, and yet not be performed.
The earth seems to stand still and the sun revolve around it.
This false appearance results from our position on the earth,
and our not perceiving its revolution because we are carried
along with it.   So, without careful thought, other things
which do not exist may appear to be realities.   Some facts
are beyond our comprehension; but, even if we cannot comprehend them, it is still our privilege to ask, To what shall we
liken facts which constitute that basis of truth?   For truth
must be in exact conformity with actual facts.

Truth has a different appearance according to the position
from which it is contemplated.   For instance, views of the
moon differ, and its light varies, with the position of the observer: at one time it is small, faint, and crescent-shaped,
and only at its full can we get a complete view of its beautiful globular shape; and yet the moon itself remains the
same, while to our vision it seems to change.

Let me represent familiar illustrations of some partial
views of truth held by various religious denominations and

scientific schools, for the views of all are in some measure restricted.

The Roman Catholics, as a religious denomination, discern great varieties of opinion prevalent where free thought and free discussion are allowed, and they also see that in such a commixture of thought no absolute and universal standard of belief pertaining to church creeds can obtain. They also see the necessity for some standard authority or court of ultimate appeal in these and like matters, and as a consequence the Pope and the Romish hierarchy are with them accepted as the highest court of appeal.

Against this ultimate court in religious matters Protestant denominations remonstrate. Protestants profess to receive the Bible as their ultimate standard in spiritual matters; while the Roman Catholics appeal to the same Bible, but assert that it must be accepted as explained by their authorities. Evangelical Protestants make direct appeal to the authority of the Holy Scriptures; and yet each of the various denominations is inclined to accuse all others of making too much of certain Scripture passages, and giving them undue prominence, while giving too little consideration to other passages which, they assert, should modify their belief. The justice of this or of a similar accusation appears in a greater or less degree in relation to all religious denominations; for, if one did not give more and another less prominence to certain Scripture doctrines, these different religious denominations would not exist.

Yet in some respects all prominent religious denominations hold much of the truth. There must be some fundamental truths (which are genuine) held by every numerous sect in enlightened countries, whether these are scientific or religious sects, otherwise the leaders of these sects could not make and hold together any considerable number of converts where free discussion is allowed.

For instance, among the Protestants, the pronounced Calvinist sees prominently the justice of God and his Divine Sovereignty, and hence he receives the doctrine of Predestination or Foreordination by an unchangeable Divine purpose ; and all his theology is in some measure colored by this view.

The Arminians, followed in general by the Methodists, see the moral freedom of men, and as a consequence they have strong views of moral responsibility ; and all their theology is in a measure squared to agree with these fundamental ideas.

The Universalist sees conspicuously the love and mercy of God, and does not deny his justice as he understands it ; and all his theology is squared by his views of love as a Divine Attribute.

Unitarians and Mohammedans see the unity of God, which is a most important truth ; and with them all else must be squared by that truth.

The ancient Sadducees originally saw that virtue ought to be revered and loved for its own sake, rather than in the expectation of rewards (a very important truth), and to square that with their other beliefs (in their opinion) necessitated a disbelief in a future state of rewards or punishments ; and thus they denied the immortality of the soul. They saw that if the soul consciously exists in a future state it must be susceptible of happiness or unhappiness, and, further, that probably the condition of this consciousness must to some extent be modified by or connected with their previous moral character.

As the Sadducees did not deny the existence of a Deity

they could not deny that the consequences of deeds done in their present state of existence might in some way be felt during all conscious existence, and to avoid such a conclusion, a result so nearly equivalent to rewards and punishments, they taught that the soul must cease to exist. The Sadducees appear to be an exception to the general rule, viz., that those who believe in God also believe in immortality.

The ancient Pharisees originally were pure, and saw that purity and devotion should be prominent in the lives of men. They also saw the need of commentaries on their sacred books; but by perverting originally pure ideas, they rushed into devotion to ordinances and traditions, to the exclusion of other and more important matters. Their mistakes in this direction gave strength to the position of the Sadducees, who were mostly free-thinkers and sceptics, wealthy and powerful, and while they were never numerically large (the multitudes never going with them), yet on account of their wealth and learning their influence was great for a number of centuries. The great mass of the Jews, however, sided with the Pharisees, who were believers in a future state of rewards or punishments. After some eight or nine centuries the Sadducees substantially ran out; and yet in one sense they never ran out, for their representatives are still found among religious sceptics and scientific materialists to-day.

By way of digression it may be remarked that denominations or sects are, in some respects, like nations.

When they discover a lack of interest or cohesion they are apt to concentrate their energies in a contest with another sect, and while thus engaged they overlook their own internal dissensions.

In this way sects, nations, and denominations are often perpetuated which otherwise might crumble for want of cohesive power.

But why cannot men select genuine truths, separate them from error, and thus form scientific or religious sects embracing all that is good and true both in religion and philosophy?

Really, would not that be delightful and beautiful if it was practicable? That would indeed be a genuine broad church or perfect philosophical society. But who shall select these genuine and choice truths? Where are the men who have such extensive and infallible views of truth in its fulness that they can completely separate truth from error? Where can we find any man or any set of men who have not preconceived ideas or opinions which in some respects color their views of the full truth? Who is able to comprehend the full truth? As Pilate asked, "What is truth?"

Those who ask this question may justly be requested to define or describe the combination of facts concerning which they desire information; for truth must always have some connection with legitimate facts, or some state of facts. To illustrate, suppose we desire particular information about the sources of light, and we are told that light is always light, and that pure light is always of similar composition. But the light from the sun originates in the sun itself, while the light of the moon is not original with the moon, but is reflected light.

Rays of light may also be of different shades. Thus, when we ask What is truth? we must take into consideration every legitimate fact pertaining to the subject about which information is sought, or our views will be partial, and thus may be misleading as really as if we were to suppose that the moon is self-luminous because its light may appear to be so to careless and not inquiring observers.

Now turn to scientific schools and look, for instance, at the latest scientific theories of development. Some theory of development must, to a certain extent, be true. Of course, without development the child never would become a man, nor the egg a chick, nor the acorn an oak. What then are its limits, and where shall it commence and stop? I say commence and stop, for it takes as much power to arrest development, when it has once started, as it does to commence the development.

Shall we go with Hæckel to the moner, and through that to "spontaneous generation," for the origin of life? Shall we accept Lamarck's theory? Lamarck attempted to explain all varieties of life by development, through practice and habit, or through the laws of heredity. Or shall we accept the theory of Darwin, who, while allowing for an original creation of the lowest forms of life, asserts that all the numberless varieties of life can be accounted for under the laws of development? Or shall we agree with that class of creationists who believe that every distinct species of living creatures represents a creative thought of the Supreme Being?

There are doubtless limitations on each and every one of these theories, and I do not believe any one has ever comprehended all the truth concerning the origin and development of life. But by proper study much can be learned which contains fragments of the truth, and by putting these fragments together we may hope to come nearer the actual truth.

That there is such a thing as actual truth, and that this is opposed to all error, I cannot doubt; although some have claimed that all error is partial truth, as well as that "all evil is partial good." The only difficulty we experience in deciding what is actual and absolute truth arises from the imperfection of our mental constitutions, our defective training, or our prejudices.   There can be no doubt that the human mind has the ability to reason correctly from proper premises, if it is possible to lay aside all unreasonable prejudice and come with a simple desire to know the truth in its purity and simplicity.   But the instant one takes a stand on some particular truth to the exclusion of other truths all his subsequent reasonings are modified or distorted through the influence of that truth to which he gives undue prominence. The difficulty that here occurs is the question where the various modifications which the bearing of one truth has upon another shall cease.

For instance, a statement may contain an absolute truth, and this statement standing by itself may be absolutely true, and yet, without other things being received and considered in connection with this truth, the statement may be practically equivalent to an untruth.

The truth that man is a free moral agent is a grand one ; but if we do not also take into consideration the fact that from the very composition of man's mental constitution there are certain restrictions upon his perfect freedom of thought we shall accept as truth what is nearly equivalent to an untruth.

Here comes into action the unconscious nature of man (of which his desires, emotions, and affections are indices), and this unconscious nature works mysteriously to color all his opinions.   Our unconscious natures act upon the intellectual faculties in one respect like colored glass upon the rays of light, and our views are like light passing through this glass.   The light will be tinged or colored by the glass, no matter how pure the original ray ; and thus again it becomes us to ask, in all humility, "What is truth ?"

Yet truth, when discovered in its purity, is one of the most beautiful and enjoyable of all things in the universe. Whose heart has not thrilled with joy at the discovery of some new fact, or some new view of truth? Thus Jesus said, "I am the way, the truth, and the light." As much as to say that the light and the truth are equally necessary to man's well-being, and each is an element of great joy to the honest seekers for the right, and that He, Jesus, would in like manner be a source of joy and comfort to all who receive His teachings and make them the rule of their lives. We have the testimonies of multitudes who claim to have experienced great joy in following the rules laid down by Him whom they receive as a Divine Master.

In the last few pages I have been writing principally of speculative views, or beliefs, rather than of views of truth which can be demonstrated with the certainty of a mathematical proposition. Now there are certain truths that are as certainly demonstrable or axiomatic as any mathematical proposition can be. For example, the axiom that the finite cannot comprehend the Infinite, but that the Infinite may comprehend the finite, is indisputably true.

Again, if we decidedly hate a person, we know that fact absolutely through our consciousness ; and this needs no demonstration, for consciousness in this case is the most positive and absolute witness. So, if we greatly love another person, we know that fact absolutely. We also know that the company of some persons is agreeable, while that of others is disagreeable. Just so in regard to physical appetites, as instanced in the craving for alcoholic liquors experienced by inebriates. So also in regard to other things not directly cognizable through the senses in the same manner as material things are. We are conscious, for instance, that some truths are agreeable to contemplate, while others are not agreeable.

To illustrate, we feel assured that all men must die. To the young and healthy the consideration of this truth is generally repulsive, and there can be no doubt that they absolutely know that this contemplation is repulsive. We also know many other things which are matters of experience, unless these experiences are delusive. If we suffer pain, we feel certain that we are not deluded in regard to that experience.

But very much in our moral natures is colored by our beliefs, and our beliefs are often the result of accident of birth or education. I suppose that many who are now active Christian workers would have been zealous Mussulmans if they had been born in Constantinople and had been instructed in the religious doctrines generally taught there. Can we then be responsible for our beliefs? I answer yes, and no. In some respects we must be responsible, and in other respects we cannot help believing what seems to be reasonable. But from our very mental constitutions we must believe in something. It is a fact, however, that in most cases we readily believe what is agreeable to our feelings, and, on the contrary, our feelings are largely indices of the state of our inner natures. Each seems to act on and react upon the other. Some take pleasure in contemplating the miraculous and inexplicable, while others are much better pleased to contemplate truths which are demonstrable. Some ridicule believers in miracles and all reports of miraculous events, and assert that such a thing as a miracle never did exist or could have existed. But are such sure that in making such a sweeping assertion they are giving a proper meaning to the language they use?

Until we can truthfully assert that we fully understand all the laws of nature we have no right to assert positively that what is commonly called a miracle cannot exist. From a scientific stand-point we may doubt whether what are generally understood to be miraculous events ever occurred; and from experience we are justified in disbelieving the present working of miracles; and this is as far as we can rationally go. When one denies that anything miraculous can exist does he not forget that the very existence of both mind and matter is inexplicable? Who can explain how either of these originally came to be in existence? To say that they always existed and did not originally come into existence does not help their position, for it is as easy to imagine that they were in some way brought into existence as it is to conceive that they could have no beginning. In all ages events out of the commonly observed course of nature have been regarded as inexplicable, wonderful, miraculous; but I suppose that, to an intelligence high enough to understand the operations of the laws under which these unexplained events have taken place, they would seem no more wonderful, *i.e.*, miraculous, than the gathering of a thunder-cloud does to ordinary observers.

To assert that such a thing as a miracle never existed is going beyond what any human being has any right to assert. That designing parties, for the sake of paltry gain, or for the sake of gaining undue influence over the minds of credulous or deluded followers may, in some cases, pretend to work miracles, or be the witnesses of miraculous acts, is in accordance with experience; and hence, if a person should now appear pretending to work miracles, every unprejudiced person would be justified in believing that this pretension is *prima facie* evidence either of insanity or fraud.   It is certainly in accordance with the laws of nature for unprincipled men to lie and in many plausible ways, to deceive ; but it is not in accordance with experience that good and honest men should lie.   Thus the testimony of eye and ear witnesses to the works and words of Christ, if the men were really good and honest, and not themselves deceived, must be received as valid testimony ; and this testimony cannot be impeached until it can be shown that they either were themselves deceived, or else had some selfish motive in reporting untruths.   If the above views are rejected, the only alternative is to assume that these witnesses were bad men, and bent upon deceiving the people.

The writer has heard intelligent men who, while admitting that the miraculous acts of healing reported by the Evangelists actually took place, ventured the assertion that Jesus Christ understood certain laws of nature not before or since so well understood by any other man, and hence He was able to do what no man in any succeeding age could do.   I suppose that such have a right to believe so, if such views seem reasonable to them, but Nature herself never deceives her proper interpreters.   Some are accustomed to treat all religious experiences as delusions.   But is this treatment philosophical ?

Such men as Matthew Arnold, Herbert Spencer, and Prof. Tyndall believe that religious feelings are as really a part of man's nature as their physical appetites are.

Prof. Tyndall writes (p. 542, " Fragments of Science") : "No atheistic reasoning can, I hold, dislodge religion from the heart of man.   Logic cannot deprive us of life, and religion is life to the religious.   As an experience of consciousness, it is perfectly beyond the assaults of logic."

In this case Prof. Tyndall is speaking of religion as
an actual fact, in its substantial and pure sense, and not the
forms of religion. And is it not to be feared that with too
many religion consists more of mere forms than of genuine
substance? The agreement of these forms with religion
itself may well be questioned, for forms may be only shadows
of the substance. While one is satisfied with the shadows
he is little inclined to inquire into the nature of the substances by which these shadows are cast. And yet, when
the reality of these shadows is denied or questioned, many
think the substances themselves have been attacked or denied.
Bear in mind that the real substance exists, even if men
mistake the shadow for the substance.

When we come to understand the actual truth we are
often surprised at its simplicity. From its nature, truth
must appear simple when fully comprehended; for it is
interwoven with the very laws of nature, and these laws are
in every respect perfect. That which we know of our
knowledge is (beyond any cavil) truth. Then the absolute
truth is not, as some would have us believe, an indistinct
and nebulous thing which can only be dimly discerned; but,
when properly understood, it must appear simple. The
really important thing to decide is, whether we properly
comprehend truth. Who has not fairly wondered at the
simplicity of scientific or moral truths when he has become
able to clearly understand them? And the more simple the
truth seems to us the more likely that we really comprehend it, and thus that our views are correct. Hence, also,
those who see the truth most clearly and best comprehend it
can generally explain it in a manner so simple that other
intelligent men can understand it. Cicero asserted that those
who think clearly can also write or speak clearly. And it is

doubtless generally true that those who so puzzle us in their writings with misty or cloudy statements are themselves mentally in the clouds or mists.

Those who attempt to be teachers of truth should be clear in their apprehensions of the truth. And yet those who appear to be most positive and certain in their own minds that they see the truth clearly are not the safest to follow. The writer once heard it remarked concerning a very dogmatic lecturer, "He seems to know everything but comprehends nothing."

The writer has very often been painfully impressed with a like idea while reading the writings of that large class of writers who deal in positive and rash assertions about matters concerning which no certain or positive knowledge has yet been obtained or is obtainable through human intelligence or intellectual inquiry. And on no subject does it seem that there is need of more careful inquiry and conscientious reflection and meditation, coupled with a sincere desire to understand the actual truth, than the subjects previously discussed, viz., the problem of life, and our inherited tendencies as bearing upon our welfare during the whole of our conscious existence (be it longer or shorter), and the limits and extent of our moral responsibilities. Where do these begin and end?

INDEX.

www.ingramcontent.com/pod-product-compliance
Lightning Source LLC
Chambersburg PA
CBHW021107270326
41929CB00009B/760

* 9 7 8 3 7 4 2 8 6 7 1 2 4 *